Where Did You Come From?

And

Where Are You Really Going?

This Book Answers the Two Basic Questions

Of Life

By: Thurston Ben McCutchen

© Copyright 2009 by Thurston Ben McCutchen

Where Did You Come From? And Where Are You Really Going?

By Thurston Ben McCutchen

Printed in the United States of America

ISBN 978-0-615-33342-7

Cover Design/Artwork by Kris Rogers

Unless otherwise indicated, Bible quotations are taken from The Scriptures version of the Bible, © 1993, by C.J. Koster, Published by Institute for Scripture Research Ltd.; and The Hebraic-Roots Version Bible, © by James S, Trimm, 2001, 2004, Published by The Scriptures also at: www.isr-messianic.org; and The Hebrew Names Version (HNV) of the World English Bible, a Modern English update of the American Standard Version of 1901, and is Public Domain; and The King James Study Bible (KJV) © 1988, by Thomas Nelson Publishers, Inc., and The Scriptures (ISR) 1998 and those quotes in parentheses are my own added emphasis.

www.seedtime2harvest.com

Disclaimer

I did not seek nor have I attained agreement or endorsement from anyone whose website, names or books have been referenced, and mention of them as references does not indicate that they agree with my thoughts and ideas.

Acknowledgments

T *hank you Bonnie Ruth for loving me and marrying me! It is a joy to grow spiritually together as we seek Him. Your patience and encouragement (YHWH's special gift to you!) as I wrote and updated this book were and are appreciated! Thanks also, Sharon Zenner for editing the first edition and Eddie Rogers for many hours of editing this updated (October 2009) version. Your insight, commitment and tireless work is the only way this edition is now made available to truth-seekers all over the world! Thanks also mom- it was you who taught me to pray and believe; what a wonderful gift! Ann you are a great step-mom, thank you for helping raise me! You both are truly caring parents. I thank my dad T.C. McCutchen who taught me integrity, not to take myself too seriously and the value of doing what is right; and my step-dad Hollis Rogers who showed me how to laugh. YHWH knows I miss you both and look forward to seeing you in the Kingdom!*

Family, you have always encouraged and seen me through eyes of love- you are the greatest! Special thanks must go to my sisters; Brenda, Linda, Jessie, and Callie who endured patiently with love (and still do). I must mention our children; Courtney, Amanda, Lindsay, Shelley, Mindy, Misty; Phil, John, and Heather whose lives are lived in such a way that makes me proud and gives me undue credit. You are nine of my best friends!

Added thanks are due unmentionable numbers of other friends, you each know who you are. You all continually look for the good in me and sharpen me as iron sharpens iron. I am blessed to have each of you in my life! The mercy and love you have all shown me may I extend to others. And, foremost I thank our wonderful deliverer and life-giver Messiah Yahshua who is and was and is to come, apart from Him we can do nothing! May the Creator bless, direct and provide for each of you as we turn our hearts toward Him! Loved one, please remember that He hears heart rendered prayers!

Forward

You are invited on the journey of your life! I encourage you to open your mind to the possibility of a divine purpose for your life. That the possibility exists that you were created for a specific purpose that only you can accomplish. Attaining that destiny will give you the peace of mind and sense of fulfillment that you may have searched a lifetime for! Only a Truth Searcher will seek truth and I must caution you that very few will ever complete the journey.

Maybe you are one that has accomplished much by the standards of men. None of that really matters when you take your last breath on the earth. What sort of car you drive, how large your bank account is, or how famous you are will be inconsequential 1000 or even 20 years from today. The only significance remaining will be whether or not you fulfilled your true destiny. Indeed it is WAKE UP TIME as the day is far spent! Most on the planet have some understanding that things are not normal, whatever that definition might be to you. I challenge you to open your heart and mind to the possibility of a supernatural Creator with a specific purpose and destiny for your life. Have the courage to read and follow the instructions in this book and accept this challenge.

Ask this Creator (if He exists) to make Himself real to you and reveal your purpose as you read and follow the instructions contained in these pages. If He is real, then you will have gained opportunity to pursue your destiny! Gaining that destiny and purpose will only be obtained by your determined and enduring pursuit of truth. Again, I should warn you that most will not continue the truth-seeking journey, for wide is the path that leads to destruction and many enter there, and narrow is the path that leads to life and <u>very few find it</u>. If He (The Creator) does not really exist, then you have only lost the few hours it took to read this book. May your life be enhanced, prepared, and excited as you take this journey to your true destiny and purpose in this experience called life. Truth Searcher: *Your journey begins!*

Thurston Ben McCutchen

Table of Contents

Chapter One:
Where Did We Come From?

Some believe that the earth was not created-
only evolved from a big bang.

Those who think that the earth is happenstance must also deduct that they too evolved from the Earth's big bang. My question remains; "What created the Big Bang?" That thought process requires an enormous degree of faith and begs the question for the source of energy that created the big bang.

I recently heard a scientist say, "if the earth were any closer to the sun, the earth and all its inhabitants would burn up, and if it were any farther away from the sun, it would be frozen." This is interesting and if true, the earth is exactly where, by some exacting degree of order, it must be for mankind to inhabit and live. Maybe it didn't just happen by random chance. If that is true then there must be a Creator. Of course, before we can have any relationship or knowledge of this Creator we must realize that we ourselves did not create the earth and the heavens and all that is in them. Can we agree on that premise? Core Research, a group of scientists whose fields of expertise include physics and astronomy ask the questions, "Is the theory of evolution supported by science? Did disorder create order?" They say that the Law of Increasing Entropy states that any natural system left to itself will decay. They also say that the Law of Energy and Matter states the amount of energy and matter remains constant and due to that truth/fact, you cannot subtract something from nothing or create (add) something from nothing. Only a Creator or a being with supernatural power can do that. This research can be studied at www.am.org and www.creationists.org. Other websites of interest would include: www.creationevidence.org; www.icr.org www.creationresearch.org; and a video set available *Unlocking The Mysteries of Life* at www.creationresource.org. In addition, a good book available in Christian Bookstores is *Creation*, by Grant Jeffrey. It is a collection of recent scientific discoveries via the Hubble Space Telescope. Were you there when He hung the moon and stars? I sure was not. Then if we did not do the creating, it stands in the line of reason that there is a Creator and we are not Him.

> **Furthermore, if there is a Creator, is He or she *kind enough* to have created us for a purpose and given us some guidelines to live by, that we may achieve that purpose or destiny?**

If we can agree that's a possibility, then hear what is accredited to the Creator as saying to you in the Book of Jeremiah in the Scriptures, "I know the plans I have for you, declares Yahweh, your Creator, plans to prosper you and not to harm you, plans to give you hope and a future..." The Creator designed us for living a certain way that we may receive His plan of blessings. Here's what He says about His instructions to you in 2 Timothy 3:16-17 "(16) All Scripture is given by inspiration of Yahweh and is useful for teaching, correcting and training in righteousness, (17) so that the person who acknowledges Yahweh and His Son Yahshua, may be empowered and supplied for every good work."

The Scriptures are of no private interpretation according to 2 Peter 1:20-21 "(20) Know this first, no prophecy of the Scripture is of any private interpretation. (21) For the words came not in old times by the will of man, but as Holy men of Yahweh spoke as they were moved by the Holy Spirit."

How can we actually believe and know that the Scriptures were actually inspired by the Creator?

Over forty authors wrote down their specific parts of the Bible over a fifteen hundred year time span. Most of these authors could not possibly have known one another yet their writings all agree and lend themselves to affirming the other writers.

Additionally, there are new and ongoing scientific discoveries that have shown the Bible to be correct when past scientific knowledge disagreed. You may want to look at the charts in the websites listed above. Why use the name Yahweh (Father) and Yahshua (Son) for this Creator-God? There were Ten Commandments or instructions for blessings from Yahweh that were given to a righteous man named Moshe (Moses) and they were recently found, hidden safely in the country of Israel in the language of ancient Paleolithic Hebrew. You may study this at www.Eliyah.com and other archeological biblical discoveries at www.wyattmuseum.com. There, you will find information discovered on the Red Sea crossing, Noah's ark found and other amazing biblical finds.

I believe the first of the Ten Commandments from your Creator reads something like this:

> **My Name is Yahweh. Do not forget My Name. Call on My Name. Have no other gods or instructors before Me!**

Take the word hallelujah, pronounced hallelu<u>YAH</u>, it still means today- praise is to Yah, a shortened form of Yahweh. Yahweh means *I*

AM and I will be in Hebrew. Interesting that Satan or someone he deceived changed the "y" in hallelujah to "j" to hide the real name so that the inhabitants of the earth would not know His name and therefore could not call on His name for help and instructions. There were no j's anywhere prior to around 1500 and none found in the Scriptures until the second edition of the 1611 King James Bible. This fact is easily researched on the Internet. What if I know I have had great results and power using the name Jesus? I can tell you if that's the only name you know then you can and will have His results using that name. That is the name most Christians have learned and used with great success. But it stands to reason that if there were no j's prior to the second edition of the King James Bible, then that could not possibly have been His name. The Greeks worshipped Zeus, and it is possible that they were using Hay Zeus (hail Zeus) or Jesus as that name of a false deity would have been more acceptable among the Greek conquered culture. The King James translators probably had no evil intentions, as they did not realize the Scriptures were originally written in Hebrew and Aramaic, a dialect of Hebrew, spoken by Hebrews and recorded by Hebrew speaking people. They only had Greek copies and they did the best they could with the information at their disposal.

There is a principle throughout the Bible that requires accountability once you learn truth. That is something Yahshua taught in His message to the Pharisees in John 9:41 "If you were blind you would not be guilty of sin, but now you claim you see and so your sin remains."

If you understood your best friend or spouses' name was "Dog's Breath" and you lovingly called them that for most of your life but then you found out their true name was Bill or Susan, etc., and you then discovered the name you had been using was less than flattering, would you continue to use it? I don't think so, not if your heart was determined to truly honor that person. Others may think His name is Jehovah, so let's take a look at that. If "Je" is supposed to stand for Yah and in Hebrew "hovah" means mischief, ruin, wicked, and evil one, that couldn't possibly be His name. According to the Encyclopedia Britannica 1991, under the heading "Yahweh" here is how the name "Jehovah" came into being:

"The Masoretes, who from about the 6th to the 10th century worked to reproduce the original text of the Hebrew Bible, replaced the vowels of the name YHWH (Yahweh) with the vowel signs of the Hebrew word Adonai or Elohim. Thus, the artificial name Jehovah (YeHoWaH) came into being."

YHVH (the Tetragrammaton, YHWH is pronounced Yahweh the true name, since in Hebrew the V is pronounced like a W;) has been found in ancient copies of the Septuagint in ancient Paleo Hebrew script dated between 50 BCE and 50 CE (A.D.) and www.Eliyah.com is an available study site. What is the truth concerning His name? I would encourage you to search for yourself, as you are the one who will benefit or give account one day. Over and over throughout the Scriptures, we are reminded to call on His name. *His Name*, not an adjective describing Him, although it is certainly okay to use adjectives and titles in our praise and conversation with Him. Examples of this would be, "Wonderful," "Lion of the Tribe of Judah," "Counselor," "King of Kings," "Most High God," "Good Shepherd," "Ancient of Days," "Healer," "Provider," "Messiah," "Author of our faith," etc. These are all titles and adjectives about His works. However, they are not His name. Don't just say, "In your name." Let's study together, find out to our satisfaction, and **then use His name!**

Since *believing or faith comes by hearing His instructions,* then it would be helpful for us to understand what denies us those instructions and keeps us away from a right relationship with the only one who knows what our purpose and destiny is. Hebrews 11:6 says: "Without faith it is impossible to please Him, for whoever comes to Him must believe that He exists and is a rewarder of those that diligently seek Him."

Additionally, we have an enemy. Reportedly, there was a servant of our Creator that rebelled, a spirit being without flesh as you and I have. His name is Satan or Lucifer. He is described as a thief, the evil one, the dragon, the snake, the father of lies, the serpent, and the devil, etc. but very real and very evil for sure.

Satan, being cast out of Yahweh's dwelling place in heaven because of his rebellion and pride was thrown to the earth. He now makes war against humankind. His desire and plan is to deceive us into worshipping him...or at least deny us the relationship that comes from following the instructions of our Creator, Yahweh. This instruction book, called the Bible or the Scriptures, says Yahweh sent His only begotten son to deliver us from this evil being and from Satan's evil purposes, restoring us to a right relationship with our Creator. An angel appeared and announced the event to a teenage girl named Mary who was chosen to birth this Son of Yahweh. This begotten Son's name was called Yahshua, which means Yahweh saves in Hebrew. The Son's name Yahshua can also be rendered Yeshua, Yahushua or just Y'Shua. For the purpose of this book, I will use the spelling "Yahshua" (pronounced Yah-shu-uh) for the Messiah and the only begotten Son of Yahweh. Not because I am sure that is the only correct rendering, but because it is reasonable since Yah (יהוה Elohim) is the root name of the Tetragrammaton found in ancient manuscripts and pronounced by many Hebrew scholars as Yahweh.

Chapter Two:
Personal Restoration and Forgiveness

The first step in restoring for yourself this right relationship with your Creator, Yahweh, is to acknowledge the Son He sent to deliver you. You see, the Bible, Yahweh's instructions, say that the wages of sin which is disobeying His instructions, is death. That means that someone had to receive that punishment. You can pay that just payment, death, or you can acknowledge that Yahweh sent of Himself His only begotten Son (Yahshua) on your behalf. If you receive His righteousness, the right standing with our Creator, then He received your punishment death, for your sins. You may call on His name (Yahshua- The Lamb and Son of God) and approach Yahweh and acknowledge you are a transgressor of His Commands (sinner) because you have either rejected His Commands by choice or rejected them from a lack of knowledge.

In John 10:10 Yahshua (Jesus) says: "The thief (Satan) comes only to steal, kill and destroy, but I have come that you may have life, and have it more abundantly."

Yahshua also said you must be born again so that you may receive His life nature to help you understand Yahweh's instruction for restoring a right relationship between you and the Father Creator, Yahweh. Yahshua states that His Words, the Bible, must be spiritually understood or discerned. To do that you must be born again by His Holy Spirit. You may do this by speaking that you believe in Him and desire to have Him as your Lord and Savior, and be forgiven of all your transgressions against His instructions. Romans 3:3 says: "The righteousness of Yahweh comes through faith in Yahshua, to all who believe."

You may confess Him and receive that righteousness for yourself by continuing:

I believe that Yahshua is the only begotten Son of Yahweh the Creator; I believe He died for my sins, shortcomings and rebellion and I confess that He is alive forevermore. He rose from the dead the third day, in accordance with the Scriptures, and sits at the right hand of the Father- Yahweh and I submit to His instructions. It is my desire to obey Him. I reject Satan and his plan for me. The Creator knows my thoughts and actions and as my Creator, I cannot deceive Him. Yahweh, because Yahshua died in my place I ask you to forgive me for all my sins. The Scriptures say when I do this with a truthful heart, the old person in me, is changed- behold, I am a new spiritual person. I am born again in His image. I now can understand the Scriptures and obey them. Since this loving, merciful Creator said that I am required to forgive others their trespasses or sins against me or the Father would not forgive me- I speak these words right now.

Father, I forgive everyone You now bring to my mind that has done evil against me. Just by speaking this, I am obeying, for words are spirit. I do this, not because their forgiveness is deserved, but because I am commanded to forgive and I desire to obey my Creator-Yahweh! I am born again and I will not listen to Satan's lies otherwise. Yahshua has promised me in His Word, that whoever calls on Him, believing that He came from the Father and died and rose again in accordance to the Scriptures, would have eternal life. His Word is The Way, The Truth and The Life. I have eternal life and I'm now born again!

One of the quickest ways to lose your blessings and the promises Yahshua came and died for is to allow unforgiveness in your heart toward someone. Don't allow even the thoughts to get a foothold. When someone offends you, quickly speak his or her forgiveness so that it has no hold on you. Unforgiveness is disobedience and allows the enemy to do harm to you. Not forgiving someone does not hurt the person who offended you nearly as much as it allows avenues of attack against you! The prayer you just spoke has effectively cut the cords that bound you and stopped those attacks.

You are now "born again" spiritually. The Scriptures attest to this in 2 Corinthians 5:17-18 "(17) If anyone be in Messiah, he is a **new creation**, old things are passed away; behold, all things are become new. (18) And all things are of Yahweh, who has reconciled us to Himself by Yahshua the Messiah, and has given us the ministry of reconciliation."

Maybe you don't look or feel like a new creation but you are. You are a *spirit* being created in the image of Yahweh, you have a soul which is your mind, will, intellect and emotions (personality) and you live in a body which is of course, physical and what you see. It is your *spirit* that became a new creation instantly when you were forgiven, because you asked Messiah Yahshua to be your Lord and Master, to forgive you of all your iniquities and reconcile you to Yahweh, your Creator. That is why you don't think of yourself as older, because the Scriptures declare that our spirits are renewed day by day, but the flesh is dying. The spirit person or what the Scriptures call the *hidden man of the heart* doesn't die or age. It was created in Yahweh's image. It will spend eternity somewhere, either in Heaven, in the Creator's Kingdom and presence, or cast into fiery torment of Hell. Hell was not created as a place for you; it was created for Satan and those angels that rebelled with him. You choose to go to hell for mankind's rebellion by choosing to not receive Yahshua's legal payment for your sins. That is why we make the effort to get *born again.* Since all flesh was made from dirt, all flesh will go back to dirt. If your body was overweight when you got born again, it's still overweight, and if you were slender, you still are, because it was a *spiritual* rebirth. Now you may choose to renew your mind (soul realm) in the word of Yahweh, and this allows Him to change you from the inside out. You bring your body in subjection by renewing your mind in the Scriptures according to Romans 12:1-2 "(1) I urge you therefore brothers, by the mercies of Yahweh, present your bodies as a living sacrifice, set apart (Holy) and acceptable to Yahweh, which is your reasonable service. (2) And do not conform to this world's culture and direction, but you be transformed and changed by the renewing of your mind (soul), that you may prove that which is the good, pleasing, acceptable and perfect will of Yahweh."

As you renew your mind in His Word and humble yourself to change, you will grow in His image and have authority over your body and flesh nature. This will allow you to flee those areas of vulnerability toward sin. Sin is disobedience and always produces destruction and ultimately death, so it is wise to flee those areas that you have been vulnerable in. The question is, do you really want to flee sin or do you think that your results will be somehow different? Do you have hidden sin? Proverbs 13:13 says: "Whoever despises the Word (instructions) shall be destroyed, but he who fears the Commandments shall be rewarded."

And Proverbs 13:15 states: "good understanding gives favor, but the way of the transgressor is hard." Proverbs 28:13 addresses this: "The person who covers (hides) their sin shall not prosper, but whoever confesses and forsakes them shall have mercy." Yahshua addresses this on teaching about the religious in Luke 12:1b "Beware of the leaven of the Pharisees, which is hypocrisy." What is He speaking of here?

> **Hypocrisy is appearing to be free from sin but only hiding our sin.**

That is what many of the religious leaders were doing in biblical days. It is what many religious people still do today. Then Yahshua continues to teach us what will happen to those that cover up and hide their sin in Luke 12:2-5 "(2) For there will be nothing covered that will not be revealed; and nothing hidden that will not be made known. (3) Therefore, whatever you have spoken (or done) in darkness shall be heard in the light; and that which you have spoken in secret, shall be shouted from the housetops. (4) And I say to you my friends, be not afraid of them that kill the body, and after have no power to harm you. (5) But I forewarn you whom you should fear: fear Him Who has power after you are dead to cast you into hell, yes, I say again, fear Him."

The hypocrisy of sin is, that it is not really "hidden" at all. You may have fooled all your friends, co-workers, and even your intimate family members. Most of us cannot fool ourselves. However, the Scriptures indicate that *we can even fool ourselves* in 1 Timothy 4:1-2 "(1) Now the Spirit speaks specifically, that in the last days some shall depart from the faith, giving heed to doctrines (teachings/actions) of devils and seducing spirits; (2) speaking lies in hypocrisy, having their conscious seared with a hot iron."

If we continue to hide and cover up our sin and do not ask for forgiveness and turn away from that sin, we become seared or hardened.

We then begin to compare ourselves with others who may do worse than us and think that makes us heaven bound. 2 Corinthians 10:12 addresses this thought: "For we dare not add ourselves to that number, or compare ourselves with some that commend themselves; but they, measuring themselves with themselves are not wise."

Your Heavenly Father knows everything and He has power to cast you into hell fire. Satan also knows your secret sin and he wants you cast into hell fire. If we will stop and consider how Satan uses our flesh nature to keep us in bondage with sin, we will confess our sin and turn from it. Numbers 32:23 confirms this: "Be positive of this, your sin will find you out."

You will choose to uncover your sin yourself and in so doing destroy sin by not letting it rule your body, or sin will destroy you! Yahshua tells us in John 14:30 "the prince of this world (Satan) comes, but he has no hold on me."

The devil had no hold on Yahshua, because Yahshua was without sin. The only way you and I can truthfully say that, is to confess our sins and turn from them. Romans 6:16-17 says: "(16) Do you not know, that whoever you yield yourselves to obey, you are his slaves and servants; whether to sin, which leads to death, or righteousness, which leads to life? (17) But Yahweh be thanked, you were once servants and slaves to sin, but now you have obeyed from your heart the doctrine (teaching/doing) that has now been delivered to you."

That doctrine is to ask forgiveness, turn from sin and reject Satan's plan of deception against you. Then, we too, can say, "The devil has no hold or secret sin on me, and he cannot keep me in bondage." Satan is condemned and wants to put his condemnation on you. The only way you allow this, is by having hypocrisy or hidden sin. So now, we must answer the question, since our sin is not really hidden anyway. Who do we give the authority over our future to? Satan, who has plans to kill you with hidden sin, or, our merciful and loving Heavenly Father? The only reason your sin has not been uncovered by Satan already is because he is waiting for the best probable time, to do the most evil and hurt to you and the ones you love.

Remember, John 1:29 says that He came to take away the sins of the world. The decision for peace and a life of blessings is up to us, as He will take away our sin and even the desire to sin. He offers us help, redirection, and reconciliation to our heavenly Father. We will stop making provision for our flesh nature to rule us. Call out to Yahshua *now* and He will blot out your sin. Proverbs 13:3 says: "Hope deferred makes the heart sick, but when the desire comes, it is a tree of life."

Don't make your heart sick loved one, confess and receive His peace and His righteousness now! Romans 6:23 says: "the wages (product) of sin is death, but the gift of Yahweh is eternal life through Yahshua the Messiah."

> *Flee sin as though your very life depends on it—because it does!*

Yahshua taught us the principles of prayer in teaching the disciples His prayer in Matthew 6:9-13 "(9) Our Father which is in heaven, Holy is Your Name, (10) Your Kingdom come, Your will be done, on earth as it is with You in heaven. (11) Give us this day our daily bread. (12) And forgive us our trespasses as we forgive those that trespass against us. (13) And lead us not into temptation, but deliver us from the evil one: For Yours is the kingdom, and the power, and the glory forever. Amen."

We can learn much from this simple prayer about our method of fellowship with our Creator, Yahweh. First, Yahshua declares that Yahweh is our Father now and His Name is Holy, set apart, and precious.

Second, that we should pray that the earthly Kingdom would become like His heavenly Kingdom, where no lack, poverty, disease or death exists! Third, He cares for us and will provide for our needs. Fourth, we need forgiveness but must give the same forgiveness we request to receive any forgiveness ourselves. Fifth, that we would not be allowed any temptation to transgress or commit sin above His help to deliver us from the evil one's schemes and finally, that our Heavenly Father has a Kingdom of power and glory forever! Then the Scripture restates the requirement to forgive prior to receiving any forgiveness from Yahweh. You now walk in forgiveness and you are an obedient child of Yahweh the Creator and have a restored relationship with Him because you forgave others and trusted in Him.

How can you know you are now *born again*? Because the one thing Yahshua, the Word, cannot do is lie. He is The Truth. The Scripture tells us in Romans 8:16 "The Spirit Himself bears witness with our spirits, that we are the children of Yahweh."

We will know we are "born again" because He is faithful to witness that Truth to our spirits. You can now benefit from your obedience because the Creator promises with obedience He will bless you. He will show you favor and help you when you call for His help in any and every situation, especially if Satan is attacking you. You can always know that an attack is from Satan if things aren't as Yahweh promised. Ignorance of Yahweh's instructions and promises allow Satan to attack and destroy you and the blessings Yahweh intends for you according to Hosea 4:6: "My people have perished for lack of knowledge. Because you have rejected knowledge, I reject you from being priest for Me. Since you have forgotten the Torah (Law/Instructions) of your Elohim (Hebrew God plural), I will also forget your children.

I caution you to flee sin and the scheme that Satan has set against you. You may think you have gotten away with disobedience and hidden sin but you have not. The Scripture gives us Yahweh's warning promise in Numbers 14:18 "Yahweh is patient and of great mercy, forgiving iniquity and transgression, and by no means clearing the guilty, visiting the iniquity of the fathers upon the children unto the third and fourth generation."

Even when we think we've gotten away with some hidden and dark sin it is not really hidden. As we see from this Scripture, the curse or judgment from Yahweh is visited on our children and grandchildren and even great and great-great grandchildren. To reverse and stop these curses we have to repent (Confess and turn from our sins).

You have been given gifts or talents specific to you and what His plan and purpose for your life is, and only you can fulfill the purpose you were created for and destined for. Yahshua admonishes us in Matthew 10:8 "...freely you have received, freely give."

You will receive more gifts as you freely give. These gifts are in all three realms of your life and are designed and given for you to give and help others. The spirit realm allows for nine gifts for the benefit of others as recorded in 1 Corinthians 12:1-12; the soul realm refers to your mind, will, intellect and emotions, which make up your personality. A few examples would be to give a smile or kind word to someone. You will receive more back. Comfort someone who is hurting, and you will be comforted. Lastly, the body refers to the physical realm, which may include your giving and sharing of your finances or material things you have to help others. You may say I just barely have enough for myself and my family. Why would He give you more in any area when you do not obey and freely give? How can He bless you, as He really wants to? Read the story of the wise steward who went and produced more for His master in Matthew 25:14 and remember that the fearful servant did not use his talent but only buried it. That fearful servant was called wicked and lazy by his master and was thrown into outer darkness where there was weeping and gnashing of teeth, which sounds a lot like hell. Use what you have been freely given and *freely give!*

Satan, the evil spirit being, has a host of fallen spirit beings under his command that hate you as Yahweh's creation on the earth. So, it is imperative that you study to find out for yourself what your Creator's instructions are and then obey them, so that He may protect you from Satan. Luke 4:19 mentions areas of our lives where Satan uses his resources to keep us from producing spiritual fruit for our Lord: "..and the *cares of this world*, and the *deceitfulness of riches*, and the *passionate desires of other things* enter in, choke the Word (of Yahshua) and it becomes unfruitful."

Just making a living and keeping the standards sold to us by advertising on television keeps most people from doing the works of Yahshua. Drugs, alcohol, sexual habits, gambling, eating excessively, etc. are all areas Satan will use if he cannot stop you with just making a living. We must not allow hidden and dark things room to grow in us. We must be alert and confess our sins, get forgiveness and deliverance and then repent and turn away from these areas of vulnerability in our lives.

Some of my earliest memories are of my sisters and me praying the simple bedtime prayer our mother taught us as soon as we could talk. It went like this:

> *"Now I lay me down to sleep,*
> *I pray you Lord my soul to keep,*
> *If I should die before I wake,*
> *I pray you Lord my soul to take."*

Afterwards, the seemingly endless prayer for every member of the family including all aunts, uncles, cousins, and grandparents along with anyone else that would come to mind. Many of you readers knew and said this and similar bedtime prayers. Teaching a child to pray a simple prayer teaches them several things. First, that there is a Creator or God. Secondly, that our lives could end unexpectedly, even during the night and lastly, that we could have a relationship and carry on a conversation and even make requests of this Creator. We never attended church as a family but when I was about thirteen or fourteen I was invited by a wonderful family, the Bundy's, to attend church with them. I was a friend of the sons and they also had two beautiful daughters, which increased my desire to attend. Looking back today, I can see the loving methods that a loving Creator uses to bring us to Him. We learned some Scriptures along with the Apostle's Creed which was a simple statement of faith saying you believed in God and Jesus (Yahshua), His only begotten Son and that He was crucified, died and buried and rose again the third day to pay for our sins and overcome death. *Overcome death!* Now that seemed like a really good idea to me, since I had grown up praying and knowing that my time here on the earth could end at any time. Not expected- but a possibility anyway. There were several of us about the same age who memorized this Creed and were to recite it as a reflection of our beliefs in front of the whole church assembly. The day came and the recital happened without much personal fanfare.

I remember walking out on the church lawn and looking up to heaven and saying,

> *"Lord, I'm not sure I felt anything really happened back there (for to me it seemed to be mental assent only) but I really mean it, I want you to be my Lord."*

Then something strange happened, as though the heavens were opening and acknowledgement of the answered prayer was happening instantly! I have thought about it since and have come to believe that at that instant my name was recorded in the **Lamb's Book of Life** because Yahshua is The Sacrificial Lamb. Yahweh's Spirit is the Holy Spirit sent by Him to those who accept Yahshua as Messiah and Lord and His Spirit seals us unto the day of redemption. Ephesians 4:30 states: "Do not grieve the Holy Spirit of Yahweh by Whom you were sealed for the day of redemption."

Now in the particular church denomination that I attended as a young boy we were not taught any depth of the power of the Bible so I didn't learn that I had an enemy and that I needed to study and grow up spiritually. The result of this lack of understanding kept me a spiritual baby and certainly on spiritually dangerous ground. That is to say, you really couldn't tell much difference between me and an atheist or unbeliever. Within six months of my newfound faith in Christ as my Lord I was busy being accepted as a teenager and fitting in. My parents divorced about that time and I was hurt and disillusioned about the goodness of life and gave little thought to living for this God and His Son I had confessed.

The Bible says that as soon as the Word is planted, Satan comes immediately to steal the Word in Mark 4:14-20 "(14) The sower plants the Word (of Yahshua). (15) And these are they by the wayside where the Word is planted; but when they have heard, Satan comes immediately and takes away the Word that is planted in their hearts. (16) And these are they also that are planted on stony ground; who, when they hear the Word, immediately receive it with gladness; (17) And have no root (understanding) in themselves, and so endure for only a short time afterwards when *affliction and persecution come for the Word's sake* and immediately they are offended. (18) And these are they (hearers) that are planted among thorns; such as hear the Word. (19) And the cares of this world, and the deceitfulness of riches, and the lusts of other things enters in and chokes the Word (of Yahshua) and it becomes unfruitful (unproductive). (20) And these are they (hearers) that are planted in good soil, those that hear the Word and receive (humble their thoughts and preconceived religious ideas) and bring forth fruit (doers of the Word of Yahshua) some thirty fold, some sixty and some one hundred fold."

Please note that persecution and affliction come for the *Word's sake.* Why would Satan want to steal the Word from us? Of course, the answer is simple. It is because the Word of Yahweh will produce fruit for the Kingdom of Heaven, spiritual fruit that will remain. Satan is not afraid of you and me, but He is petrified of Yahshua's Word and the power it wields against his kingdom of darkness and death.

> *I have come to realize that hurting people-hurt other people, and they usually hurt them with words and the actions that follow.*

I certainly have hurt others while being in a state of pain myself. When a person is hurting, all attention turns to self for protection and the grieving process. We tend to get more selfish, and of course that promotes more hurt for others and Satan's kingdom is served. A valuable lesson for those who are hurting is to recognize the trap being set by Satan to continue his spiral of pain and suffering at the very time your pain has made you vulnerable. Decide to obey the Commands of your Creator by blessing those that curse you and praying for those that spitefully use you. Make a conscious decision to stop the cycle of pain by forgiving those that hurt you. Words are spirit and the Bible says there is a cloud of witnesses to hear what you say. All of Heaven's Kingdom and Hell's entire kingdom wait to see whom you empower with your words. The hurt has already been done to you so why continue for Satan and help him to hurt others like he has hurt you?

That is what I've learned by studying the Scriptures but that is not what I did as a fourteen-year-old boy. I remember my mama saying she wouldn't ever get married again just after my parents divorced. That she just needed her freedom and some time to think. Looking back, I am sure that may have been her intention but within six months, she was remarried. I was crushed and felt if I could no longer trust her- then there was no woman I could trust. I remember making the decision to be the one who did the hurting and not the one who was hurt in the future. I grew more selfish and unwilling to allow others, especially females, into my heart. I would just love them and leave them, so to speak. Besides, I thought my mom didn't deserve forgiveness because she had split up our home and my three sisters moved out with her while I stayed with dad. I felt that since I didn't make the decision to divorce, I would just stay where I was. I continued down that road of "protecting self" throughout my college years. I did forgive my mama though, because even then, at the height of my rebellion and self-preservation, my Heavenly Father whispered, "you must forgive and restore your relationship with her." I knew it was Him because I had no intention of forgiving her. I had even made the decision known to others that I would never talk to her again. That short and simple message from heaven gave me a glimpse of the mercy of Yahweh God. I realized that my mother, dad, nor I was perfect and I made the decision to obey and call and forgive her. *Realizing now that people make mistakes and need forgiveness, I suppose I was forgiving her for not being perfect!* In retrospect, it seems almost humorous but at the time, it was no laughing matter. I have a wonderful relationship with my mother and did with my step dad before his passing on to the Kingdom in 2008! I also had a wonderful relationship with my dad who also passed on to the Kingdom in 2005 and still do with my step mom who is also alive and well!

I openly forgave and that certainly helped cure my heart pain. I did not, however, turn again to the Lord and His Word to grow up spiritually and *follow Him* as He has commanded in Matthew 4:19. I was still following me, and concerned mostly with how I could have the most fun, be happy, and still look the best I could possibly look. I got married after college, and became very goal directed in my business. I had started a cattle feed business, which was prospering, and then I was offered a really good career opportunity with an insurance company. I operated the biblical principle in Mark 11:23 that states if you believe, you can have whatsoever you SAY!

I didn't know it was a biblical principle and works whether or not you are serving God. Every area you become a *doer* of the Word of God you will get His wonderful results! You don't even have to be born again. You can be operating according to His principles and be blessed in that particular area. That is why you can see the wicked seemingly prosper. Of course, they may prosper financially and pile up wealth as it becomes their god and their source of supply, but they have *no eternal life and no peace.*

To get and keep peace, you have to know the Prince of Peace, Yahshua!

Philippians 4:6-9, 13 and 19 gives the keys to Yahshua's peace: (6) "Do not be anxious or worried about anything, but in all things by prayers and petition *with thanksgiving*, let your requests be made known to Yahweh. (7) And the peace of Yahweh, which passes your logic and understanding, shall protect and guard *your heart and your mind* through Yahshua the Messiah. (8) Finally, brothers, whatsoever things are honest, just, pure, and lovely, and whatever agrees with the good report; if there is any virtue or anything worthy of praise, think on these things. (9) Those things which you have learned, received, and heard, and seen in me, do them, and the peace of Yahweh shall be with you. (13) I can do all things through Yahshua the Messiah who strengthens me. (19) But my Elohim, (God) Yahweh, shall supply all your needs according to His riches in glory by Yahshua the Messiah."

We must keep our minds from focusing on the evil report or the plan of Satan and focus our thoughts on the good report, the plan that your Creator desires for you and the plan Yahshua paid for! We focus on the report the Scriptures promise. When you are anxious or worried you are disobedient (sinning), so repent by casting all your cares on Him for He cares for you according to 1 Peter 5:7. Notice also that you are giving thanks for something you petitioned for. That means you believe you have the thing you asked for and that puts the matter over into the realm of Yahweh's problem. You have given the problem or need over to the Creator of all things and He is quite capable of bringing it to pass. That is a great formula for peace!

Those not trusting Yahweh become busy piling up their wealth and even busier guarding it from those that want to take it from them. They are moved by fear and the more they seem to accumulate, the more worried and enslaved they become to their stuff. In reality, they have a poverty mentality because they are always fearful that they will not have enough. Because of this fear of lack, they are driven to horde and often become stingy people. Now understand it is okay to have things and be a believer. Just don't allow things to have you. Be free enough to give it all away if He tells you to. Yahshua said, "Don't pile up treasure on Earth that thieves can break in and steal, but rather pile up treasure in heaven." You do this by producing fruit that will remain. Every time you obey His Word and do His Commands, His Word will produce fruit that is spiritual and will remain. This is what glorifies the Father, increasing His Kingdom! Heaven and Earth will pass away but Yahshua promises His Word will endure forever.

Where your treasure is, there will be your heart also. You cannot serve God and money. Realize that it is not money that is the root of all evil but the *love* of it! You cannot be a giver and help orphans and widows and help finance the growing and nurturing of the Kingdom of God, without having provision enough for your own family. Some however, equate godliness or favor from Yahweh with material wealth. The Scriptures deny this thought in 1 Timothy 6:5-10 "(5) Perverse disputings of men with corrupt minds and destitute of truth, supposing that *gain is godliness*: from such withdraw yourself. (6) But godliness with contentment is great gain. (7) For we brought nothing into this world and it is certain we will carry nothing out. (8) And having food and clothing let us be content. (9) For those who desire great wealth fall into temptation and a trap, and many hurtful passions and desires which drown men in destruction and hell. (10) For the <u>*love of money*</u> is the root of all evil: although some have coveted after, they have erred from the faith, and pierced themselves with many sorrows." These that passionately desire riches and great wealth become what they think about because the Scriptures tell us that as a man thinks, so is he.

Wealth or true riches is to be able to walk uprightly and humbly with faith, hope, love, and patience in Yahweh. The ability to trust your Creator in all situations for provision and help in trouble is far better. Understand that wealth and riches are for serving Yahweh and helping others anyway. In Genesis 12:2 Abram (soon to be Abraham) was <u>blessed to be a blessing</u>, and in Genesis 13:2 the Scriptures mention that Abram was very rich in cattle, in silver, and in gold. What was the purpose of the wealth? Of course by looking at the Scripture it is obvious, Abram was *blessed to be a blessing* -to help others. Just like you will be if you keep His Commands and help widows, orphans and those Yahshua tells you to help. On the other hand, some believe it is evil to prosper; they seem to be of the opinion that godliness is poverty. They are just as wrong as those that think godliness is gain. How can you help the down and out with your witness if you don't obey with your giving? A poverty mentality also restricts you from being a giver and sharing what you have. Remember, your gift is acceptable according to what you have, not on how large or small your gift is; it is accepted based on the willingness of your heart to give. Deuteronomy 8:18 gives warning: "For you shall remember Yahweh your Elohim, for it is He that gives you power to get wealth that *He may establish His Covenant* that He made with your fathers, as it is this day."

Our heavenly Father even promises to give seed to the sower to help the giver plant into the Kingdom of Heaven in 2 Corinthians 9:10 "Now He who gives seed (Yahweh) to the sower (giver) and gives the sower provision will multiply (increase) your seed sown and increase the fruit of your righteousness."

Even the dumbest farmer in the world would probably not eat all of his seed, surely he would plant some. *Are you eating all your seed?* A person who expects different results while continuing to perform the same actions could be properly described as insane! If you just barely get by financially, why not try something different? **Start Giving**. *I realize it makes no sense to your mind, but to win spiritually, which will always manifests later physically, you must trust and obey the Scriptures.* Start helping the widow, the orphan and those that spread the truth of the gospel of Yahshua of Nazareth! The purpose of the blessing of wealth is to spread the gospel, feed the hungry, clothe the naked, and feed the widows and orphans, or in other words, to establish the Covenant of Yahweh on the earth! If we want supernatural help financially, we will have to obey the

Scripture in 1 Timothy 6:17-18 "(17) Command them that are rich in this world not to be high minded, nor to trust in their riches which are uncertain and untrustworthy but in the living Elohim Who gives us richly all things to enjoy; (18) **that they do good and be rich in all good works, ready to give and distribute and willing to share.**"

Malachi 3:7-12 gives insight: "(7) Even from your father's days you are departed from my Laws (Teachings and Instructions) and have not kept (obeyed) them. Return to Me and I will return to you says Yahweh. But you ask, how may we return? (8) Will a man rob Yahweh? Yet you have robbed Me. You ask, how have we robbed you? You've kept My tithes and offerings. (9) You are cursed with a curse because you have robbed Me, even this whole nation. (10) You bring all the tithe into My storehouse, that there may be provision in My house, test Me on this now and see if I will not open the windows of heaven and pour out such a great blessing that you will not have room to receive it. (11) And I will rebuke the devourer for your sakes, and he will not destroy the fruit of your field, neither shall your vine cast fruit before its time, says Yahweh. (12) And all nations shall call you blessed, and you shall be a delightful land, says Yahweh."

Some would have you to believe that their church or denomination is the storehouse of Yahweh. Actually, I suspect the tithe is not for building denominations and buildings. You, not your denomination or a television evangelist, are accountable for *His* tithe. This does not mean you cannot give your tithe to your denomination, a television evangelist, or to any ministry you see fit. Just pray first and looking for spiritual fruit, be motivated by the peace in your heart. The tithe is for His provision to the widow, orphan and the Levite or one who is called to preach the everlasting gospel and does not covet things. When you obey by giving the tithe, which is Yahweh's, and your freewill offering, which is yours, the

Creator of the universe removes the curses, and rebukes Satan, the thief and liar. He asks us to test Him on this matter, and guarantees He will pour us such a blessing from heaven that we will not have enough room to receive it all!

I was operating in the biblical principle of goals, and speaking the desired results of Mark 11:23, I would just think of *goals I wanted to attain, write them down on paper and confess them as accomplished every day*. Habakkuk 2:2 says: "Write the vision, and make it plain upon tables, that he may run that reads it."

The vision is your goal or target of what you want to obtain or become. You will never have what you are not willing to target and pursue. Of course, I was unaware of these Scripture promises. Proverbs 29:18 says: "Where there is no vision (plan) the people perish: But he that keeps the Torah (Law, Yahweh's Teachings and Instructions, the *plan* of Yahweh), happy is he."

Surprisingly, within a few short months, I was promoted and my income continued to leap upward. Next, we desired our dream home, so we found and made the down payment on some land with a spring fed creek and bought house plans. Do you see the action to our faith? Faith is still faith without action to back it up, but according to the Bible it is dead faith and likened to the body without the spirit being inside. We then started confessing and seeing ourselves in our beautiful new home. Within months everything came into place and we were starting construction on our dream home. We were continuing to prosper financially but I knew something was still missing. Over the next several years we became a family as we had three children, a son and two daughters. We were quite blessed and appeared to be chosen up and comers. It seemed like everything worked perfectly for us. Certainly, our family and friends indicated that to us. One of my goals was to own and pilot an airplane. I did what worked and that too was accomplished in a short span of time. Once in 1982 when flying from Florida back home to Texas in our small plane we ran into violent weather. We had our small four and a half year old son in the back seat. I can still remember being afraid that he would hit his head on the ceiling as we were being tossed around. The clouds totally encompassed us and it grew dark. So dark and stormy that we could barely see our light strobes flashing on the wings. Water started coming inside the plane coming up through the floor and brake pedals! I really didn't have any remnant of a personal relationship with Yahshua or Jesus at this point in my life but I remember praying with my wife that the clouds would open up and allow us safe passage through them. To our surprise, it seemed like a tunnel opened up within the dense and dark cloud cover! We must have flown like that for over an hour with just enough room inside our direction heading to give us about fifty feet on either side of the wingtips to fly! I have mentioned this story to remind you that even when I thought I didn't need Yahshua, and considered myself *self-made*, He was mercifully watching over His Word to perform it. ***He will do the same for you, because He was and is merciful and His mercy endures forever!***

I wanted to start my own company and have more freedom. That goal was accomplished quickly also. I remember thinking if I just had a hundred thousand dollars in the bank, (remember this was way back in the early 1980's) then I would have peace and contentment! Surely, I would then have peace of mind from this accomplished goal! The day arrived quickly when that goal was achieved, but where was the peace and satisfaction that was supposed to come with it? Would there ever be an accomplishment that would bring this peace and contentment? Keep in mind that I was attending a church regularly but this denomination was not much different than the one I had been in as a boy and had no understanding or teaching of the power of God and His Word. I was a little surprised that I hadn't attained the peace and fulfillment I desired and expected from my success of attaining one hundred thousand dollars in the bank and I immediately reasoned that maybe my goal needed to be higher, possibly $500,000 or even one million in the bank. Pondering these thoughts I discerned that the whole process seemed to be too much trouble and could take longer than I wanted to commit to. Even if I accomplished these sums they still might not be the magic number I was looking for and bring satisfaction. In 1985 I went to my dad's ranch in Robert Lee, Texas to go deer hunting. I was going to stay in his cabin ranch house and hunt early the next morning. My dad had a ranch foreman who had **"Ye shall know the truth and the truth shall make ye free"** written above his front door in giant letters.

I questioned myself, "What is Truth really?" By this point in my life I really had no remnant of faith in a living savior or Jesus (Yahshua) as I had been taught as a boy. I was pretty much an agnostic, not denying there must be a Creator, but certainly not acknowledging the only way to this Creator was Yahshua, His only begotten Son. I asked myself again, "What really is Truth?" It didn't appear to be achieving my goals. That night in the ranch cabin I built a fire in the pot-bellied stove to keep warm and sat down in a comfortable chair. I picked up a blue book lying nearby written by Tom Landry and Roger Staubach of Dallas Cowboy fame. Being a football fan of the Cowboys and Coach Landry, I glanced at the title which was something like: **My Greatest Achievement in Life**. Expecting to read about football I started reading. This famous coach and his star quarterback told of their relationship with the Messiah, Jesus Christ and the absolute *Truth* of His promises. I remember reading the scripture; "You shall know the Truth and the Truth shall set you free!"

That night I read that book from cover to cover and the end of the book was a direct challenge from both of them, *"Read the gospel of John first and then read the entire Bible and find for yourself the undeniable Truth taught there."* I was excited. Could the gospel I heard as a young boy really be absolute Truth? Could this supply the peace and contentment that reaching my goals had left undone? I accepted their challenge and decided to read the Bible and find out for myself. Thankfully, I recommitted myself to Him shortly thereafter and began learning how to obey and know Him. I read how the Bible says in Hebrews 4:12 "For the *Word of Yahweh is living* and powerful, and sharper than any two edge sword, dividing even the soul from the spirit, and the joints from the marrow, and is *a discerner of the thoughts and intents of the heart.*"

A light bulb went on. I thought if the Word is alive then that must be what John Chapter One meant when it spoke of Yahshua being The Word made flesh. Furthermore, if He is the Word and is alive and He is really discerning my thoughts and intents, then that must mean *He is reading me while I read Him!* I was startled and thought, so that is how He brings us to change. Suddenly I realized when we declare Him as Lord over our lives and start to obey Him; He convicts us of areas of our lives that we must change. We get uncomfortable with our old patterns of selfishness. We become born again in His Spirit and the cleaning up process begins.

Where Did You Come From?
And Where Are You Really Going?

Chapter Three:
Staying Alive

s the cleaning up process in me continued, I grew hungry for more truth. I started hearing from Him as He dropped in thoughts and unknown words of Scripture, even telling me where they were in the Bible occasionally. There were times when He would give me a Scripture chapter and verse and I didn't even know there was a book named that, or a verse and chapter with that high a number assigned to it! He brought to mind many times when I should and would have died, had He not intervened. He said that because I had asked Him to really be my Lord as a small boy, He had kept me alive so that I would have the opportunity to repent and serve Him. He would help me turn from my sinful and self-directed way of living and learn to obey Him and not go to hell! I was saved *UNTO* the day of redemption. In other words, He kept me alive so that the day would come when I would follow Him. Of course I could have rejected this truth and the Bible says He will allow me to turn away from Him and reject Him and go to hell if I so chose. *He would never abandon me*, I alone could separate myself from Him, and only by rejecting the only one who paid the price due for my sins and rebellion against His Commands. In Revelation 3:5 Yahshua warns: "He that overcomes shall be clothed in white garments, and I will <u>not</u> blot out his name from the Book of Life, but I will confess His name before My Father and His angels."

It certainly appears from this Scripture that we can have our names blotted or removed from the Book of Life! I was certainly headed in that direction, having little if any belief in Him left, but He woke me up and redirected me just in time!

As a witness and testimony for you I will share several of the times He intervened and kept me alive as He Commanded His angels concerning me:

(1) After my parents' divorce I had gone swimming in a lake by Del Rio, Texas and dived to the bottom in murky unknown waters. I found myself down about eight to ten feet tangled in barbed fence wire and out of oxygen. I grasped and tugged at the wire in my skin and swimsuit but it would not budge loose. I could see up where the water seemed to be lighter and realized that was how far up I needed to be to get air, but I could not free myself. I remember thinking, *so this is how I will die and felt this was a really stupid way to die.* Suddenly, it felt as though strong hands were on each shoulder and shot me upward to the air! I had just been rescued by an angel but only understood that fact much later as He reminded me of the occasion.

(2) While in my first year in college, I drove toward home to our high school football game. It was just getting dark and I came around a curve to see five or six bales of hay in the middle of the road. I swerved to miss them and lost control of the car. I remember sliding into a large tree on the driver's side and the car wrapped itself around the tree. I crawled out of the car on the passenger side without a scratch!

(3) The night of my wedding rehearsal dinner for marriage to my college sweetheart, I was driving away from her home having let

her off. Driving fast, I came over the top of a hill. Suddenly, I saw the reflection of eyes all over the road and started hearing and feeling the breaking glass and crunching of the car. Coming to a stop, I looked around and saw large grown black cows all over the road. Three of them had just died and three or four more seemed sprawled about the road. I was untouched with not even a scratch!

(4) Shortly after our wedding, we were out celebrating Independence Day with friends, my college buddies and their cousin, the deputy sheriff. We were in a remote area on their uncle's ranch and started shooting at beer cans on top of a dirt livestock- watering tank. My friend had a six-shooter pistol and was shooting. I told him I could shoot that well so he gave me the pistol. I fired off a few rounds and wasn't doing so well when I decided maybe he was doing pretty well at shooting after all. Before handing him the pistol back, I thought I would entertain him and spin the pistol like I'd seen done in so many westerns. The gun went off and shot me in the stomach. At first, I couldn't believe how stupidly I had just acted. Immediately, I reached for my side where blood was oozing out and realized I was paralyzed from the waist down. They carried me to the deputy's patrol car and shouted for my wife to come as they told her I had accidentally shot myself. She piled in the back seat with me and we determined to head some forty- five miles to the hospital in San Angelo, Texas. About half way to San Angelo our car started smoking and quit. We tried to restart it but could not. Prior to this smoky breakdown, we had just met an unmarked car that resembled my dad's unmarked immigration patrol car and somehow I knew that we should try his sheriff's band radio. If it was dad, then it was certainly possible that he would have his Sheriff's band radio on along with his federal radio. That car was already out of sight and we could raise

no other Sheriff's officers or help of any kind. I somehow knew or at least hoped it was my dad as I remembered he came up to check on his cows on his ranch every few weeks from a town about one hundred miles from here. My deputy friend tried the Sheriff's band radio after I mentioned the thought that came to me as I was in the back seat and trying not to panic but sensing my life was in danger. My dad answered the call and turned around to pick us up and radioed ahead to clear traffic signals for the emergency route to the hospital. Upon arriving at the hospital it was determined that they needed to do an emergency exploratory surgery immediately. That was the last thing I remembered until I looked down from above my body and saw the emergency room nurse joking and flirting with the surgeon. I was enraged at them and started trying to talk to them and was telling them to get serious but they could not hear me. I didn't understand how I could get outside my body to watch this turn of events but knew I was utterly helpless. Suddenly, I saw myself reentering my body through the head but to this day don't understand the significance of that, except that we are created as spirit, soul, and body. A spirit being created in Yahweh's image, we have a soul that is our mind, will, intellect and emotion, and we live in a body. I looked around from inside my body again and tried to breathe but there was no oxygen and I could not speak, although I knew I was out of oxygen and couldn't last but another few seconds. I saw a nurse and realized I was being wheeled on a table of some sort. She caught what I determined was my dying look, and slapped an oxygen mask on my face. I gasped for air and started to breathe again. How sweet was that breath! I pondered these things back in the recovery room but didn't understand anything that had just happened.

(5) We were traveling in our plane from Florida back to Texas when we were overtaken by a violent storm. I have discussed this miracle in a previous portion of this book.

(6) Once we were traveling in our plane to Las Vegas and had the trip all mapped out: where the places to stop for avgas were, where backups were, radio contacts, times of operations of the field base operators and the like. Upon arriving at one of the legs where we were scheduled to buy avgas we landed but found it closed. No problem, we had a second option. Flying in the mountains of the western states is known to be hazardous and requires the diligent planning we had done. We flew directly toward the new heading for avgas that showed to be about a thirty- minute flight. About fifty-five minutes later we still had not spotted our back up avgas field base operator. We had started to sputter some and knew we were running out of avgas (aviation gas) when we crossed a mountain and saw the landing strip. As we landed, we were literally running out of gas. We had surpassed our fuel range for the airplane some fifteen minutes earlier! It is good to know that we have a loving and miraculous Savior!

(7) There were five other times he showed me but I will end with this experience. We had recently done the annual on our plane, the required mechanical and service check up. The night before, I had flown to Waco, Texas to take the wife of a business partner to meet with her husband. We'd flown back to Midland, Texas with no problems indicated at all. My wife and I, along with a friend and his wife, were all loaded up in the plane to fly and attend the Texas Tech and Texas A&M football game. Having run through

my preflight checkup without any indication of problems, I did the engine run up. I saw no problem in the compression check and started the taxi for takeoff. I attained the correct speed for lift off and another uneventful take off. Climbing out, I watched as the altimeter gauge climbed to two hundred feet altitude, three hundred feet altitude, and three hundred twenty-five feet altitude and then the engine sputtered and quit! I quickly checked carb heating to try and restart the airplane. It wouldn't restart. Glancing at the airspeed I determined we could not maintain the altitude but a few more seconds as we were starting to buffet in the airplane already. Pilots realize that when you start to buffet the airplane, you are losing lift, and entering into a stall. When all the lift is gone, which is guaranteed when you lose airspeed, you fall like a rock from the sky. I turned to tell our passengers in the back seat to brace for a crash. The man's wife in the rear seat answered, "Ya'll don't be joking about that, it's my first time in a small plane." To which we replied, "We are not joking, get in a crash position!" I had one fleeting thought of desperation to God. Simply, "God help us!" I didn't even have time to voice this prayer. I knew immediately that if we were to survive I must nose the plane down to gain airspeed and lift. That, however, made no logical sense, as we had not nearly enough altitude to regain airspeed in time to make a controlled landing. I thought if I can just gain a little air speed, maybe we could flare the wings out just before ground contact and gain some lift before hitting. There would be no second chance if it didn't work, because we were going into an imminent stall and nearing the rock falling stage. Down we went and at the last second I flared the wings on the urging of God. We hit ground hard and I felt the tail crunch. Back in the air from the bounce we were turned around backwards with no control whatsoever as we went through mesquite trees backward. Finally coming to a stop, we asked if everyone was okay. Not a scratch on one person! However, the plane was destroyed and would never fly again. Getting out of the plane, I made the comment that now we would have to drive to the football game, so we better get loaded into the car and get a case of beer for our journey. In retrospect, I am sure the angels were discussing among themselves, "That boy is a little slow, do you think we saved the right airplane?" What a merciful and patient Messiah!

My purpose for sharing these experiences with you is not to make you think that I am special for I am not. My purpose is to have you *know* that Yahweh God is special, and He desires that you fellowship and know Him intimately. I am no one special as He is indeed no respecter of persons. He loves you and wants you to know that you can have a deeper, more personal and intimate relationship with Him, but only to the extent you hunger and desire Him. He knew you and loved you before you ever knew Him. Get hungry for Him. If you don't have that hunger, ask Him for it and He will mercifully grant it! Remember Yahshua's Scripture promise in Matthew 5:6 "Whoever hungers and thirsts for righteousness shall be filled!"

Where Did You Come From?
And Where Are You Really Going?

Chapter Four:
Heavenly Help & Protection

Yahshua has plans and desires to equip you against Satan's attacks if you seek Him with all your heart. As Joel 2:28-29 and Acts 2:17 state: "(28) And it shall come to pass afterward, that I will pour out My Spirit on all flesh, your sons and daughters will prophesy, your old men shall dream dreams, your young men shall see *visions*, (29) and also upon the servants and upon the handmaidens in those days will I pour out my spirit." So as you yield your flesh and natural man to *seek* Yahweh and His righteousness you will go on to dreams and visions from Him.

About fifteen years ago, I experienced a vision that may shed some light on the schemes of the enemy of our souls. This type of vision is much like seeing a giant movie screen in front of you and you may or may not interact in it while you are wide-awake. Here is the vision, as it was not really happening in the natural or physical realm: I was sitting on a couch in front of an older black and white television, the kind with one knob and twelve channels that must be turned at the television because there was no remote. Suddenly flashes of color streaked out of the black and white picture. I got up and changed the channel by walking to the set. As I began to turn the knob to change channels, the colors coming out of the black and white television changed. Finally, having exhausted all twelve- channel options, I turned off the television. The Lord then spoke to me, "what you have seen are the spirits of adultery, homosexuality, murder, hate, deceit, covetousness, pride, sexual immorality, witchcraft, death, and rebellion. These are the spirits that Satan is unleashing on America now."

Looking back over the past fifteen years, we can now see the results of these spirits at work. We now have removed even the Ten Commandments and any mention of God from public display, but it seems perfectly fine in our corrupt society to welcome witchcraft, homosexuality, widespread adultery and the like. There are even some believers who watch their horoscope and get their futures told, dabble in the new age mysticisms and the study of witchcraft such as Harry Potter. These are all entries into witchcraft and sorcery and will bring judgment by Yahweh and attack by Satan. They are popular because they demonstrate some power over the known and natural realm, and because you and I were created to walk in power according to the instructions our Creator has for us.

We must learn to protect our eye gates and ear gates, which are the windows of our souls. Be careful what you watch and listen to because what you consciously or sub-consciously store in your mind will produce results of some sort.

You can test this- just listen to sad songs all day for a week or so, and then be prepared to experience and live it! You will find that these sad songs will find a way out of your mouth and what you are doing is pronouncing your future! Better yet, listen to uplifting songs or praise songs and test the difference for yourself!

Remember the importance of what you speak. You may say, "I don't really mean that." Your mind does not know the difference, because words are spirit and bring you life or death, depending on what you speak and who you are agreeing with! You can find out how much affect secular television programs, news, and sitcoms are having on you, and how much you are addicted to the schemes and patterns of this world by turning off your television for a week, and then try a month. You may find you are more captive than you thought. Spend at least equal time fellowshipping with your Creator and studying. You may want to rethink your listening and watching habits, as they will produce the lifestyle you program for.

> **Your results in your life will be a direct product of what you've read, watched, and listened to, and then spoken! Proverbs 18:21 confirms this, "Death and life are in the power of the tongue, and they that love it shall eat the fruit of it."**

Those that guard their tongue shall have good fruit and those that refuse to align their tongues with life and prospering words will continue to experience the less than desirable results. *They cannot explain it, but for some mystery to them, they continually have bad luck!* Yahweh is no respecter of persons (He has no favorites) but is a rewarder of those who diligently seek Him and do His Word, because He watches over His Word to perform it. Learn to speak only words of blessings on yourself and loved ones!

Also, He has nine *Supernatural Power* gifts available for those who believe and obey Him as taught in 1 Corinthians 12:1-11 "(1) Now about spiritual gifts brothers, 1 do not want you ignorant. (2) You know that when you were unbelievers and pagan you were influenced and led astray by mute idols, (3) therefore I tell you that no one speaking by the spirit of Yahweh, calls Yahshua cursed, and no one can say Yahshua is Messiah except by the Holy Spirit. (4) There are different kinds of gifts but the same Spirit. There are different kinds of service but the same Messiah. (6) There are different kinds of workings, but Yahweh works all of them in all men. (7) Now to each one the manifestation of the Spirit is given for common good. (8) To one there is given a message of wisdom by the Spirit, to another the message of knowledge by the same Spirit, (9) to another faith by that same Spirit, to another gifts of healings by that one Spirit, (10) to another workings of miracles by that same Spirit, to another prophecy, to another discerning of spirits, to another speaking in unknown tongues, and to still another interpretation of tongues. (11) All these are the workings of the same Spirit, and He gives them to each one as He determines."

These are all supernatural gifts given to believers as He determines our need and belief. We don't control these gifts, for they are given as *He wills*. However, as you study them and believe them, you will begin to experience them yourself.

Once while ministering in Thailand, it was a Sabbath and the annual *March for Jesus Day* in America and other parts of the world. We were traveling toward the Cambodian border where the infamous "Killing Fields" of the slaughter of thousands of intellectuals had taken place a few years earlier. There were about nine or ten of us in the van and this included Lindsay, my daughter who was fourteen at the time. We were driving up a mountain to arrive at this Temple (Hindu or Buddhist- I can't remember) at the peak of the mountain. The whole mountaintop was filled with this giant structure (much like a pyramid), with statues of ogres and demonic looking creatures all around it and on it. We had determined to march for Yahshua (Jesus) around this temple on this *"March for Jesus Day!"* We could do this without offending anyone since we would speak to these demonic strongholds in English. We were planning to march around the entire complex seven times like when Israel brought down the walls of Jericho according to the biblical account. After having marched around this pagan temple once, we knew it took about ten to fifteen minutes to complete the circle. We were singing praise songs, commanding the pagan gods to depart, and for the temple and the demonic authority to come down!

Receiving a word of knowledge from heaven and the gift of supernatural faith, Roger my missionary friend spoke loudly and boldly, "Lord- if this is pleasing you, us marching around and praising you and pulling down the authority of these demon gods, give us a sign; put a rainbow in the sky when we come back around!" Still faithless after all the miracles I had seen and been involved in, my stupid religious thinking kicked in as I thought and muttered, "I can't believe he's saying this...he will destroy these new believers' faith!" Lindsay Ann, my daughter was not a new believer but our interpreter and van driver certainly was. Obviously, I hadn't thought this through; because no one would speak this without hearing from heaven, as no one can at will, put a rainbow in the sky except Yahweh! As we turned the corner, to my surprise there was a rainbow! Of course, sanity or possibly unbelief entered in again and I thought, "how lucky, I guess there was going to be a rainbow about this time anyway." I can't speak for the others, but I was relieved to see the rainbow. Then, as we started around again, to my disdain, I heard Roger speak again, this time even louder and bolder than before, "Lord if we are really pleasing you, give us another sign- put a second rainbow beside the first one!" Now that was too much! We would surely now lose all of our believers or at least they would think we are phony when this didn't come to pass. The Scriptures tell us that a prophet is false and has not heard from heaven and to not fear them if the thing spoken does not come to pass. When we had marched all the way around and preparing to turn the final corner I was still muttering, "I can't believe he said that." Turning the corner, we all looked skyward. There they were: *Two rainbows side by side!* I heard from heaven then, "Your unbelief did not help!" Surprised and saddened by my own lack of faith I apologized to Yahshua for my carelessly muttered words. Lindsay Ann raised her Kodak Instamatic camera that was draped around her neck and flashed two quick pictures of the side by side rainbows, as we continued our final four trips around the temple dancing and much bolder in our faith now! Sometimes, in spite of us, Yahshua does mighty acts of deliverance through the gifts of the Spirit! Several months later, we received a newspaper clipping from Roger that showed the temple was crumbling and engineers were concerned about the soundness of the structure!

This is a good time to share another experience I had concerning an *open vision* Yahshua gave me during a time of great trauma and personal hurt. I must state up front that I had never experienced nor did I really believe such an experience could or would happen to me, nor was I praying for it. I had just been informed that the person I had been praying salvation for wanted nothing to do with me, and in fact, wanted to end the relationship that we had. I walked into my Great Room (large living room) with tears in my eyes and reminded Yahshua that He had promised her salvation. As I stood there sobbing and saying, you promised, you promised, I looked up facing the East. As I did, I saw Yahshua coming in the room at a forty-five degree descent. Thinking I must have fallen asleep standing up and dreaming or hallucinating, I glanced to my right to see if my two-story rock fireplace was still there, and it was! Not understanding what was happening, I glanced quickly to my left to see if my staircase was still there and it was! By this time I looked forward and Yahshua was just to my left, still descending and about four or five feet above me. He appeared to be about 6'-2", with a long white robe on, a full dark beard, a smile, and eyes that pierced my very being. When He arrived at my side, He spoke, "You've done well, son!" I was thinking, "I will go anywhere with you," as the peace and goodness emanated from His presence. Then, to my horror He disappeared at the same forty-five degree slant and continued downward through my solid wood floor!

I remembered the scripture that said, "Test the spirits to determine whether they be from God or not." I quickly thought: if You are the Spirit of Yahshua that was born of a Virgin Mary, was crucified under Pontius Pilate, died and then three days later rose from the dead, then either come back and talk to me… or take me with you. Immediately, I was going through my wood floor following Him. Out of my body or in my body I could not determine, but it seemed as though all of my body was present. Following just behind Yahshua by some power I did not know, we traveled down into the earth at a high rate of speed at the same angle of descent. It seemed dark and occasionally I would sense the presence of sinister beings. Suddenly, we arrived at what seemed to be two giant gates or doors that seemed to spread twenty feet high and about forty feet wide each and met together in the center, much like a barn door might.

When we arrived, Yahshua stepped toward the doors in the center and I heard what sounded like an explosion, **BOOM!** The giant doors flung backwards and opened all the way. Standing on my toes to see over Yahshua, as I was directly behind Him, I saw a large cavernous room with monkey-looking beings that seemed to stand about seven to eight feet tall and were scattered about the room in disarray. They had shocked and terrified looks on their faces and immediately they each started dragging their right foot toward Yahshua. I looked to see what the matter was, why they didn't walk properly. Each of them seemed to have a clubfoot or it was cut and had a chain or something on it. At any rate, it seemed turned under their ankle somewhat and they could not walk without dragging it. Surprisingly, as they approached Yahshua they couldn't look at Him but looked down and aligned themselves on either side of Yahshua forming a line out from Him of about six on each side, back into the cavernous room. They were standing at attention, much like you would expect a military guard. I thought at the time- so these are what demons in hell look like. They are terrified! They reminded me of the monkey beings on the Wizard of Oz if you ever saw that movie. After they had lined up in great submission and respect toward Yahshua, He took about two steps toward them. As He did this He blocked my vision, as I did to not move when He did, and He was several inches taller than me. Trying to see and look over Yahshua's shoulder I thought, Lord I wish I could see, I wish I could see. Immediately, I was up behind Yahshua and able to see. Yahshua was standing between the first two beings which formed lines headed backwards into the cavernous room of two rows back away from Him. Yahshua extended His hand outward as though expecting something to be given to Him. It was then I saw His hand had no hole in it and it worried me. Later, I learned that He was pierced in the wrists, at the edge of His hand during crucifixion. What happened next surprised me as I saw the person whom I had prayed for and their hand was being placed in Yahshua's hand. Then He turned and we three went upward at the same angle and I found myself standing in the same place I had been in my Great Room with no Yahshua around and the person gone also. I quickly asked the Lord, "What just happened?" He replied with a question, "What do you think happened?" I said, "I don't know but it looked like you just saved her from hell, but she isn't dead yet."

My religious thinking had determined that no one was in hell until they died. I had apparently never really thought about the fact that until you are born again, you are (your spirit man) a citizen of hell because of Adam and Eve and mankind's fall. Yahshua responded sternly and quickly, "The gates of hell will not prevail against my praying believers!" I spoke again, "But Lord she's not dead yet." Then He spoke again saying, "She had been taken captive to do Satan's will." I answered again saying, "But Lord, you don't save people against their will." I had been under the false belief that everyone had a free will. He replied patiently, "No one wants to go to hell son, if they had a free will they would choose to be freed." I replied with testing, "Lord, I don't see anywhere in Scripture where you saved anyone against their will." He retorted quickly, "what about Saul of

Tarsus? He was breathing murderous threats against My people, son, and you know that out of the heart the mouth speaks. But Ananias and the believers in Damascus knew he was coming to do them great harm and they were praying that I would open Saul's eyes that he might really see My Truth. When I hit him with light he called Me Lord. That was the first time he had a free will, son. No one wants to be a prisoner of Satan in hell, they have been taken captive."

I didn't know Yahshua was quoting Scripture until I started trying to confirm, test, and prove by the Scriptures that everything I experienced was true. The *gates of hell Scripture* is in Matthew 16:18. The *taken captive by the devil* to do *his will* Scripture is 2 Timothy 2:26. The *out of the heart the mouth will speak* Scripture is Matthew 12:34 and the Scripture about Saul of Tarsus being converted is Acts 22:4- 21. So, dear believer, it is up to you also to **pray and believe for your loved ones**. Someone who loved you prayed you into the Kingdom also. I remember asking Yahshua later after I had learned these truths, "Yahshua, who prayed me into freedom and your Kingdom?" His answer was gentle as He brought a picture of my grandmother to mind, and I knew in my spirit that her prayers had been answered. Your prayers are extremely important. Pray and give Him thanks for His wonderful works! Yahshua didn't promise me that He would *save our relationship*, but He had promised that He *would bring her to salvation*. He was true to His promise. You may ask, is this really true? Did this all happen as you say? I can unequivocally answer: Every word is true. All liars will have their part in the lake of fire in hell and I would not care to join them by exaggerating one word spoken to you. The spiritual realm is more real than the physical realm anyway, as the physical realm is passing away, but the spiritual realm will remain.

I believe that visions are one of the nine power gifts of the Spirit, which is called Discerning of Spirits. This gift allows us to see in the spirit realm. There is no gift called *a discerning spirit,* nor is there a *gift of discernment,* which so many erroneously report. This gift is to *discern spirits, to recognize spirits, or in other words to be able to see in the spirit realm.* Spirits sometimes can even be angels, which the Scriptures call *ministering spirits to the heirs of salvation.*

Chapter Five:
Fleeing Sin

Since the Messiah Yahshua died for our sins, our transgressions against His instructions, "Let not sin reign in your physical body, that you should obey it and its passions and desires" according to Romans 6:12. Continuing in Romans 6:16-18 "(16) Know you not, that to whom you yield yourself servants to obey, his servants you are to whom you obey; whether of sin toward death, or of obedience toward righteousness?" (17) "But Yahweh be thanked, that you were the servants of sin, but you have obeyed from the heart that form of doctrine which was delivered to you." (18) "Being then made free from sin, you became the servants of righteousness."

The Holy Spirit will always warn us and help us flee the temptation to sin. The question is do you want to flee? Your answer to that question will determine whether or not you receive blessings or curses from this day forward. Stop and make the decision and determination for life! Say, "I choose to flee all manner of sin." If we will quickly obey His warnings, we will escape all the traps of Satan and it will become more difficult for him to trap us with his schemes. If we give in to our flesh nature, we become hard hearted and soon cannot even recognize sin. Yahshua warns us in Hebrews 3:13-19 "(13) But exhort one another daily, while it is called *today*, lest any of you be hardened through the deceitfulness of sin. (14) For we are made partakers of Christ, if we hold the beginning of our confidence steadfast until the end; (15) While it is said *today* if you will hear His voice, harden not your hearts, as they did in the rebellion, (16) for some when they had heard, did rebel: however, not all that came out of Egypt with Moses. (17) But by whom was He grieved forty years? It was with them that sinned, whose dead bodies fell in the wilderness. (18) And to whom did He swear they would not enter His rest, but to them that did not believe? (19) So we see that they could not enter in because of their unbelief."

Flee sin today, which means immediately. One critical area Satan has been allowed a foothold to destroy our ability to flee sin is in the area of unforgiveness. We tend to not want to forgive others. We want forgiveness ourselves, for sure, but for some reason don't want to extend that mercy to others. We may say we forgive them for offenses, but then we will not *forget*! Of course, the result is the same. You might still be capable of remembering mentally, but it must have no more hold on you, because that opens the door for Satan's attack against you. Do check yourself out in this area, because that means you are obeying Satan, not your Heavenly Father. Remember, if you don't forgive others, you will not be forgiven, as Yahshua explains in Matthew 6:14-15 "(14) For as you forgive men their trespasses against you, your Heavenly Father will also forgive you: (15) But if you will not forgive men their trespasses against you, your Heavenly Father will not forgive you."

If you are not forgiven, you should expect that Satan will hold you in bondage and blindness with all manner of the operations of the flesh nature, spoken of in the book of Galatians Chapter 5. All of the areas of the flesh nature listed there can bring judgment for hell fire. Flee this critical area of sin by *forgiving and forgetting* by giving it over to Yahshua, He will repay them much better than you could anyway. Pray for those that have offended you and break the cycle of curse off of yourself and your loved ones! *Flee sin today!*

Galatians 5:19-24 gives us those manifestations or results of obeying the desires of our flesh or obeying the instructions of Yahweh: "(19) Now the works of the flesh are evident, which are: adultery, fornication, uncleanness, lewdness, (20) idolatry, sorcery, hatred, contentions, jealousies, outbursts of wrath, selfish ambitions, dissensions, heresies, (21) envy, murder, drunkenness, revelries, and the like of which I tell you beforehand just as I told you in the past, those that practice such things will not inherit the Kingdom of Yahweh." Most people who produce these fruits of the flesh nature sincerely believe that they will still inherit the Kingdom of Yahweh or heaven. According to the Scripture, they are sincerely wrong! "(22) But the fruit of the Spirit (spirit of a born again person) is love, joy, peace, patience, kindness, goodness, faithfulness, (23) gentleness, and self-control. Against such there is no law (instruction)."

There are no instructions against these. 1 Corinthians 1:18-21 further states: "(18) For the message of the cross (Yahshua's death for you) is foolishness to those who are perishing, but to us who are being saved it is the power of Yahweh. (19) For it is written: I will destroy the wisdom of the wise; the intelligence of the intelligent I will frustrate." This may be the reason that it is difficult for extremely gifted or intelligent people to become like small children and believe the Scriptures unto life. Continuing, "(20) Where is the wise man? Where is the scholar? Where is the philosopher of this age? Has not Yahweh made foolish the wisdom of the world? (21) For since, in the wisdom of Yahweh the world in its wisdom did not know Him; Yahweh was pleased through the foolishness that was preached to save those who believe."

Galatians 5:24-26 further testifies: "(24) And they that are Messiah Yahshua's have crucified the flesh with its passions and desires. (25) If we live by the Spirit, let us also walk in the Spirit, (26) Let us not become conceited, provoking one another, envying one another."

If we really understood Satan's plans to use our own flesh nature to destroy us, we would flee from all manner of sin. We are given pictures of the fun and excitement of sin, but never really look at the results of sin. If we really study the attributes of the flesh nature in Galatians 5 above, we could better understand the product and the wages of sin. Sin only produces *DEATH and DESTRUCTION*, while purporting to bring only excitement and pleasure. Yahweh's Spiritual Laws are the rules that were written by our loving Creator to protect us and provide for us. Our obedience to flee sin brings His blessings. It is *grace*, which gives us power to flee sin and allows us to escape sin. Some seem to think that grace allows us to continue to sin without the results and wages it produces. The Holy Scriptures couldn't disagree more in Hebrews 10:26-31 "(26) For if we sin willfully after we have received the knowledge of the Truth, there remains *no more sacrifice for our sins*, (27) but a certain fearful judgment and fiery indignation that will devour His adversaries. (28) He that despised Moses Law died without mercy under two or three witnesses: (29) How much greater punishment will He find you worthy of after you have trampled under your feet the Son of Yahweh, and counted His Holy blood of the covenant agreement by which you were cleansed an unholy thing and have ridiculed the Spirit of Grace? (30) For we know Him that has said, Vengeance belongs to Me, I will repay, says Yahweh. And again, Yahshua shall judge His people. (31) It is a fearful thing to fall into the hands of the living God."

Chapter Six:
Hearing from Heaven

The instruction of Yahweh further declares that He will talk with you. Yahshua (Jesus) states, "My sheep (followers) will hear My voice, they will not listen to the voice of a stranger." (Thief, liar, Satan) Does Yahshua (Jesus, the Lord) still speak to people? Of Course! He is true to His Word. He tells us that He is no respecter of persons. In the Scriptures, the book of Malachi, the Creator, Yahweh, says, "I change not." Additionally, Hebrews 13:8 speaks of Yahshua the Messiah (the only begotten Son of Yahweh), and states: "He is the same, yesterday, today, and forever." Many have asked the question: How can you be sure it is the Holy Spirit speaking to you in your spirit? The answer is rather simple. You will only have three sources of hearing; The Holy Spirit who is the Spirit of Yahshua or Yahweh (or an angel sent by Him); Satan and his camp of demons; and lastly, your own flesh nature. Yahshua speaking to you through the Holy Spirit will always *agree with what the Holy Scriptures say.* The Holy Spirit will always exhort, encourage, help, and caution you. So will an angel sent by Yahweh. Satan and his camp will *always disagree* with what the Holy Scriptures say. This camp will accuse the believers, belittle believers, and lie to take away or diminish the power that is available from Yahweh to help and deliver you from every trap or circumstance. They will use a partial Scripture and twist it (making it wicked) so that those who do not know the Scriptures might easily be deceived. Their plan is to always bring fear, condemnation, failure and death. Remember, Satan even challenged Yahshua during His forty day fast with partial Scriptures. Challenged Yahshua, Who is The Word made flesh! Finally, your flesh man will always decide in favor of your flesh nature and what is pleasing to the flesh. Recently, I heard a man say, "**One word from Heaven can change your life forever**." It is so true. Further, He states to Jeremiah 1:12 "You have seen correctly, Jeremiah, I am watching over My Word to perform it."

So when you obey Him, you will start to hear more and more, and be revealed more and more Truth, as you decide to yield your heart to His instructions, because He is watching over His promise to bring it to pass. Why would He talk more with you if you won't obey what you already know to do? That would require Him, your merciful Creator, to bring judgment on you, and He is long-suffering (patient) toward you that you would not perish. It is His desire you live, and that you live more abundantly. Furthermore, If He is talking to you and you are so preoccupied with your life and *your* plans, how could you possibly hear Him?

Recently, I heard of a young man attending a Bible study. The teacher said that our Creator Yahshua still talks to people. He admonished them to pray to Him, listen, and then obey Him. That night, on the way home from the Bible study, the young man prayed, "If You still talk to people, talk to me, I will do my best to listen and obey." Driving on home he felt he needed to stop and buy a gallon of milk. He didn't need milk. Could this be the Lord he wondered? This wasn't much of a requirement for obedience so he thought; I'll just stop and buy some.

Is that you, Lord? He bought the milk, thinking that it wouldn't go to waste, and he could always use it. Then as he was approaching Seventh

Street he thought he heard, "turn here." That wasn't the way home, so he kept driving. Before he reached the next block he felt again strongly that he had to turn on Seventh Street. Turning the car around, he said, "Lord, if that's not You I am really looking stupid here." He drove a few blocks when he felt he should stop here. He stopped the car and looked around. All the lights were off in the homes and he felt sure they were all in bed. A very average neighborhood, certainly not the best area of town, but not the worst either. Then he thought he heard, "take the milk to that house across the street." Glancing there, he noticed all their lights were off also. He stayed in the car, feeling foolish. Again, he felt the urge to take the milk across the street to that house. Grudgingly, he said, "Okay Lord, but if this is not You, they are going to be really mad at me for waking them up." He got out of the car, crossed the street, and knocked on the door. He heard a man shout gruffly, "who is it?" He was about to flee when the man opened the door, asking, "What do you want?" "Here," the young man said, pushing the milk into his hand. The man looked at the young man, took the milk and began shouting in Spanish as he disappeared down the hall. A woman came saying, "We had many large bills this month and had no money left to buy milk for our baby. We just prayed to the Lord that He would show us how to get some milk for our baby. We asked Him to send an angel. Are you an angel?" The man returned following his wife carrying the crying baby down the hall toward the front door where the young man stood talking to the woman. The young man reached in his pocket and gave them all the money he had to help them. So, you tell me, does Yahweh (God) still talk to people? Pray to Him, listen and obey, and you, too, will find out. Start talking to your Creator through the relationship made available by His Son, Yahshua. As you study the Scriptures you will find promises made to you about His provision: peace, joy, life everlasting, healing, protection, food, shelter, clothes, abundance in finances to allow you to be a giver, wisdom, and direction for your life. Basically, His provision for any need you have in life, including miracles. He confirms His Word with signs and wonders when we become a *doer* of His Word according to Mark 16:20. I have, and now you will experience His miracle working power, as you become a doer of His Word by putting action to your faith!

One time while I was fishing above the Galilee on the Mediterranean Ocean, I had an interesting experience. I was just below the U.N. checkpoint about one mile from the border of Lebanon. It was a very beautiful place, with about seventy-five yards of white sand for miles and miles. On the land side of the beach was a picturesque park area. After casting several times, I heard *"Get you out of here!"* I turned to see who spoke, and there was no one present, so I continued to fish. I cast a few more times and heard a little louder, *"Get you out of here!"* Looking behind me, and very aware of Muslim extremists from the area, I scanned the area again but saw no one. Could that be the Lord, I wondered? Surely not, since He knew I was planning on fishing here today. I continued to fish. The water was truly beautiful and I was enjoying the tranquil beauty of the place. Once again I heard, "Get you out of here!" this time stern and loud. Sensing this had to be the Lord as no one else was around, Alarmed, I quickly obeyed. Besides, no one I knew talked like that. I reeled in, loaded my pole and tackle box, and drove toward Jerusalem. After driving several hours, I decided to stop on Mount Carmel, the mountain where Elijah challenged the false prophets. It was a rugged, forest-like area. I pitched my tent and settled in, as it was getting dark. I then heard something just outside my tent... animals of some sort. I peeked out to see several large wolves circling my tent! These were large enough to pass for German shepherd dogs! I sensed that Yahshua was showing me the spiritual condition of Israel. Even though I am a black belt in Karate, I felt helpless and defenseless against these wolves. Maybe I should not have been, but I was fearful! I thought to myself, everyone in Israel seems to have a machinegun except me- I have a butter knife! Although that amused me it was a long night. So, at sunup the next morning, I broke camp, quickly packed and left. (I probably broke all records for time in breaking camp) Driving back toward Jerusalem, I stopped about sundown, determined to camp out at the park area at Emmaus, near Jerusalem. I found several great campsites, but was given no peace as to where to camp. It was nearly sundown, and I was frustrated that the Lord had given me no peace concerning a campsite, because it was Friday and nearly the Sabbath. He kept bringing to mind a nice couple that had invited me to stay in their home at Bet Shemish, if and when, I returned from the Galilee. Finally, I said, "Okay Lord, I will call them."

I found their phone number and drove out of the park area to a pay phone. I dialed to hear them exclaim, *"Where are you? We have been praying for you for three days. The Lord told us to pray, because your life was in danger!"* I answered, "Well, thank you for praying." Then I told them where I was and I was only five minutes from their home! Upon arriving, I walked in to their beautiful home and they had satellite television. It was an English CNN newscast of the ongoing missile attack by Muslim extremists on the area where I had been fishing! I turned to watch, and was surprised at the devastation to the area I had just come from. We serve a loving and miraculous Redeemer! Thank goodness He still talks today!

I know He talks to believers, so I will share with you an earlier experience I had in the early part of 1993. I was walking down the hall of my offices to join another believer to pray in our boardroom for the salvation of someone that I had prayed for every day for about six months. As I started down the hall, I heard, "Don't pray for their salvation again today." Immediately I said, "I rebuke you Satan!" I thought I heard a chuckle and then the words, "You can't rebuke Me, son." I said, "Lord if that is You why would You ask me not to pray for her salvation?" He replied, "Because, either you believe I can save them or I cannot, what do you believe?" I replied, "Of course I believe you can, I sure wish you would!" He asked, "Do you believe it is My will that she be saved?" I replied again, "Of course it is Your will Lord. It is Your will that none would perish." He patiently spoke again, "Do you believe I have heard you?" I said, "Of course I believe You heard me Lord, I believe You hear all my prayers, or else I would not even pray." He then spoke something so profound and different to my thinking and I didn't even realize it was a direct quote from Scripture in 1 John 5:14-15 "(14) If you ask anything according to My will, you can *know* I've heard you, (15) and if you *know* I've heard you, you can *know* you have the thing you asked for."

He said, "What would you do if you really *know* you have this thing you've asked for?" Continuing, He answered Himself saying, "You would be thanking Me! You would dance before Me! I want you to start thanking Me!" Lord, I replied, "I don't see the results of that salvation and from my perspective; it looks like she's worse." He replied softly this time and said, "You are required to walk by faith and not by sight." I remembered the story of the unjust judge in Luke 18:2-8 and remembered that by much asking the lady had gotten her request. I had thought that by continuing in persistent prayer, He would finally act on my behalf. He quietly and firmly said, "I am *NOT* the unjust judge!" He requires an action that shows your belief. You don't have to believe in your head, but you must believe with your heart. The Bible says that whatever is stored in the heart; the mouth will speak, according to Matthew 12:34. Store His promises in your heart and head by memorizing and meditating on the Scriptures. Of course, there have been innumerable times when I had a question, He would just drop the answer into me and I would know. Sometimes He would give a

Scripture for an answer and I would have to go look it up to see what it said. Once He did that when I asked Him where America was in the Scriptures. His reply went against everything I believed up to that point. He said, "Go to Revelation 17:1 and read, son, there you will see America for who she really is." What a shock it was when I read, "Mystery Babylon the whore- who rules over many *waters*." (Peoples or nations) Mystery, as it has only been a nation for a few hundred years. He showed me the reason it is not easily recognized by believers in America is that we don't really like the name He has given us. It is contrary to our thinking. There are three Babylon the Whore's: (1) A government, (2) a church religious system and (3) a land and they all receive Yahweh's wrath. Needless to say, that was a surprise, but not nearly the surprise He told me regarding the fate of America. In the year 2000, I was camped out all alone with my Bible on the Sea of Galilee in Israel for eleven days. I asked Him where a safe place would be in America when Jacob's trouble started. I won't shock you with His answer, I'll save that for later, but you should know it is extremely important that we work on our intimacy with Him, **Now**!

He hears heart rendered prayers!

I heard a famous preacher say once, "If God (Yahweh) doesn't judge America, He will need to go back and apologize to Sodom and Gomorrah!" Of course, He is not going to apologize; He is and will be righteous and right ruling. Revelation 18:2-5, 8, 17, and part of 18 gives us a glimpse: "(2) And the angel cried mightily with a strong voice, saying, Babylon the great is fallen, is fallen, and is become the habitation of devils, and the home of every foul spirit, and a cage of every unclean and evil bird. (3) For all nations have drunk the wine of the wrath of her fornication, and the rulers of the earth have committed fornication with her, and the merchants of the earth have become rich through the abundance of her delicacies. (4) And I heard another voice saying, Come out of her My people, that you do not partake of her sins, and that you would not receive her plagues. (5) For her sins have reached heaven, and Yahweh has remembered her lawlessness (transgressions). (8) Therefore, shall her plagues come on her in one day, death, and mourning, and famine; and she shall be utterly burned with fire: for strong is Yahweh who judges her. (17) For in one hour such great riches are come to nothing, and every ship captain, and all the company of the ships and sailors, and as many as trade by the sea, stood far off, (18) and cried when they saw the smoke of her burning."

Chapter Seven:
What Are You Saying?

The Scriptures are the foundation for your prayer requests. Find a Scripture promise concerning your need, and pray what He promises. In Mark 11:23-24 Yahshua states: "(23) For truly I say to you, whoever says to this mountain (problem), Be removed and cast into the sea; and shall not doubt in his heart *(your mind might still doubt as that is where the battle for rulership is)*, but shall believe that those things which he says shall come to pass, he shall have whatsoever **he says**. (24) Therefore I say to you, whatever you desire, *when you pray, believe that you receive* them, and you shall have them."

Hopefully, you can see that what you *say* about a situation is extremely important. You must have words that agree with your Creator to get His results for your life. You must *say* what He *says* and stay in agreement with His promise, and not agree with the current facts, especially if the current facts don't line up with what the Scriptures promise. Ephesians 4:29 says: "Do not let evil words come out of your mouth but only what is edifying for the hearer."

Surprise, <u>you are always a hearer of your own words</u>. Evil words are those words that don't agree with the Truth, which is the Word of Yahweh, the Scriptures. Beware of "careless" words and phrases.

71

Examples of these ungodly and extremely careless phrases of speech common today are; "I wish I could just die," "It just kills me," "It just makes me sick," "I'm always broke," "I never have enough," "I always catch the flu," "I'm so tired," "I always eat too much," and "I'm not going to make it." Guard your tongue! Remember, life and death is in the power of the tongue, according to Proverbs! Desire to have your words agree with His because He never said He would follow you, He Commands each of us to *follow Him!* Yahshua affirms the importance of your words agreeing with His in Matthew 12:36-37 "(36) But I say to you that every careless word that men shall speak, they will give account for on the Day of Judgment, (37) for by your words you will be justified and by your words you will be condemned."

We are Commanded to fight the good fight of faith in 1 Timothy 6:12 by taking hold of our confession, or in other words, what we speak agreement with.

> **Have you been speaking about your problems and obstacles or speaking to them?**

If you have been speaking about the problem, you are affirming or agreeing with the enemy of your soul to establish his plans against you! *Speak to your problems!* Speak what Yahshua, The Word, says about them. Then you will have guaranteed victory! Romans 10:8 says: "What does the Scripture say, (referring to Deuteronomy 30:14), the Word is near you, even in your mouth and in your heart (spirit) which is the Word of faith, which we preach."

Understand that you can have no lasting victory in the physical realm, until you have victory in the spiritual realm, and that starts in your heart and is spoken from your mouth! Yahshua said in John 6:63b "My Words are Spirit and Life."

All words are spiritual, but words that do not agree with Him produce destruction and ultimately death.

Remember, it is what you believe in His Word (Yahshua) **speak and do** that brings His power and deliverance according to Romans 10:9 "If you confess with your mouth Yahshua (who is The Word) and believe in your heart that Yahweh raised Him from the dead, you shall be delivered."

The Greek word for delivered is *"sozo"* which means "to be saved, healed and made whole." This Scripture refers to so much more than just getting born again and becoming heaven bound, it is also about our deliverance and healing from every attack by hell's plan. We are commanded in 2 Corinthians 5:7 to "Walk by faith and not by sight." Just as real as the law of gravity is in the physical realm so is His Word Spiritual Law in the spiritual realm. Whether or not I believe in gravity or not, if I jump off the roof of a building it is safe bet that I will go down and not up. Since Yahshua's Words are Spirit and Life, if you appropriate them by believing them and speaking them, you will receive life or His results every time.

You may not see the results yet, continue to speak them and give Him thanks. The god of this world (Satan) will do everything in his power to show you just the opposite of what you pray for. He wants you to give up and speak his results-failure, defeat, sickness, lack, poverty, death, etc. You see, Satan has been condemned and he wants you to have the same destruction that has been promised him. Remember what Romans 8:1 says: "There is now no condemnation to them which are in Yahshua the Messiah, who walk not after the flesh nature but after the spirit,"

Remember the story of Peter in Matthew 14:27-31. Yahshua had walked on water and when Peter saw Him he was afraid and asked if it was really Yahshua. Furthermore, if it was really Yahshua, Peter asked for Yahshua to call him to walk on the water toward Him. This gave Yahshua only one answer to give Peter saying, "It is I, come." Peter got out of the boat and walked on the water toward Yahshua. Immediately a storm arose and Peter being afraid began to sink, and cried out to Yahshua, "Save me!" Yahshua stretched forth His hand, caught Peter and spoke to him, "You of little faith. Why did you doubt?" We can see from this example that Yahshua expected Peter to stay focused in faith on what His instructions were, "Come." If we will keep our eyes focused on Yahshua, who is the Word, we can overcome the storm. We also notice that Yahshua did not cause the storm, but Satan did, because when they got into the ship, the storm ceased. It is my belief that every time you determine to obey Yahshua, Satan the enemy of our souls will also send you a storm, a distraction that is designed to be large enough to get your eyes and thoughts on the distraction and get you to fearfully speak the evil report of the greatness and vastness of the storm. Satan's plan is to get you to take your eyes off of the instructions from Yahshua and His Scripture promise you are standing on. The storm seems to get greater so as to manipulate us to only see the storm. If we become blinded by the storm, we lose focus on what we know to be Yahshua's instruction. If Satan can get you over into the physical, flesh realm, he can beat you. However, if you'll wage the war against him spiritually, with your mouth continually agreeing with the Word of Yahweh, you'll beat him every time. Because Yahshua has destroyed the works of Satan according to 1 John 3:8b "For this purpose was the Son of Yahweh manifested, that He might destroy the works of the devil."

I remember reading the Scripture in Isaiah 54:17 "No weapon formed against you shall prosper and I will refute every tongue that accuses you. For vengeance belongs to me, I will repay declares the Lord."

I said, "Lord, if no weapon formed against us believers will prosper, how come all my believing friends are losing jobs, getting divorces, and going through all manner of torment? This Scripture doesn't appear to be working!" Yahshua replied, "No weapon formed against you will prosper." I replied again, "they sure seem to be prospering against us!" Yahshua replied again, "I destroyed the works of Satan!" I replied, "If that's really so, then why are all these bad things allowed to happen?" Yahshua answered, "I destroyed the works of Satan, but not *your tongue!* The power of life and death is in *your tongue!* He (Satan) shows you the storm and you agree with it with your mouth rather than speaking My Word!" Hosea 4:6 confirms this as Yahweh speaks, "My people perish for lack of knowledge."

Since faith (trust) is how we are Commanded and instructed to walk, it is important that we find out what Yahweh's definition of faith is. Hebrews 11:1 says: "Now faith is the substance of the thing hoped for, the evidence of things not seen."

What is the thing you hope for? Of course it is the Scripture promise you are standing on, and requires no faith if you can already see it. Hebrews 11:6 goes on to tell us: "Without faith it is not even possible to please Yahweh, because whoever comes to Him must believe that He exists and is a rewarder of those that diligently seek Him."

Faith comes by hearing and hearing the Word of Yahweh according to Romans 10:17. Amos 3:3 asks: "Can two walk together except they be agreed?"

In other words, you cannot follow the Messiah and say whatever you want. You must train your tongue to agree with Him and His Words. Every time you depart and speak careless words, you have departed from Him! He is still the Truth. I remember, I asked Yahshua what a *careless* word was once. His answer was, "Every word that disagrees with Me is careless!" Once again, In Matthew 12:36 Yahshua warns us: "But I say unto you, that every careless word that men shall speak, they shall give account for on the Day of Judgment, for by your words you will be acquitted and by your words you will be condemned."

Chapter Eight:
Stand! Give Thanks & Receive!

A dditionally, the Scripture in Psalm 100:4 says, "Enter into His gates (His presence) with thanksgiving, and enter into His courts (intimacy) with praise." Learn to give thanks in any and every situation, as He is watching over His Word to perform it. Wouldn't you thank Him if you really believe you have the thing you are hoping for? Will you be one who will have the corresponding action that says you believe His promise? 1 John 5:14-15 says a beautiful promise: "(14) And this is the confidence that we have in Him, that, if we ask anything according to His will, He hears us: (15) and if we know that He hears us, whatsoever we ask, we know that we have whatsoever we ask of Him."

Arc you asking according to His will? His Word and His Will are the same. So give Him thanks and stand until you see the thing hoped for! Don't throw away your confidence just because you don't see the results you desire yet. Remember, whoever believes in Him (His Word) will never see shame according to Isaiah 8:14 and Romans 9:33. Shame only comes with failure and you cannot fail if you stand on His Word! Learn to praise Him for all the wonderful blessings and provision He has made for you. Praise Him (Yahweh) because He alone is worthy to receive blessing and honor and glory! Man cannot receive praise, honor, and glory, as it will bring forth pride, and the scriptures say that pride always leads to a fall. Pride is what made Satan fall. Do not allow men to praise you, as it will make you fall also.

Men (or women) who are *free* do not starve. Remember Moses' words from Yahweh to Pharaoh, "Set My people *free* that they may come and worship Me." Free men and women have learned how to worship. Yahshua confirmed to me what another believer and servant of Him had been told, "Since the time of My man Adam, not one man has ever starved to death, while praising Me." Many have starved to death, but not one man has ever starved who would worship Him! Raise your hands to Heaven, worship Him by singing praises to Him and saying words of thanks and praise to Him. Learn to give thanks and praise to Him in any situation you find yourself in. He is the answer to lack and defeat. His greatest desire is that you are free and know Him intimately, that you may come and worship Him. **Ask Him to make you free**. Whom the Son sets free is free indeed!

> *When the grocery stores are empty, praise Him!*
> *When it appears hopeless, praise Him!*

What do you do when the scripture promise doesn't seem to be manifesting or happening? 2 Corinthians 1:24b says: "By faith you *stand*." Ephesians 6:11-13 declare, "(11) Put on the whole armor of Yahweh that you might be able to *stand* against the schemes of the devil. (12) For we wrestle not with flesh and blood, but against principalities, powers, against the rulers of the darkness of this world, (Satan's army) against spiritual wickedness in high places, (13) therefore put on the whole armor of Yahweh that you may be able to *stand* in the evil day and having done all, to *stand*." Colossians 4:12b says, "Laboring fervently for you in prayers, that you may *stand* perfect (mature) and complete in all the will of

Yahweh." Hebrews 10:35-36 admonishes us: "(35) Cast not away your confidence, (in the Scripture promise) which has a great reward. (36) For you have need of patience, that, after you have done the will of Yahweh, you may receive the promise."

Fear is the opposite of faith and the primary enemy of faith. I am not talking about the fear of the Lord. That kind of fear is actually a Holy awe and great respect. The Proverbs tell us the beginning of wisdom is to fear Yahweh, to hold Him in high esteem and reverence. The enemy of your faith is the kind of fear that worries you. Just like faith has power to bring or manifest results that our Creator meant to bless us, fear has power to bring forth Satan's results to harm us and do evil. In 2 Timothy 1:7 we are told: "Yahweh has not given us a spirit of fear, but of love, power, and a sound mind."

Fear is spiritual; it is faith in Satan to bring about his plan. The reason Satan brings the storm or those apparent manifestations of results, which are the opposite of the promise you are standing on or praying for, is to get you to speak agreement with him. When a synagogue ruler was given bad news about his daughter being dead, Yahshua told the ruler immediately, "*Fear not, only believe*, and she will be made whole." It is important that we put fear down immediately by finding or remembering and speaking Yahweh's promises rather than looking at the natural situation and allowing fear to continue against us. How important is it to banish fear from your mind? Revelation 21:8 speaks of fear as an attribute that will bring judgment for hell: "But the *fearful*, and unbelieving, and the abominable, and murderers, and whore seekers, and sorcerers, and idolaters, and *all liars* shall have their part in the lake of fire which burns with fire and brimstone: this is the second death."

Some demonic schemes against you will only be destroyed by prayer and fasting. **Fasting gets rid of your unbelief**. When the disciples could not cast out a demon for a father from his son, they were surprised. Yahshua had given them (and you now) authority to cast out devils, and they had been doing just that. They asked Yahshua privately why they couldn't, and He answered them in Mark 9:23, *"because of your unbelief,* this type only goes by prayer and fasting." Remember, in Mark 11:23-24, Yahshua assures us, "if you *can believe*, all things are possible to him who believes." So fasting puts your spirit man in control and brings the battle out of the physical realm where Satan cannot win as the god of this world. *Fasting gets rid of unbelief.* Fasting and prayer are an unbeatable combination for Satan. Learn to fast gradually by skipping a meal, then two meals, then a day, week, multiple weeks, etc. Learn how to prepare your body for a fast by not eating sweets, drinking coffee, cokes, etc. prior to your fast. Study your Bible on fasting and read books on how to fast and how to end your fast safely. Putting your spirit man in control over your flesh will bring you great rewards. Why would *I tell you* that He gives authority to cast out devils? Luke 10:19 says: "I give unto you power to tread on <u>all the power of the enemy</u> and nothing shall by any means hurt you."

You have power given you now to overcome *ALL* the power of the enemy. Mark 16 says that believers will cast out devils. Also, He said. "No one born of woman (flesh), is greater than John the Baptist, but the least of those *born again*, are greater than John the Baptist." Are you born again? You are if you meant it when you said your prayer earlier. You have Yahshua and His nature living inside of you. We will discuss in more detail casting out devils later.

Isaiah 58:6-14 gives some of the benefits of fasting: "(6) Is this not the fast that I have chosen? To loose the bands of wickedness, to undo the heavy burdens and to let the oppressed go free, and that you break every yoke? (7) Is it not to give your bread to the hungry, and bring the poor that are cast out into your home? When you see the naked that you cover him; and that you hide not yourself from your own flesh. (8) Then shall your light break forth as the morning and your health shall spring forth speedily and your righteousness shall go before you and the glory of Yahweh shall be your rear guard. (9) Then shall you call and Yahweh shall answer; you shall cry and He shall say, here I am. If you will take away from yourself the bondage, and stop pointing your finger with blame and speaking vanities, (10) And if you draw out your soul to the hungry, and satisfy the afflicted soul; then shall your light rise in obscurity, and your darkness be as the noonday; (11) And Yahweh shall guide you continually and satisfy your soul in drought and make your bones healthy, and you shall be like a watered garden, and like a spring of water whose waters never fail. (12) And they that are of you shall build the old waste places. You shall raise up the foundations of many generations. And you shall be called the repairer of the breach, the restorer of paths to dwell in. (13) If you turn away your foot from the Sabbath, from doing your own pleasure on My Holy Day and call the Sabbath a delight the set-apart day of Yahweh, honorable and honor Him not doing your own pleasures nor speaking your own words. (14) Then you shall delight yourself in Yahweh and I will cause you to ride upon the high places of the earth, and feed you with the heritage of Jacob your father, for the mouth of Yahweh has spoken it."

When you fast according to your Creator's design you will loose the bondage of wickedness and remove heavy burdens from people. That's what Yahshua did after His fast as recorded in Mark 1:13-28—He started His ministry on the Earth, cast out devils, healed the sick, and taught with authority. Note also in verse eight, your own health will break forth speedily. There are physical rewards to fasting. Your body isn't so busy using all of its energy to digest food and can rest and heal itself. When you obey verse nine, and stop pointing your finger to blame others for all of your own problems and weaknesses, then Yahweh won't have to judge you because you are willing to judge yourself. When you feed and help others as mentioned in verse ten, and then His light will be your light even in the darkest times. Verse thirteen says when you stop doing your own thing and your own pleasure on His Holy Sabbath (Friday sundown to Saturday sundown). As you honor Him, He will cause you to be honored and exalted because verse fourteen says you will rise up on the high places of the earth. He will give you all the inheritance promised to Abraham, Isaac, and Jacob, or *ISRAEL*. He guarantees these benefits for He has spoken it! So, you decide, should you be fasting? Yahshua said that when He is gone away, then His disciples *WILL FAST!*

In Daniel chapter 10, we read that Daniel fasted for 21 days giving up some foods. And on the 24th day, Daniel saw an angel who came and instructed him on questions that he had. Daniel's fast was apparently only a partial fast. Daniel had no pleasant bread, meat, nor wine. I am not positive of the fast being meatless only though, because many times in the King James and other translations, meat is translated for grain or food. Daniel's fast was possibly a vegetable and water fast but probably a water only fast. When the angel arrived he assured Daniel that he had been sent by Yahweh on the very first day of Daniel's fast, exactly when Daniel had afflicted his soul and set his heart to chasten himself and began seeking to understand the Words of Yahweh. But a regional demonic strong man or power, called the Prince of Persia, withstood the angel until the 24th day. Michael, the archangel, was sent to help the angel and successfully broke him through and the angel arrived saying, "And now I am come to make you understand what shall befall your people in the last days." The point I want to make here is that angels are dispatched from the throne room of Heaven when you fast and pray. So when you need Heavenly results and answers, you would do well to fast and pray. These two are the power twins—in the spirit realm—fasting *and* praying. Don't leave off either. To fast and pray removes all unbelief. I mentioned earlier the plans your Creator has for you are good to give you hope and a future. Continuing in Jeremiah 29:12-13 "...then you will call upon Me and come and pray to Me and I will listen to you. (13) You will seek Me and find Me when you seek Me with all your heart." Get hungry for His Truth. Seek and desire Him with all your heart.

Do not be ashamed of the gospel or the Words of Yahshua for it is the power of Yahweh to deliver, save, provide for, make whole and heal everyone who believes them according to Romans 1:16. Another important reason to make a choice to abandon all shame of His Word and power is that Yahshua clearly warns us in Mark 8:38 "Whoever is ashamed of Me and My Words, him will I be ashamed of before the angels and My Father (Yahweh) in heaven."

As you change your thought patterns to line up with the Scriptures, you are repositioning yourself to receive His blessings. You will have to make the decision for yourself to let Him increase in you that you may decrease. John the Baptist made that decision and announced, "He must increase and I must decrease." He will not force His Ways on you. He spoke in Matthew 5:6 saying: "Blessed are those who hunger and thirst for righteousness, for they shall be filled."

This repositioning will show you what position you are in Him. You are justified *in Him* or *declared righteous*! Not going to be in the future-you are declared righteous *now*. Remember the Scriptures say in Hebrews 13:8 that, "Yahshua is the same, yesterday, today and forever." Most of us have no problem believing the miracles and the power of Yahweh happened back in the biblical times or yesterday. Most of us have no problem even believing we will be with Him in heaven, and the promises will all be true tomorrow or in the future. Where we must grow is the *today* part, the *Now* faith. Not tomorrow or someday "in the sweet by and by" faith. Understand we *are* positioned *in Him now. Today* is the day of deliverance; *today* is the day of victory. "*Now* faith is the substance of the thing hoped for" as is recorded in Hebrews 11:1. When you can *see* something, it no longer requires faith, but faith is required *until* you can *see* the thing hoped for, according to Romans 8:24-25.

Faith is not *producing* faith at all and will not bring results for you until you believe it <u>*NOW* and *not going to be* in the future</u>! Faith without action is dead, just as the body without the spirit is dead according to James 2:26. It may still be faith but it is *dead* faith and can produce nothing. *Act as though you believe the word or promise you are praying!* Remember He is *I AM* that *I AM*- not only am going to be in the future. He answered Moshe (Moses) in the desert when Moses asked Him "Who should I tell Pharaoh Who sent me? Tell him *I AM* sent you!" Sometimes people pray for needs and concerns continuously, but they are praying future tense. Please, Father do this for me *someday*. That kind of prayer is vague and has no faith. Sadly they are wasting their breath because He is limited by His own Word and He cannot go against Himself. He requires you believe Him and give Him thanks as though you already have the thing hoped for, according to Mark 11:23-24. It may not have physically manifested yet but you must know you have the victory already. We walk by faith and please Yahweh and we do not walk by sight.

I will share a few experiences of ministering in Thailand in 1997. We were praying for the sick, lame, and diseased in the jungle close to Buriram, Thailand. They led us to a lady for prayer that was on a mat and unable to walk. The interpreter said that the doctors there had told her they did not know what was wrong with her but that she had tumors appearing on various places of her body. They directed my hand to her stomach. It was extraordinarily large and at first glance it appeared she was pregnant. Knocking my knuckles against her stomach, I felt it was as hard as a rock, like you might expect a cast to feel but there was no cast. Looking at her left leg, I saw it was twice the size of her normal right leg, and it too, was hard like a cast. I was certainly no miracle worker, but I did and do know the Messiah Who is! We prayed the prayer of faith and laid hands on her according to Mark 16. I cursed this obvious operation of Satan and commanded Satan to be loosed from the lady in the name of Yahshua. His Word teaches us that whatever we bind on earth is bound in heaven and whatever we loose on earth is loosed in heaven in Matthew 18:18-19 it says: "(18) Truly I say to you, whatever you bind on earth is bound in heaven and whatever you loose on earth is loosed in heaven. (19) Again I say to you, that if two of you shall agree on earth as to touching anything, it shall be done for them by My Father in heaven."

Then, a word of wisdom from our Messiah came from heaven and admonished her to agree with us and not say anything contradictory to this prayer request, only to stand by faith and start thanking Him for absolute victory before she saw the desired results of this Scripture promise! She agreed and we walked away from the area with her apparently in the same situation as we had found her. Thank Yahweh that He keeps His promises! Two weeks later she was up and attending the assembly of believers worship service after having walked many miles to the service! She had spoken agreement with us continually and given thanks for her healing. Yahshua came and healed her, as He always will, when we believe in our hearts and confess with our mouths that He is God come in the flesh and confess His promises! He is the answer to all our needs; healing, salvation, and lack, because He is our Deliverer, our ever- present help in times of trouble.

Another time, we were in the jungle and they brought us to a paralyzed Buddhist to pray for. I had the interpreter tell him that our God was alive and was a healing God. I asked him what Buddha had ever done for him. He replied nothing that he was aware of. I told him that our God, Yahshua, would heal him if he would receive our God as his Lord, Savior and Healer. He said that would certainly be agreeable to him. This man was paralyzed from a stroke and bedridden. Not much of a bed really as it was a wooden ply board raised up about two feet off the ground with dirt all around and under it. We placed our hands on him as Mark 16 says that believers will lay hands on the sick and they will recover and we certainly qualified as believers. We prayed the prayer of faith for him confessing the Scripture promise. Immediately, he was up on his feet praising and walking about through the chicken poop on the dirt all around us. Nobody had to instruct this man to raise His hands to heaven and worship in thanksgiving. He knew and did this instantly dancing and praising! We all had taken off our sandals, as this was a sign of respect of entering their area or home even though there was no floor anywhere or even walls, as the tree house was nearby and was used only in the rainy season. So we all rejoiced with the man that was healed instantly by believing the Words from Yahshua that He is Healer and Lord over all. It didn't really bother any of us to dance barefooted in the chicken poop but I was certainly ready to clean my feet and put my sandals back on!

Without exercising and developing our faith it is not even in the realm of possibility that we can please Him, according to Hebrews 11:6. You may ask why and the answer is simple. It is because He gets great pleasure in blessing us with His results and plans for us. Jeremiah 29:11-13 says: "(11) I know the plans I have for you, speaks Yahweh, plans of peace and not evil, plans to prosper and do good to you. (12) Then you shall call upon Me and pray to Me and I will hear you. (13) **And you shall seek Me and find Me when you seek Me with all your heart**."

Yahshua said in John 15:8, "Herein is My Father glorified, that you produce much fruit, so shall you be My disciples." This is how we bring glory to our Heavenly Father- produce fruit for His Kingdom! If we will not exercise our faith and trust Him more and more, how will we receive the wonderful plans and blessings He intends for us? In John 15:9, Yahshua continues: "As the Father has loved Me, so have I loved you, continue in My love."

Remember, John 14:21 teaches us that loving Him is synonymous with obeying Him. As you obey Him your faith will be tested and you will grow in faith and be continuing in His love. This is the way to put yourself in position to receive His blessings for your life, your family, the people you come into contact with, and even those you pray for and don't even know.

> ***You become a doer of His word and He backs it up with signs and wonders following!***

Where Did You Come From?
And Where Are You Really Going?

Chapter Nine:
Religion vs. Relationship

B eware of Satan's schemes to take you to hell if you already belong to a religious denomination or affiliation! Please, be sober and alert! We are warned in 2 Timothy 2:15, "Study to show yourself approved, rightly dividing the Scriptures, a workman that need not to be ashamed at Messiah Yahshua's appearing." Sadly, most churchmen will be ashamed at His appearing. **Religion** is without relationship and is <u>*DUTY*</u>. It looks good for appearance sake, but leaves a person having made no real inner changes, empty and yet full of hypocrisy. Yahshua told the religious leaders of His day that the drunks and whores would enter into Kingdom before they would in Matthew 21:31b; "Truly I say to you, the drunks and the harlots will enter the Kingdom before you do." The religious think that by their own righteous living they will enter the Kingdom. They cannot enter in because of their self-righteous pride. They will not humble themselves and repent because they think everything is fine. The drunk and the harlot, however; know they are sinners. When they hear the Truth they are much more apt to humble themselves and repent. What about you and me? Do we also believe we have no areas in our lives to humble ourselves and repent of? You may fit in socially and be a believer according to your denomination or affiliations' standards, but Yahshua may have a totally different standard! He defines *believers* in Mark 16:16-18 "(16) He that *believes* and is baptized shall be saved; but he that *believes not* shall be damned (cast into hell). (17) And these signs shall accompany those that *believe*; In My Name they shall cast out demons; they shall speak with unknown tongues (pray in the spirit), (18) they shall take up serpents (power over the demonic realm) and if they drink any poison (unintentional of course) it shall not harm them, and they shall lay hands on the sick and they shall recover."

Yahshua certainly has a different perspective for defining *believers* than most of our religious affiliations do. Since He is the One we stand in front of on Judgment Day we all need to be very open to grow up spiritually and change into His image! It is surprising how many people trust in a religion that has not properly met His test. If there is no supernatural power and results that confirm His Word (their prayers answered), no casting out of the demonic spirits, no supernatural healing, no miracles, no prayer language in unknown tongues, then according to Mark 16:20 one should deduct that there is about a 100% possibility that they have missed the mark somewhere. Saul's (Paul) prayer in Acts 4:29-31 affirms this: "(29) And now Messiah, behold their (religious rulers) threats: and grant Your servants all boldness that we may speak Your Word. (30) By stretching forth Your hand to heal; and that signs and wonders may be done in The Name of Your set apart Son, Yahshua the Messiah. (31) And when they had prayed, the place was shaken where they assembled together; and they were all filled with the Holy (set apart) Spirit and they all spoke the Word of God with boldness."

Yahshua told the religious leaders of His day in Matthew 23:27-28 "(27) Woe unto you scribes and Pharisees, you hypocrites! You are like white washed tombs, which really appear beautiful outwardly, but within are full of dead men's bones and of all uncleanness. (28) Even so, you also appear righteous to men, but inside you are full of hypocrisy and iniquity."

The outward appearance looked fine, but they never got "born again" and let Yahweh clean them up from the inside out! We see why the process of being *born again* is so important in John 3:1-7 "(1) There came a man of the Pharisees named Nicodemus (A religious leader in Yahshua's day), a ruler of the Yehudans (Jews), (2) the same came to Him at night and said to Him, Rabbi, we know You are a teacher come from Yahweh: for no man can do these miracles that You do, except Yahweh be with him, (3) Yahshua answered him saying, Truly, Truly, I say to you, except a man be born again, he cannot see the Kingdom of Yahweh. (4) Nicodemus replied, how can a man be born again when he is old? Can he enter a second time into his mother's womb and be born? (5) Yahshua answered, Truly, Truly, I say to you, except a man is born of water (natural birth and also references the water of the Word) and of the Spirit, he cannot enter the Kingdom of Yahweh. (6) That which is born of the flesh is flesh; and that which is born of the Spirit is spirit. (7) Marvel not that I said to you, you must be *born again*."

> *Understand this truth, you can go to church every day the door opens and be "good" all of your life and end up cast into hell! You must be born again!*

A **True Relationship** with Yahshua is based on *DESIRE* and receiving forgiveness and new life where there is peace and a new hope for the person. Then the cleaning up process begins in that person with a new spirit in them, and they go to work on their souls (mind, will, intellect, and emotions) by studying Scriptures, and making lifestyle decisions of change. Religion without relationship with Yahshua is without power and equals zero *anointing*. The *anointing* is tangible power delivered from Heaven and comes when we abandon ourselves to study and grow in Him and His Word. It is His anointing that breaks the yoke (bondage) from us. We can receive more and more of His Holy Spirit and anointing when we surrender to His Plans, His Words, and His Commands to us. As we surrender, even to the point of raising our hands in worship without anger toward anyone or doubt, as is commanded in 1 Timothy 2:8, He is faithful and just to use us and *anoint* us with His power for service to others. Think of raising your hands in surrender to Him, much like a surrendering army might raise their hands. The beauty of this surrender is that it is one of choice. Yahshua quoted Isaiah 61 in Luke 4:18-19, saying: "(18) The Spirit of Yahweh is upon Me because He has *anointed* Me to preach the good news to the poor, He has sent Me to heal the broken hearted, to preach deliverance to the captives, and recovering of sight to the blind, to set at liberty them that are bruised, (19) and to preach the acceptable year of the Lord."

What Yahshua left off was the remainder of the verse in Isaiah sixty-one, which is "and the Day of Vengeance of Yahweh." It was not the time while Yahshua was still on the earth yet for the Day of the Lord or Day of Vengeance, the repayment to Yahweh's enemies who are the disobedient and unbelieving ones. We will look into this matter of the Day of the Lord and His vengeance later by discussing His bowls of wrath. For a short time, this is still the Day of Deliverance as John 3:16 states, "For Yahweh so loved the world that He sent His only begotten Son, that whosoever would *believe* on Him might be *SAVED*." As I previously mentioned, the Greek word for *saved* is *"Sozo."* It means "to be saved, made whole, *delivered*, and healed." The kind of *believing* mentioned here is absolute humbling of one's self to receive the Words of Yahshua like a small child, by asking Him to change us into His image, with actions that reflect that belief and trust.

Many religious people have been socially accepted in their group or denomination and they have never considered what the Scriptures really say. Most of the "Church" has never really scrutinized what they believe so they are easily led down the wide path of destruction. That is why a refiner's fire or testing such as the Great Tribulation is needed, so that we may establish what we believe. Not every action that seems religious and good in our eyes will produce fruit that will remain. It is in the realm of possibility that our understanding or our denomination's understanding of the Scriptures might be incorrect and not really agree with His Word established in heaven!

I have an acquaintance who was a Pastor and leader in a respected denomination. He lost a great deal of blood from his body when the main trunk artery to his heart ruptured. The doctors said it just was not possible for him to live, having lost the amount of blood that he had. He reports having an after life experience, after he was pronounced dead in the ambulance in route to the hospital. He has lived to tell the story. In his book, "Placebo," he tells of the last days' church being warned by the Lord that they have taken a placebo of religion as accepted doctrine, instead of a Right Spirit of relationship between the Creator and the created. He warns that the last day's believers are not even close to being ready to stand in the Lord's presence. One of the amazing things he was shown was the born again believers going home to heaven. *What shocked him, was of those dying on the earth, less than 3% had made it to heaven!* You can order the book at (601)736-4955 or write Howard Pittman, P.O. Box 107, Foxworth, Miss, 39483. You can also order an audio cassette taped account of his story and they are 2 for $5. It is an astonishing wake up call for believers!

There are many new Bibles being translated and paraphrased but beware! Most of them leave out or change Scriptures that are vital to agreeing with what is established in heaven. If the words you invoke as prayers don't agree with the Scriptures that are established in heaven, you cannot possibly get heavenly results. An example of this would be in

Matthew 17:21. The King James has *fasting and prayer* are both necessary for getting rid of our unbelief and casting out devils; but the NIV and other paraphrases of the Bible leave off *fasting*! So, you the reader are left powerless against the devil, because all the Scripture requirements are not met. There are literally hundreds of places in the many new Bible translations, where vital information necessary to fight and beat the devil, are twisted and omitted from The Word that is established in heaven! Study to show yourself approved! This is the famine of the Word mentioned in Amos 8:11 "Behold, the day is coming says Yahweh, that I will send a famine on the land, not a famine of bread or water, but a famine of hearing the Words of Yahweh."

This is clearly in the last days as Amos 8:9 states: "And it shall come to pass *in that day*, says Yahweh, that I will cause the sun to go down at noon, and I will darken the earth during the daytime."

Remember, *"in that day"* is an idiom that always refers to the *"Day of the Lord"* or the seventh millennium and the darkening of the sun is recorded in the Book of Revelation in the Bible. According to 1 Corinthians 3:12-15 "(12) Now if anyone builds on this foundation gold, silver, precious stones, wood, hay, or stubble; (13) everyone's work and their intent will be revealed for The Day shall declare it (the Day of the Lord), because it will be revealed by fire; and the fire (fiery trials of tribulation) shall test everyone's work for what manner it is. (14) If anyone's work shall remain on the foundation they have built, they shall receive a reward. (15) If anyone's work shall be burned up, they shall suffer loss: but they shall be saved; even through the fire." We can understand that wood, hay, and stubble will not withstand the fire. These might be acts from misguided understandings of Scripture or possibly acts done with selfish purposes and intentions.

Yahweh knows the motives of our hearts! Check your motive. Are you doing these righteous acts and good deeds to be seen and acclaimed by men? Be honest here, because Yahshua promises if that is your real reason for doing them, you have received your reward in full! There is no reward left- not heaven, not a robe of righteousness, nothing! These actions will burn up and not remain. The righteous acts done with obedience, a correct understanding of His Word, which is already established in heaven, and done with compassion and *unselfish motives*, would equate to the gold, silver, and precious stones. These actions would not burn up, but only be refined in the fire. Many religious people are not really open to His Commands and His Truths, so their sin remains. Understand that Yahweh, our Creator, is a consuming fire according to Deuteronomy 4:24 and Hebrews 12:29. John the Baptist confirms this in Matthew 3:10 "And now also the ax is laid against the root of the trees; therefore every tree that does not produce good fruit, will be cut down and cast into the fire."

Many have been given explanation and commentary on what their particular sect of Christianity believes as Yahweh's doctrine. They have never asked the Spirit of Yahweh for truth on any given tradition or Scripture. Some have never heard from heaven even one time! They must not believe Yahshua's promise that His sheep would hear His voice. There are actually ministers and pastors who have never really studied the whole Bible by themselves and asked the Creator to reveal Truth to them. They just blindly accepted what their denomination's seminary taught them through commentary. Yet, unbelievably, these same leaders become teachers of His Word. Sadly, it is the blind leading the blind and they will both fall into a ditch! Much of today's "church" are busy winning souls or followers of their denominations *for their denomination* but that is not The Command of the Father! Matthew 23:15-16a states: "Woe unto you, scribes and Pharisees (religious), you hypocrites! For you devour widows' houses (they use all your tithe and gifts to support the "church" system) and travel sea and land to make one proselyte (follower of your denomination) and when he is made, make him twice the son of hell as yourselves. (16a) Woe unto you blind guides..."

Sadly, some "believers" have never won even one soul for the Kingdom of Heaven, although they may have won many to their church denomination. They don't understand that they must produce *fruit for the Kingdom* or be cast into the fire themselves according to Yahshua in John 15:5-8 "(5) I am the vine, you are the branches: He that abides in Me, and I in him, the same produces much fruit; for without Me you can produce nothing.. (6) If a man does not abide in Me, he is cast out like a branch that is withered, and men gather them and they are cast into the fire and are burned up. (7) If you abide in Me, and My Words live in you, ask what you will and it will be given you. (8) Here is how the Father is glorified, that you produce much fruit, so shall you be My disciples." James 1 explains what Yahshua's definition of True Religion is: James 1:26-27 "If any man among you seems to be religious, and does not control his tongue, he deceives his own heart, and that man's religion is in vain. (27) Pure (acceptable to the Father) religion is this, to visit the fatherless and widows in their affliction, and to keep yourself from being polluted by the world."

> **If you consider yourself religious, please, I implore you to open your heart and mind to search for truth.**

We are not promised tomorrow, but the Scriptures warn us in Hebrews 3:13 "But exhort one another daily, while it is called Today; lest any of you be hardened through the deceitfulness of transgressing His Commands and Torah (instructions)." Understand, you may think you are obeying and not transgressing His instructions and commands, but the probability is extremely high that we all are missing it in some areas. Don't allow your heart to be hardened.

Why did the religious leaders of Yahshua's day not see that He was the Messiah? They certainly were expecting Him. Let's look at some of the prophecies they had. First, they knew Messiah Yahshua would come as a man (or in flesh) according to Isaiah 9:6. Second, they knew He would be born of a young virgin woman according to Isaiah 7:14. Third, they knew He would be born in Bethlehem according to Micah 5:2-5. Fourth, they knew He would arrive in Jerusalem riding on a colt according to Zechariah 9:9. Fifth, they even had a detailed account of the Messiah's betrayal in Psalm 41:9 and Zechariah 11:12-13. Sixth, Psalm 22 gave the details of His death, and Seventh, Isaiah gave us the reason for His death in Isaiah 53:1-12. Lastly, He was declared to be the Son of Yahweh by resurrection power in Psalm 16:10. Did they just not understand these prophecies? Of course they *understood* the prophecies; they had debated and memorized all the Scriptures from birth. Could it be that a religious spirit had them blinded? Remember, Sha'ul (Paul) was blinded until the scales were removed from his eyes when Yahshua hit him with His light. Could we, too be blinded in some critical areas? Most likely, so let's look at the normal life and character of a Pharisee or any religious person. They probably did not cheat on their spouses. They probably never murdered anyone. They were not particularly mean people. They probably loved their families. They were probably not habitual liars or drunks. I doubt they were gossipers. I expect, like us, they were well accepted in their denominations and religious affiliations. Their families, friends, and co-workers probably respected them, and agreeing with them, had the same *understanding* of the Scriptures. But something went drastically wrong, because they missed the time of their Heavenly visitation! Maybe, like some of us, they had a *hidden* minor sin or two. We could probably understand that, as they, like us, would want to appear to their friends, family, and peers to be righteous, godly men. Could the hypocrisy of *hidden sin*, allow Satan to cause spiritual blindness in them, and maybe *even in us?* Is it in the realm of possibility, that we also have some misunderstandings, and some misconceptions of the Scriptures? Maybe our friends, associates, and families agree with us on the Scriptures. Why did most of the believers and followers of Messiah Yahshua come from common people, and not from the leaders and teachers; the Sadducees and the Pharisees?

> **Is it possible that these teachers and leaders had much to lose? Their positions of acceptance, provision, favor and authority were all at risk! Could history be repeating itself with us? Would Satan set the same traps for us?**

Possibly, but his traps don't have to snare us. Ask Yahshua to make your heart and mind like putty in His hands because we are the clay and He is the potter. Ask Yahshua to guide you into All Truth. *A religious cult would be best described as following a follower and not searching the Scriptures diligently and obeying them yourself!* Diligently study with an open mind, especially, when we realize that we have had much added to and compromised from the time of Constantine's rule. This sun god worshipper changed many of the dates and seasons and commands of Yahweh to fit his system of church *UNDER* government. Deuteronomy 4:1-2 states: "(1) Therefore hear and obey Israel (believers and followers of Messiah Yahshua), the Commands and Statutes which I teach you, do them that you may live and possess the land (and promises) which Yahweh your Elohim gives you. (2) **You shall not add to The Word which I give you, neither shall you diminish anything from it, but you shall keep** (do/obey) **the Commandments** which Yahweh your Elohim has Commanded you." <u>We are not to add anything, especially pagan rituals, or take away anything, especially His Commands from His Word</u>.

Some "believers" openly admit that they do not believe in miracles, casting out devils, laying hands on the sick and seeing them recover or speaking in unknown tongues! *One might need to ask: what then are you a believer of?* They are *mouth professing but not heart possessing!* Do you believe in some denominations' doctrine that denies the availability and accountability as True Believers to do these things, according to Yahshua's own definition of a believer? A few things are certain: If you don't believe in miracles you will never see one! If you don't believe in casting out devils then you better have a state owned and managed insane asylum, because it will be full. If you don't believe in Yahshua healing the sick through the laying on of hands by believers and/or the anointing by oil as James 5:14 commands, then you better have plenty of doctors, nurses and hospitals! If you don't believe in praying in the spirit (unknown tongues) then be prepared to never have the prayer life and results you should have. You won't have to worry about praying in unknown tongues anyway, because you never will. You must desire truth and believe *before* receiving any of His promises and help. What sort of oil do you anoint with as a believer? Of course the power of Yahweh is available to the spirit-filled believer. The oil is symbolic of the Holy Spirit, so you can use any oil. However, in biblical times they used essential oils as they had a much better understanding of them. There is a great book out called "<u>Healing Oils of the Bible</u>." You may order this book and many therapeutic essential oils at <u>www.younglivingworld.com</u>. You will be amazed at the book's documentation of biblical references of the use of spices and essential oils. Samples of essential oils are frankincense, hyssop, myrrh, rose of Sharon, rosewood, sandalwood, cedar, eucalyptus, cinnamon, and the like. Remember, the wise men brought Yahshua frankincense and myrrh for His anointing. These oils in a pure form were valuable aids to healing different maladies and illnesses of the body. They still are!

Scientific research has discovered that therapeutic grade essential oils contain healing properties that can rebuild cells on a molecular level and even reprogram the DNA to repair itself!

Doctrines of devils have crept in amongst believers. What are some of these tricks Satan uses to keep us away from the anointing and the power of Yahweh? The anointing is the power, which is extended us through Yahshua to do the things He did. Healing and setting captives free and preaching the good news mentioned above in Luke 4:18-19. Understand it is *good news* to a blind person to be allowed to see, it is *good news* to a impoverished person to have life abundantly, it is *good news* for the demon oppressed and possessed to be set free, it is *good news* for the maimed and sick to be made whole and healed, it is *good news* for the dead to come to life again, and it is certainly *good news* to us all to have life eternally with Him. The doctrines of devils are what take away from the power and magnificence and unending mercy of Yahweh towards mankind when He sent Yahshua. They would say that Yahshua is not the same, yesterday, today and forever. They would tell you that His promises are not for you. They would tell you all the supernatural powers and miracles are passed away. They would pray something like this, "if it be your will Father, heal them." That prayer is a doctrine of devils because they have determined that it might be Yahshua's will for you to stay sick and die. They do this because of their own spiritual pride, not wanting to look bad if the person doesn't get healed because of unbelief. They have never *seen* a miracle so they don't believe. They don't understand that you must first believe then receive from heaven, not see and then believe. Think about it with me: They think that it might have been Yahshua putting this sickness or some cancer or disease that could kill on them to teach them something! I wouldn't, and I'm sure no loving parent would put a sickness or disease that could kill their children on them to teach them a lesson of some kind. I would take it myself before I would put it on them. Yahshua came and took it on Himself, also. He loves you more than you love your children if you are a parent. Yahshua never once said it is My will that you don't be healed or set free from some oppression of Satan. That is the reason He came. Once a leper came to Him declaring Yahshua could heal him *if* it was His will. According to Matthew 8:3 "Yahshua put forth His hand, and touched him saying, *I will*; be you clean. And immediately his leprosy was cleansed." **Learn this truth: Yahshua came to deliver, make whole, heal and set captives free and according to Luke 10:19, He has given you that same authority**.

Isaiah 53:4-6 says it better: "(4) Surely *He* has borne our sicknesses and carried our pain, yet we did esteem *Him* stricken by Yahweh and afflicted. (5) But *He* was wounded for our transgressions; *He* was bruised for our iniquities (lawlessness): the punishment for our peace was upon *Him*; and by *His* stripes we are healed. (6) All we like sheep have gone astray, we each turned our own way; and Yahweh has laid on Him the iniquity (rebellion and lawlessness) of us all." From this Scripture we know that all of our sickness, disease, pain, poverty, and death due us was placed on *Him*. Paid in full by *Him*.

There is a law called <u>Double Jeopardy</u> in our legal system that states that no one can be tried and punished for the same crime twice. In the Kingdom and courtroom of heaven, the accuser of the believers, Satan, is putting these things on us but he has no legitimate or legal right to do this, because Yahshua paid the punishment for us. Of course in Hosea 4:6 Yahweh states that His people perish for lack of knowledge. You can stop him and reverse the plan and schemes of Satan, and the doctrines of devils, by standing and saying what Yahshua said, paid for, and promised you.

Remind Satan that he is the condemned one, not you! Yahweh inhabits the praises of His people, so Satan cannot stay around when you praise Messiah Yahshua!

Chapter Ten:
Traditions of Men

Matthew 15:3 Yahshua (Jesus) answered them, asking, "Why do you transgress the Commandments of Yahweh (God) with your traditions?"

Matthew 7:9 and Yahshua (Jesus) said to them, "full well you reject the Commandment of Yahweh (God) that you may keep your own tradition."

Matthew 15:6 "...thus you have made the Word of Yahweh (God) of none effect by your traditions."

Matthew 15:9 "but in vain they do worship Me, teaching as doctrine the commandments of men."

Deuteronomy 12:32 "Whatever I Command you, you shall observe (keep/do) it; you shall not add to or take away from it."

Christmas, Easter, Lent, etc. consists of taking pagan, heathen festivals and applying them to the worship of Yahweh (God). Scripture condemns this practice. We should not ascribe a clear satanic practice invented by demons and assimilate it to the worship of Yahweh (God)! 1 Corinthians 10:21 "You cannot drink of the cup of Yahweh (God) and the cup of demons; you cannot partake of Yahweh's table and the table of demons."

103

Jeremiah 10:2-4 clearly states: "(2) Hear the Word the Lord speaks to you. Thus says Yahweh: *Learn not the way of the heathen,* and be not dismayed at the signs of heaven, for the heathen are dismayed at them. (3) For the <u>customs</u> (traditions) of the people are vain. For one cuts a tree from the forest, the works of the hands of the workman, with an ax (4) they deck it with silver and gold, they fasten it with nails and with hammer that it move not."

Clearly, this is the practice of the Christmas tree. Why was there concern about the signs of heaven? The winter solstice- December 25th, was the birthday of every sun god. This included the Egyptian, Assyrian, Roman, Babylonian, and even Nimrod's birthday. At this time each year the sun would start to return in size, as it would get closer to the earth. *We can absolutely be sure that our Messiah and Savior was not born on this date.* To better understand the origin of pagan traditions that have crept into Christianity get the book called "<u>Fossilized Customs</u>" available at <u>www.fossilizedcustoms.com</u>. A quick example would be a summary of Lent. Lent was the 40 days of weeping for Tammuz, the Babylonian and Syrian sun god, mentioned in Ezekiel 8:14. It seems he was hunting on his 40th birthday and was gored to death by a wild hog. So, they would weep for Tammuz for 40 days, then kill the wild hog on the 40th day and have it for their Ishtar or Easter ham. Ishtar or Astarte was later called Easter, and was the wife of Tammuz, and was also known as Mother Nature and the fertility goddess. It was and is an abomination to Yahweh. She was also known as the Queen of Heaven.

So, why would we want to come out of paganism and celebrate the Feasts of the Lord? Because Yahweh Commands us throughout *all* your generations! Some would call them *Jewish* Feasts but the Word declares they are **Feasts of the Lord**. Yahshua actually fulfilled the Spring Feasts down to the day and hour when He came the first time, and He will fulfill the Fall Feasts when He comes again, also down to the day and hour. Understanding the Feasts of the Lord gives us insight to His actions and Words. Also, remember that the Feasts of the Lord and all of what is commonly called the *Old Testament* are a shadow or a rehearsal of things to come. They teach us what is to come, and what to expect. For example, the Exodus from Egypt by Israel, and their great and miraculous deliverance by Yahweh, was an example for us for our soon coming *great exodus from the world during the Great Tribulation.* That alone is a compelling reason to study and keep the Feasts of the Lord, which include the weekly Sabbath.

> **They are a pattern of what is to come! They teach the rehearsals and Appointed Times of Yahweh.**

What about the Feast of **Hanukkah**? This feast is not a command of Yahweh, but it is certainly one the Messiah kept. It is the Feast of the Dedication of the altar. In 167 BC, Antiochus Epiphanies was overthrown as he sacrificed the pig on the altar and commanded the Jews to eat and worship the pig at the threat of death. Of course, you probably know that pig is a biblically unclean animal and NOT food, whether you and I say it is food or not. So it was an abomination for them to be forced to eat it and for it to be placed on the altar. The Jews, led by the Maccabee's, revolted, restored, and rededicated the Temple on this day. This is a season of dedicating ourselves. 1 Corinthians 3:16 says "know you not that you are the temple of Yahweh (God) and that His Spirit dwells in you?" We are to let our lights shine before men. Some may remember the childhood song: "this little light of mine, I'm gonna let it shine!" The secular humanistic culture of the heathen was being forced on the Jews and those who wished to obey Yahweh. Today, the culture of self and pleasure seeking is being forced on us by the courts (removal of 10 Commandments, homosexual rights, etc). We even now have homosexuals demanding to be married!

Matthew 24:37 offers a sobering reminder, when Yahshua, the Son of Man returns, it will be as the wickedness of the days of Noah were! Judgment by water of the flood came then, this time we are promised judgment by fire!

> *Since Yahweh is a consuming fire according to Hebrews 12:29 and Deuteronomy 4:24, it is sensible to ask Him to burn everything up in us that's not from Him. NOW! Why wait until you have to stand before Him and give account? If He doesn't show you changes you must make then at least you will have an excuse and answer for Him when you stand before Him. You may rest assured that all of us have hidden areas that we are probably not aware of or haven't properly understood, repented from, or were improperly taught.*

We are instructed to come out of that self-pleasing, pleasure seeking culture and walk as a light in a darkening world, or we can disobey and just be "normal" and not be a testimony or light to anyone. In 1 Corinthians 3:1-5 we read: "(1) Know this also, that in the *last days* perilous times will come. (2) For men will be lovers of their own selves, covetous, boasters, proud, blasphemers, disobedient to parents, unthankful, unholy, (3) without natural affection, trucebreakers, false accusers, incontinent, fierce, despisers of those that are good, (4) Traitors, heady, high minded, lovers of pleasure more than lovers of Yahweh (God) (5) having a form of godliness, but denying the power thereof, from such turn away."

We can certainly see that these are the last days. Today self- pleasure is most desired in our society. Who are those who are lovers of pleasure more than seekers of Yahweh (God)? Just about every one of us should probably take stock. Who are those that have a form of godliness?

Certainly not the unbelievers... the whores, liars, thieves, pimps, drug pushers, etc- they don't have any form of godliness. I suspect the living God is speaking of believers here. Possibly churchgoers or professing "Christians" but they are "luke warm" at best. They just want to fit in and be accepted by our culture (traditions), their family, friends, and peers more than they want acceptance of Yahweh (God)! Verse five of 1 Corinthians 3 states that *these believers have a form of godliness but deny His power*. They don't want anything to do with casting out devils, speaking with new tongues, miracles, or laying hands on sick people and seeing them recover as Mark Chapter sixteen defines a believer in Yahshua's own Words. They really don't understand that these gifts and miracle working power from Yahshua are necessary for His plan and people to overcome the forces of darkness. Otherwise, Yahshua would not have made them available.

They are deceived into believing that they can overcome by their own righteous living and can obtain victory over Satan without these gifts from Yahshua. Apparently, they believe these gifts are passed away or at least not necessary for personal victory and that Yahshua and His people are no longer at war with Satan. Nothing could be farther from the truth. This is the work of the antichrist or anti- messiah spirit. The spirit of religion is the demonic spirit that encourages "believers" to deny the power of Yahweh. "Believers" are encouraged to be good people and it is basically man trying to achieve acceptance and heaven, based on how our lives appear to others and compared to others. 2 Timothy 3:5 warns us of the last days' people, "Having a form of Godliness but *denying His power*, from such turn away." We need and must appropriate by believing and receiving His gifts. Especially the powerful Spiritual Gifts available to His body of believers mentioned in first Corinthians chapter twelve, verses eight through eleven. He says He does not want us ignorant of them. Of course, most of us are just that, ignorant of them. For some thoughtless reason, we believe that He is not the same today, yesterday and forever in that area. Remember, He is no respecter of persons, and He watches over His Word to perform it.

What about you and me? Who will we obey? Will we come apart and be holy as He Empowers us and Commands us to be?

> ***Or will we, too, fall in the trap set by Satan and follow man's traditions taught as Yahweh's doctrine?***

Will we determine that if so many other believers including our friends, families, and maybe even our now deceased family lines followed and obeyed these traditions that are extra biblical, then it couldn't be bad for us? Surely they searched these matters out you say. Precious believer, if this is your line of reasoning for not keeping His Feasts, His Sabbaths, His Commands, and His Laws, then you are on thin ice. Simply put, you may be in danger of hell fire. Deuteronomy 4:2 **Commands us to not take away nor add to His Commands!** Study these matters out for yourself and seek His plan for your life.

Learn to be a giver and tithe your ten percent. Luke 6:38 says your good measure will be shaken down, pressed together and men will bring it back to you piled up to your chest. For with the measure you give, not grudgingly, more will be given back to you. The tithe is for the widows, the orphans and the Levites or the ones who are preaching the Truth and winning souls for the Kingdom! It is not for piling up wealth for your own kingdom or denomination. Since you are the one who has to give account, ask Him where to give. You and the receiver will be blessed. Also, give what you've been given. Has He empowered you to lay hands on the sick and expect them healed? If you are a *believer* He has. Give away what faith and anointing you have and your power and faith will be increased! Become a *Doer of His Word!* Give and it will be given unto you!

I remember once I was in a certain church where my friend was the Pastor. On a bulletin board in the hall I saw a picture of an evangelist from Africa. Passing on by I heard the Lord say, "I want you to send $1,000 to that evangelist back there on the bulletin board." I replied, "Lord you know I don't have $1,000 to give right now, and I proudly continued, I gave a $1,000 last week to such and such ministry." Yahshua replied, "Yes, I know you don't and I would appreciate it if you would *wait until I tell you where to give!*" There I was stupidly waiting for an "Atta Boy," and what I got was correction! You too will give account for how you handle *His Finances*, the tithe. Hopefully, you are not so gullible to think the tithe is *your* money and you can give it wherever you wish, without so much as a prayer as to where He wants you to give it. Ask and listen, and be moved by the peace in your heart. Remember where your heart is, there your treasure will be also! Learn to help the down and out, and let Him mold and change you.

You will have the opportunity to stand before your Maker someday. This could be the greatest decision you make in your life:

> **Ask Him to change you in every area that is not now, nor will be, acceptable to Him when you must stand in His presence and be judged.**

It has always seemed strange to me why "Christian" believers wouldn't ask Yahshua to make changes in them so they might stand at His appearing unashamed. Believer- do it now!

> **What is the danger of not changing and being conformed to His image by learning to obey Him?**

Yahshua is speaking to you and me and warning us in Matthew 7:21-23 "(21) Not everyone that says to Me, Lord, Lord, shall enter the Kingdom of Heaven; but he that does the will of My Father Who is in heaven. (22) Many will say to Me in that day, Lord, Lord, haven't we prophesied in Your Name? And cast out devils in Your Name? And in Your Name done many wonderful works? (23) And then I will tell them: depart from Me, you workers of iniquity."

Iniquity is synonymous with Lawlessness or disobeying Yahweh's Law. Some translations use the word "lawlessness" here. What Law is Yahshua referring to? Man's law? Are these robbers, pimps, drug pushers, killers and breakers of mankind's laws He is referring to? No, those types of people are not out doing many wonderful works and casting out devils in His Name. Yahshua is referring to the Torah or the Commands given by Yahweh on Mt. Sinai to Moses, which are the first five books of the Bible. Some "believers" think if they avoid all miraculous or supernatural signs and don't do any wonderful works in His Name they will avoid this Command to depart from Him on Judgment Day. No, we are Commanded to do what Yahshua did, and He says in John 14:12 we will do even greater things than these, for He goes to the Father. What we must avoid is lawlessness or what is Torahlessness. Study for yourself Leviticus and all the first five books of the Bible, the Torah, given to Moses on Mt. Sinai. Remember, in the beginning (Genesis or Bereshit; pronounced beare-e-sheet in Hebrew) was the Word and the Word was with Yahweh and the Word was Yahweh. (John 1:1) Basically, we can now see it was not some graceless Elohim before Yahshua, it WAS Yahshua the Word speaking at Mt Sinai, prior to being made flesh. Anyway, Noah found grace in His eyes, so we can know He changes not.

Yahshua said in Matthew 5:17 "**Do not think that I am come to destroy the Law** (Torah or the first five books of the Bible) or the prophets (The major and minor prophet's books of the Bible) I am *not* come to destroy but to *fulfill*."

To fulfill means to rightly interpret, empower or make usable and give the ability to do, which is also a definition of grace. He would not command us to do something without giving us the power and ability to do it. That would not be fair and just. In biblical days if a Torah (Bible) teacher correctly interpreted the Scripture he was said to *fulfill* the Scripture. If he misinterpreted the Scripture, he was said to *abolish* it. Yahshua did correctly interpret the Scriptures and made the religious Pharisees mad, but never would He abolish His own Word and Laws. So how is it possible that so many Christian pastors and leaders teach that the Law is done away with? Too many of them have not understood *"think not."* No beloved, the Curse of the law is done away with by obedience. We now have been given the power (grace) to obey from the giving of the Holy Spirit. These Commands are no longer burdensome, they are now written on our hearts! Jeremiah 31:33 says, "For this is the Covenant I shall make with the house of Yisra'ĕl after those days, declares יהוה: (YHWH) I shall put My Torah in their inward parts, and write it on their hearts. And I shall be their Elohim, and they shall be My people." The curse of the law is the results for not obeying the Law listed in Deuteronomy 27:15-26, now written on our hearts. The Law itself is not done away with or abolished. Yahshua says in Matthew 5:18 "Until heaven and earth pass away, not one jot or tittle (smallest Hebrew pronunciation marks) shall by no means pass away until all is *fulfilled*." Since we still have heaven and earth, this should be a "no brainer" for us. When it is *all fulfilled* Messiah Yahshua will be reigning in Jerusalem!

The blessings for obedience still remain. Yahshua continues in Matthew 5:18-19, "For truly I say to you, until heaven and earth pass away, one jot or tittle shall in no way pass away from the Law, until all be fulfilled. (19) Whosoever therefore shall break the least of My Commandments, and shall teach men to do so, he shall be called least in the Kingdom of Heaven: but whoever shall do and teach them, the same shall be called great in the Kingdom of Heaven." Maybe keeping the Sabbath is the least of these Commandments. I don't think it is, but for this example let us pretend that it is the least of His Commands. Is it worth being *least* in the Kingdom to disobey this command and teach others to disobey it? We have far too many Pastor Least's teaching that the Law has been done away with! If it were done away with why would Yahshua say that He did **not** come to do away with the Law? You cannot just pick any Sabbath you want, or make up your own Sabbath. You cannot just cafeteria pick which commands you are to obey. Just obey them, He has sent His Holy Spirit to guide you into all Truth and to help you obey. Please don't misunderstand my point here. I know Pastors are gifts to the body of believers to train and build up the body of Messiah for ministry to one another, and I don't necessarily desire to be in their shoes. If they are erroneously teaching that the Law is done away with, it is most likely what they were taught. Additionally, they have much to lose by opposing their religious denomination. They lose their incomes, their retirements, their children's college educations, and usually even the respect of their peers, so it is a difficult thing to ask anyone to do. Of course, they lose much more if they don't oppose the plan of Satan and his "church system." The Holy Scriptures say in James 3:1, that teachers would be held in stricter account, because they have power to lead many of His flock astray. They have *inherited lies and things that don't profit* according to Jeremiah 16:19-21 "(19) O YHWH, my strength and my stronghold, and my refuge in the day of distress, to You the nations will come from the ends of the earth and say, Our fathers have inherited nothing but falsehood, Futility and things of no profit. (20) Can man make gods for himself? Yet they are not gods! (21) "Therefore behold, I am going to make them know, This time I will make them know My power and My might; and they shall know that My name is YHWH."

The problem is, they don't know they have inherited lies and things that don't profit, because of the nearly seventeen hundred years from the Emperor Constantine's combination of church and government in 325 A.D. He actually killed believers who kept Yahweh's commands and set up pagan government holidays for the new "church." So, we have a compromised system from a pagan church, whose traditions have been passed down. Sometimes these pagan traditions and holidays were enforced by penalty of death by the "church."

Even later when the protestants determined that the just shall live by faith they still maintained nearly all the paganism, Sun-god-day worship, Christmas, Easter, Lent, etc. Of course, you can worship every day you desire, just keep His Sabbath holy and set apart by obeying Him! When we study just the *New Testament* as a stand-alone book and do not realize that eighty to ninety percent of it is direct quotes from what is commonly called the *Old Testament*, we are taking it out of context and come up with totally different meanings and understandings. We will especially detour, if we learn from the Hellenistic or Greek mindset, instead of the Hebrew mindset, which contains idioms and understandings that come from keeping His Sabbath and Feasts (His culture and traditions). Even doing the best we possibly can it would be lacking to say the least. When we take scriptures out of context we err. We cannot just end the scriptures and call them *Old* Testament, and think that everything Messiah lived and kept of the Law and Feasts are done away with. Let's look at some Scriptures starting with the Lamb who blots out our sins and transgressions and Who also has power to blot us from the Book of Life.

The Old Testament or Moses and the Prophets is considered *the Law* by many. Some believe and act as though it is *passed away*. Some say the Law was nailed to the cross. Really, is that what ordinance the Scripture is referring to? Let's look at the Scripture to determine the answer in Colossians 2:14 "Blotting out the handwriting of ordinances that was against us, which was contrary to us, and took it out of the way, nailing it to His cross."

What was nailed to the cross, *the Law* or the ordinances or debts against us? It was customary to write up ordinances or papers of indebtedness in biblical days. What were removed were the judgments, curses, or *DEBTS* due us for our transgression (sins) against the Law- the Commands of Yahweh. The Law was not done away with or nailed to the cross, as that would have removed our instructions. Also, sin is transgression against the Law and Commands, so that would have also removed sin, if there is no Law or Command to disobey. Let's look also at Colossians 2:16 "Let no man judge you in food or drink or in respect of a Holy Day (Feasts of the Lord), or of the new moon or the Sabbath."

The Holy Spirit inspired Sha'ul (Paul) to write this letter of instructions. Who was this letter written to? The letter was written to *Torah observant believers who were keeping these Feasts*. They were eating kosher or biblically approved foods, (sanctified; remember food must first be sanctified (declared food) by the word and then prayer 1 Timothy 4:1-5) according to the Commands of a loving Father who knew what was suitable for healthy living. The recipients of this letter were also keeping the Sabbath and the Commands of *the Law* just like Messiah Yahshua did. New converts who had been pagan were joining the body of believers and beginning to outnumber the Yehudans (Jews). What the Holy Spirit was saying was- don't let anyone judge you or challenge you for keeping the Commands of the Sabbath, eating kosher foods that are *biblically* fit to eat, and keeping the Feasts and the New Moon. Notice that now, from Christian traditions of nearly 17 hundred years of paganism due to Constantine, this understanding was completely twisted from the original instructions and their meaning, to these Torah obedient believers. What have been done away with are the **debt and the sacrifices** for forgiveness of sins.

> *There are other oblations or free will offerings and sacrifices that have NOT been done away with.*

On a side note, I expect soon we will see the city of Jerusalem divided up and the Jews in Israel will start up the Altar Services and sacrifices as they get part of the Temple Mount in the peace treaty or as a result of war. Many, even Christians will, but *DO NOT* speak against this altar. Remember it is the antichrist or anti-messiah who STOPS the sacrifices and boasts great things about himself being God. This starts the 42 month Great Tribulation. Do not have your words agree with the antichrist about this altar!

Yahweh, through the prophet Isaiah, says: Isaiah 43:24-27 "(24) You have bought Me (Yahweh) nothing sweet with your money, neither have you filled Me with the fat of your sacrifices, but you have made Me to serve with your sin, and have wearied Me with your iniquities. (25) I, even I, am He that blots out your transgressions for My sake, and will not remember your sins. (26) Put Me in remembrance today (His Word) and let us plead together, that you may be justified, (Speak His Word and do His Laws and instructions *in agreement with Him*) (27) Your first father has sinned, and your teachers have transgressed against Me."

Those that sinned here are those whose fathers and teachers strayed from keeping His Commands and Laws. They inherited lies and things that do not profit. They had listened to the teaching of Balaam, which is to disobey the instructions and Laws of Moses and the Prophets. They had left the *sure foundation* of Moses and the Prophets. 1 Timothy 1:6-7 "(6) From these things men have erred and turned aside to empty words (7) in that they have sought to be teachers of the Torah (Moses), while not understanding that which they speak or which they dispute." 2 Timothy 4:3-4 says, "(3) For the time will come when they will not endure sound doctrine; but following their own desires (i.e. denominations and purposes), will lay up for themselves teachers, having itching ears; (4) and will turn away their ears from the Truth, and turn to fables and myths." Isaiah 28:9-10 gives us the reason for the last day (Laodicean) teacher's and pastor's failure, "(9) Whom shall He teach knowledge? And whom shall He make to understand doctrine? Those who understand, who are weaned from milk and drawn from the breasts. (10) For precept shall be upon precept; line upon line, line upon line, here a little and there a little."

Understand Yahshua did not come to do way with the Law of Moses and the Prophets. Moses and the Prophets are the *sure foundation* of line upon line and line upon line. Jeremiah 23:1-3 gives us Yahshua's thoughts as He gathers His sheep together in the last days: "(1) Woe to the pastors that destroy and scatter the sheep of My pasture (These sheep were scattered by Yahshua because of their paganism and disobeying the teachings of Moses and the Prophets and today false pastor-teachers also disagree with Moses and the prophets and lead many astray). (2) Therefore here is what Yahweh the Elohim of Israel says to the pastors that feed My people; you have scattered My flock, and driven them away, and have not visited them: Behold, I will visit on you the payment for your evil doings. (3) And I will gather the remnant of My flock where I have driven them, and will *bring them back again* to their folds (to Torah); and they shall be fruitful again and increase."

We can understand from this that He will bring us back again to the sure foundation of Moses and the Prophets in the last days when He gathers His people. My point is this:

> *If a blind man, with the very best intentions leads a blind man, they will still both fall into the ditch.*

Since there is no biblical command to keep Yahshua's (Jesus') birth, why would we follow a *tradition of men*? Because it feels good and some probably think He is honored by it. Sadly, He doesn't see it that way. There is, however, a biblical command to keep and celebrate <u>His</u> Feasts!

> **In Deuteronomy 4:2 He says, "*Do not add to or take away from my commands. Don't learn the ways of the heathen.*"**

What really honors Him is to obey Him and do His Commands and His Feasts (festivals) His way! What then did He Command?

Leviticus 23:3-4 states, "(3) Six days shall work be done, but the seventh is the Sabbath of the Lord, a Holy convocation (rehearsal), you shall do no work therein: it is a Sabbath of the Lord in all your dwellings. (4) These are the Feasts which you shall proclaim in their seasons." These are not Jewish *Feasts*; they are the Feasts of the Lord! Sabbath, Passover, Unleavened Bread, Trumpets, and Tabernacles are all festivals and times of joyous gathering that we were commanded not to forget. Of course, I realize that many of the pagan holy days are festive occasions with fun traditions but we need to realize that our Creator knew of our need to fellowship and "party" with our families and created His festivals for doing that *and* remembering Him. You owe it to yourself and your eternal well being to search out these Feasts of the Lord and learn to obey them.

Keeping these Feasts will really set you free. It is a wonderful thing to have a day that is *off limits* to the world! You can kick back, sleep, study Yahweh's Word, turn off the phones, the pagers, televisions, etc., and let Him minister *life* to you! These Feasts include the weekly Sabbath and even several weeklong holidays! The tradition of men is to worship on the first day of the week. Not the last day of the week. Exactly the opposite of what Yahweh commanded. Constantine, the Roman emperor, had a coin minted in 325 A.D. His face was on one side and Solis in Victus (To the invincible sun) on the other side. He was a sun god worshipper. Some would try and tell us that he was a believer and the leader of Messiahs' body (the church), but he had many put to death for not keeping the Day of the Sun Sabbath (Sun god day or Sunday). He also had most of his own family members killed, fearing his reign or kingdom in danger. I wouldn't think anyone who searches out this matter would desire to obey this man and this tradition against your Father and Creator- Yahweh. Nowhere in Scripture are we commanded that Yahweh changed His mind, and that we could just pick any day we liked, or any and every day could be our Sabbath. Only if you are the Creator, do you have the right to do as you please concerning His Commands. We are not to add to or take away. We are to **observe and obey** His Commands. It's just that simple. Yahshua says it this way in John 14:21, "Whoever **has My Commands and obeys them**, that is the one that loves Me, and whoever loves Me will be loved by My Father, and I too, will love him and reveal Myself to him."

Amazingly, when we keep the Feasts of the Lord, we are actually keeping His ascribed and special Holy Days or holidays, and they make sense. I suspect that the Holy Spirit conceived the Light of the world into Mary on Hanukkah, the Feast of Lights and Dedication. Nine months later, when the shofar (trumpet) blew in Jerusalem to mark the Feast of Trumpets, and the start of the seventh biblical month and the harvest,

Yahshua was announced. Five days later at the Feast of Tabernacles, He was born and "tabernacled" (lived/dwelled) with men. He was living among mankind, when eight days later the Feast of Tabernacles Last Great Day arrived, He was circumcised. He was the Passover lamb, in keeping the Feast of Passover. Three days later, as was the custom of the high priest, He proclaimed the Wave Offering of First Fruits, as the graves had opened up, and He presented Himself and many others, as the sampling or First Fruits of His salvation to Yahweh. He is our High Priest. Then on Shavuot, now called Pentecost by many, He sent the Holy Spirit to empower us to walk by faith and to keep His Commands, for they are not too burdensome. *Interestingly enough, tradition claims Shavuot is the anniversary of the giving of the Ten Commandments and all the Torah on Mt. Sinai.* Matthew 7:24-25 says, "(24) Therefore whosoever hears these sayings of Mine and does them, I will liken him unto a wise man, which built his house on a rock (25) and the rains descended, and the floods came, and the winds blew, and beat upon that house; and it fell not, for it was founded upon a rock." *When* the storms of life come, *not if they come but when*, do you want to not be moved or destroyed? Then keep His sayings. He is the Word made flesh. John 1:1 says, "In the beginning was the Word, and the Word was with Yahweh (God) and the Word was Yahweh, the same was in the beginning with Yahweh." Therefore, it was Yahshua at Mt. Sinai before He became flesh and dwelled among us. The word spoken is the same yesterday, today and forever. He was not a graceless God at Mt Sinai, for we may read that Noah found grace in His eyes. You should know that the Word is Yahweh from Genesis through Revelation in the Bible. Again, Yahshua put it like this in John 14:21, "Whoever has My Commands and *does them*, that is the one that loves Me, and he that loves Me will be loved by My Father, and I too will love him and show Myself to him." Additionally, Yahshua spoke in 1 John 2:4, "The man who says I love Him and keeps not My Commandments is a liar, and there is no truth in him." *Do you say you love the Lord but you will not obey Him?*

Why should we obey Him now concerning the Feasts of the Lord?

Actually, we will be keeping these Feasts during Yahshua's millennium reign on the Earth. If they are done away with, why would the King of Kings *require* them then? The Scripture is found Zechariah 12:16-18 "(16) And it shall come to pass, that every one that is left of all the nations which came against Jerusalem shall even go up from year to year to worship the King, the Lord of Hosts (Yahshua), and to keep the *Feast of Tabernacles*. (17) And it shall be that whoever will not come up to Jerusalem and worship Him, the King of Hosts, among all the families of the Earth, even upon them shall be no rain. (18) And if the family of Egypt won't go up, they will have no rain; that is the plague Yahshua uses to punish the disobedient that come not up to keep the Feast of Tabernacles."

Some would say- it just seems like legalism to me. No loved one, it is legalism to obey the doctrines and traditions of men that have been erroneously added and subtracted and then taught as the doctrines of Yahweh! It is called obedience to obey Yahweh (God) and brings forth blessings. You see, we were freed from the CURSE of the Law. This is not saying that the Commandments or the Law is the curse. We are *not freed from the Instructions and Commands* – only freed from the curse that goes with disobedience. We either receive blessings or cursing based on whether or not we obey His Instructions. We are empowered, which is GRACE, to understand and obey because the Holy Spirit who is the comforter and helper was sent. Grace is not a license to sin as it may be falsely preached. It is the empowering by the Holy Spirit to flee sin, free from the law of sin and death.

I was fasting many days as I studied and prepared for this chapter and as I finished, this is what Yahshua told me to write to you as a love based warning of life and death, "Repent from the paganism that has in filtered My Church, My Body. It does not matter that you inherited it because now you know Truth and I will hold you accountable if you continue in your paganism and blot your name from My Book of Life! Teach men everywhere that desire Truth to walk in Truth to follow Me! Soon, you will all stand in front of Me, the Righteous Judge, and if you have obeyed, you shall hear Me exclaim, Well done you faith filled and obedient servant; you were obedient and fearless even unto death. Enter into My joy!"

This was the hardest paragraph to write in the book. It seems so harsh and hard, I did not want to write it. I can assure you though, that the warning of life or death is the purest form of love from Him. His greatest desire is that you are blessed and enter into His joy.

Where Did You Come From?
And Where Are You Really Going?

Chapter Eleven:
A Choice and a Prayer

The choice you make here will determine your destiny!

Loved one, it all sums up here. Remember, you are a loved one because you are a truth seeker, and now the choice remains for you. The choice is yours. Will you study to show yourself approved to Yahweh (God) a worker for Him, rightly dividing the Word of Truth, one who will not be ashamed at His appearing? Or will you be ashamed? The choice is clearly yours. You are the one who will suffer the curse required of the Law if you choose to disobey and keep the traditions of men and our society. You are also the one who will receive the blessings for obeying His Word. In Deuteronomy 30 He puts it like this: "I set before you life and death, blessings and curses, therefore choose you LIFE!" So what will you choose- life or death? The choice remains yours. Deuteronomy 28 lists the blessings for followers of Messiah and curses for not obeying His Commands. Read them and think on these things. His Word says that His Instruction is life to them that find them and health and healing to all their flesh.

My prayer for you dear reader: *May the life of Yahshua be in you. May He give you a hunger and thirst for His righteousness. May YHWH give* *you wisdom and revelation to know the hope of your calling and the courage to walk it out. May He establish in you His purpose for your creation, and empower you to enter in by faith the destroying of hasatan's works. May He give you peace and make you and your loved ones worthy to escape and endure the fiery trials ahead and to stand at His appearing unashamed! May He give you ears to hear Him as you obey and do His Instructions and you become an answer and help wherever there are hurting people. Finally, I pray you arise now from your slumber, and fulfill your divine purpose to your full measure, and when that is completed, enter into the joy of your Master's Kingdom! If you put yourself in agreement with this prayer, you shall have whatsoever you **say** about this so be careful what you say. "When two agree on Earth as to touching anything, it is done by our Father in Heaven." Matthew 18:19*

Where did you come from? And Where are you really going?

Hopefully, you now know you were breathed into existence by a loving and merciful Creator- Yahweh. That is where you came from. As for where you are going; He has planned a way for you to live in fellowship with Him forever. But as you now know dear reader, where you are going is totally dependent on what you decide and now do. He's done all He plans to do on your behalf without further instruction from you, and a decision to grow up spiritually. He is now at the right hand of the Father, Yahweh, waiting for His enemies to be made His footstool. His Word gives you authority to follow Him and walk in His authority and power in Luke 10:19. He is The Way, The Truth, and The Life for you if you so choose LIFE!

Chapter Twelve:
Growing Up Spiritually

Since you have chosen to follow His Commands and *grow up spiritually* as a "born again" child of the Creator Yahweh, you are especially invited to continue on the wonderful spiritual journey that your Heavenly Father has designed just for you!

Welcome! The Bible says that the angels, the spirit beings created to help and assist us, are rejoicing! You are a spiritual being, for Yahweh is Spirit and those that worship Him must worship in Spirit and Truth according to John 4:23-24. You have been recreated spiritually in His image, and born again! Remember as a newborn baby or even as a child or teenager, you are neither perfect nor trained to maturity. This is taught in 1 Corinthians 3:1-2, "(1) And I could not speak to you brothers as though you were spiritual, but still fleshly, even as babies in Christ. (2) I have fed you with milk and not meat, for up to now and even still, you cannot digest it." Just like a baby in the natural realm we are born again as babies in the spiritual realm. We must continually eat the healthy food of the Word and grow up. If you do not eat you will be malnourished at best and you could possibly die, both physically and spiritually. 1 Peter 2:2 says, "As newborn babies, desire the sincere milk of the Word that you may grow thereby." Hebrews 5:12-13 reminds us: "(12) For the time is come when you ought to be teachers, but you still need someone to teach you the fundamental principles of the Word of Yahweh; and you still need milk and not strong meat. (13) For everyone that uses milk is unskilled in the Word of righteousness: for he is a baby."

We make mistakes, learn from them and repent. We are all continually growing as He teaches us new truths, so study and grow, and do not allow Satan's lies to condemn you. Will you be corrected and chastised by the Father? Certainly yes, as He reminds us in Hebrews 12:6-9 "(6) For who Yahshua loves He corrects and disciplines every son He receives, (7) If you endure the punishment, Yahweh deals with you as sons; for what son is he that the Father will not correct? (8) If you be without correction and punishment, which you all receive, then you are not sons but bastards. (9) Furthermore, we have all had fathers of our flesh which corrected us, and we gave them respect: shall we not much more be in subjection to the Father of spirits and live?" When He uses the word "son," understand He is talking to male and female. He created man in His image, male and female. Man and man with a womb, womb-man, or woman.

How can we determine whether it is the Holy Spirit reminding us and correcting us, or the devil condemning us? The Holy Spirit will be grieved and gentle and offer hope and a way of repentance, a way out of the transgression or sin committed. He will bring to your mind the Scriptures teaching you the right way. The devil, on the other hand will offer no hope, just judgment and condemnation. Satan and his camp will continually remind you of your failure and accuse you, trying to make you believe you are not even a follower and believer in Messiah. He will try and tell you, you are not really even *born again*. Remember, if you are continually reminded about a past sin, it cannot be the Holy Spirit showing you, because the Bible says, if we confess our sins and repent, He is faithful and just to forgive our sins, cleanse of us all unrighteousness and He remembers our sin no more! If He remembers them no more, then it couldn't possibly be the Holy Spirit reminding you of the sin, unless you have not turned from the sin and repented.

I will share an experience I had in early 1992. I had just had an angry argument with my wife concerning the Lord. She was hurt and probably angry with God because her wonderful dad had died a horrible death caused by cancer. Her dad loved the Lord, so it seemed unfair that God had allowed him or caused him to die that way. It would have been unfair and unjust if I had believed for one second that God had done that, or even allowed it! I was explaining that God had nothing to do with it, that Satan comes to steal, kill and destroy, and that Hosea 4:6 says, "My people perish for lack of knowledge." I would have been wise to just love my wife because that is what she needed more than the facts. She needed comforting, but I certainly didn't give that, although that is what I wanted to give her. She snapped back at me saying you can take your "Jesus" (that's the name I used back then as it is all I knew) and stick Him! It is amazing what angry language we can use when offenses pile up and resentment, anger, and hurt toward a loved one comes out, but that is where we were. Certainly, looking back, I made so many errors and had a lack of compassion and gentleness that is easy to see these results. Now as to how I answered her, I said, "Fine! You can just go to hell if that's what you want!" And I stormed off into our bedroom. As I entered the door I was thinking to myself: I really told her off good, I guess I was thinking I got in the last word on the matter. I was extremely wrong! Entering the room and looking toward my dresser I saw a small raised cloud about seven feet up in the corner. Not sure what this meant and still being proud of how well I had just rebuked my wife, I seemed to know it was the Lord, but somehow thought He was proud of me for my strong comeback to my wife's statement. I was as wrong as anyone ever was. It was the Lord for sure, but as I watched Him move toward me, I knew I was in serious trouble. I fell on my knees, then on my face in the carpet, and said I'm sorry a thousand times, all in one second! How, I do not know, but I knew that I had. I was weeping in shame as this cloud moved over the top of me and *angrily and loudly* spoke these words:

> **YOU ARE NOT HER JUDGE! I WILL BE HER JUDGE! I COMMAND YOU- LOVE YOUR WIFE!**

I answered, sobbing and feebly, "Lord, I am so sorry, I do love my wife, but I don't even know how to show her, Help me to show her, Lord." I sensed His presence leaving and watched, as the cloud seemed to rise back toward the corner of the room and disappear. Now to my knowledge, that cloud was never seen there again. At least, while I lived there I never saw it before or after that incident.

Not everyone's transgression is as great as mine was because I purported to know the power of words; therefore, not everyone's spanking for disobedience will be as severe as mine was! The Bible had already taught me the power of life and death was in the tongue, so I received an unforgettable instruction! Of course, it grieves me to even speak of my stupidity and lack of compassion in this instance, but hopefully, it will help you to be more loving, kind, and gentle with a loved one. You see, it is love that never fails. Not your knowledge, your money, your career, your personality, your fame, your power or even your faith. Not the natural love you have for someone that loves you back, but His unconditional love is the only thing that never fails. I trust this will encourage you to continually stay in a loving mode toward your loved ones who need salvation or any other kind of prayer, and that you fellowship and receive love and compassion from your Heavenly Father to give them. They need the compassion and gentleness that flows from Yahweh's throne room. They do not need your judgment or even the facts. Judgment and vengeance belongs to the Father, He will repay.

You may be asking yourself, is he really telling the truth concerning these experiences? My answer is: Most emphatically! We both understand now that all liars are going to hell, so you will not receive any fabrication or lies from me! My job is not the hard part anyway, as that belongs to the Holy Spirit who will guide you into all Truth. My job is to come as a *teller* (messenger) only.

You see, I thought you loved someone because they acted toward you a certain way, or treated you with respect and honored and loved you. Not so, real love is what comes from the Father once we have a relationship with Him through Yahshua. The Holy Ghost sheds that love in our hearts. That love is unconditional; just like our Heavenly Father's love is without condition. You see He loves Hitler, and even the worst of mankind. That, however, is not to be confused with blessings that obedience brings. That doesn't mean that all sinners will go to heaven and have life eternally with Him. You may have a son or daughter that you feel has rebelled against you or even what you believe, but you still love them. Likewise, just because you love them does not mean they will receive your blessings, or your wisdom and instruction, especially if the relationship has been severed and none are willing to repent. Pride and stubborn heartedness always lead to a fall and destruction. Why not humble yourself, right or wrong, and allow Yahshua to raise you up and exalt you for your obedience? *Or would you rather be right and lose the blessing of a restored relationship?*

Now, let's discuss why we *must* grow up spiritually. We have an enemy by default, and two questions must be answered for us to address *why*. First, *who* is this enemy, and secondly, *what is his plan of attack or method of warfare?* This entire book is dedicated to teach you *how you may defeat him* and limit his operation against you and your loved ones.

Although most of us believers seem to be naive, we are Commanded that we are not to remain ignorant of his schemes against us.

Satan, the evil one and the demonic realm's leader, is a killer, a thief and a destroyer! We see this is in Yahshua's warning instruction in John 10:10, "the *thief* has come to kill, steal, and destroy, but I have come that you have life abundantly." How do we know that Satan is the thief mentioned in John 10:10? Let's look at what Yahshua says in John 10:1 and 10:9, "(1) Truly, I say to you, he that does not enter by the door into the sheepfold, but comes in some other way, the same is *a thief and a robber*." Yahshua continues, "(9) I am The Door, if any man enters by Me, he shall be saved and delivered, and shall go in and out and find provision." Yahshua is The Door, and the method He created for entry into the earth was through flesh. Yahshua came in the flesh. The thief came in another way. We know that Satan came as a spirit being. He hates you because you have now become *born again* and now have power to produce fruit against his demonic kingdom. Even if you aren't born again, he still hates you and will destroy and kill you after he has used you for some wicked purpose. Most "believers" do not understand and have grossly underestimated this enemy. They must think that the spiritual demons Yahshua cast out of people must have died, or disappeared somehow. No, they are spiritual beings, they do not die. Many blame Yahweh for every bad thing that happens. You will hear them make remarks like, "I can't believe in a good God with all the bad things He lets happen." They are deceived. They do not understand the basic principle of Believers 101, which is Good God-Bad Devil! Remember, every good and perfect gift comes down from the Father of heavenly lights (Yahweh), according to James 1:17. We must understand that Adam was given *dominion* over the earth according to Genesis 1:26, and was a type of the god of this world. Basically, Adam was in charge, but gave up that *dominion* when he rebelled and disobeyed Yahweh in the garden. This is confirmed later, when Satan tempted Yahshua during His forty day fast in the wilderness. He claimed that he, Satan, now had *dominion* over all the earth. Yahshua did not disagree, but only stated that He would worship Yahweh only. We can determine that Satan is the god of this world from this. He is not the god of believers and those *born again* any longer, but he certainly rules those who are not born again and uses them in his war against believers. He also has an organized army of demonic spirit beings, which includes principalities, powers and spiritual wickedness in heavenly places. That is why *bad* things happen on the earth. Don't blame Yahweh!

Ephesians 6:11-12 gives us a glimpse of his method of attack: "(11) Put on the whole armor of Yahweh, that you may have the ability to stand against the schemes of the devil. (12) We do not *wrestle* against flesh and blood, but against spiritual principalities and powers, the rulers of darkness of this world, and against spiritual wickedness in high places."

What are these schemes? He is extremely subtle and sneaky as recorded in Genesis 3:1, "Now the serpent was more subtle than any beast of the field Yahweh had made." He will not fight you and appear red, with horns and a forked tail. His spiritual army of principalities, powers, and spiritual wickedness is well organized as to operations and duties in the attack against mankind. His objective is nothing less than you and your loved ones' destruction. Satan will show you a manifestation of results directly opposite to Yahweh's plan of good for your life and your loved ones. The facts are real but will not agree with the promise of Truth, which is the Scripture. Facts are temporary and the Truth of the Scripture promise is eternal, so you must stand and declare Truth. If you are born again, it is normal that you will be challenged and confronted by Satan's warfare as we see in 1 Peter 4:12, "Loved one, don't think it is strange, concerning the fiery trial which will try you, as though some strange thing is happening to you." *Wrestling* is the most direct confrontation, in your face type of warfare! You are chin to chin, and the battle is to the death. If we operate in the physical realm where Satan is the god of this world, we will be defeated. However, we fight the good fight of faith, and it is a spiritual fight, by guarding our confession or what we speak. The Bible tells us that words are spirit, so we fight demonic spiritual beings and their schemes, with the words of our warfare agreeing with Yahshua's promises!

Chapter Thirteen:
Believer or Unbeliever?

How do most people define a believer?

Is belief in a supreme being, a creator, or a god, enough to fulfill our destiny and inherit life everlasting? Most people believe that there is *or was* a Creator or some sort of Supreme Being. They don't really *know* Him or about Him, Her, or It, but they believe there must be a higher form of being or alien civilization or something. Some even believe they are their own god, and so can live as they wish. So we could say that *most believe in some form of God*. Is just *believing* in a God or a Creator enough?

Let's look at what the Scriptures, which are the inspired Words of Yahweh, and are useful for correcting and training us in righteousness, have to say: Yahshua says in John 14:6, "I am The Way, The Truth, and The Life. There is *no other way* to the Father."

> **There are <u>not</u> many ways or paths to everlasting life. Only One died for our sins.**

James 2:19 "You believe there is one God; you do well; the devils (demons or spirit beings that rebelled with Satan) also believe and shudder." We can see from this Scripture that it is certainly not enough to

133

believe. You see, the demons believe and are aware that divine judgment awaits them for their rebellion against Yahweh and for their hateful and evil acts of terrorism against mankind. Also, for their deceptions in blinding those that do not believe. That is why they tremble and shudder in fear. In 2 Corinthians 4:4, the Bible says the evil one (Satan) has blinded those that don't believe, that they might not know the mercy and goodness of Yahweh. His glory is His mercy and goodness revealed. We can know that because Moses asked Yahweh to reveal His glory to him and Yahweh agreed. When Yahweh passed by, Moses saw His goodness and mercy revealed! Remember in John 14:21 Yahshua, who is the Savior, Lord, deliverer, provider, healer, and author of our faith, says, "Whoever has My Commands and does them that is the one who loves me... "Again, in James 1:23, the Scripture warns us, "But you be **doers** of the Word, and not hearers only, deceiving yourselves." You see, we must *hear and obey* or be deceived.

How does Yahshua the Messiah define a mature believer?

*In Mark 16:17, Yahshua speaks saying, "And these signs shall accompany (follow) those that **believe**; In My Name, they shall cast out devils, they shall speak with new (unknown or heavenly) tongues, they shall take up serpents (authority over the demonic), and if they drink any deadly thing (unintentional poisoning), it shall not harm them; they shall lay hands on the sick, and they shall recover."*

Yahshua certainly has a different perspective for defining *believers* than most of us and our religious affiliations do. Since He is the one we stand in front of on Judgment Day, we all need to be very open to grow up spiritually and change into His image!

The Scriptures aren't for us to privately interpret according to 2 Peter 1:20-21, "(20) Knowing this first, no prophecy of the Scriptures is of any *private* interpretation. (21) For the Words came not in old times by the will of man, but as Holy men of Yahweh spoke as they were moved on by the Holy Spirit." You may ask what I mean concerning private interpretation. Of course you have to interpret to understand but let the Scriptures interpret one another. The Holy Spirit will guide us into all Truth if we are open to grow and humble ourselves to change. The only reason we would not grow and change is because we were taught man's doctrine or some denominational doctrine, which will usually deny His power flowing through us personally. One may say, "This Scripture means this to me" and another says, "Well, it means such and such to me." The more we study and allow Scriptures to interpret themselves, the Holy Spirit will be our Teacher, and the more we will become in unity with His Spirit and other believers. A lack of studying and understanding, by hearing His Holy Spirit teach us His Word, combined with the lack of desire for more of His Spirit, will always cause division. That is why the body of Messiah Yahshua is divided. Denominations denominate, which means to divide. This actually establishes division in His body. This is nearly always done based on private interpretations of Scripture that deny His power, and in all probability *they have not heard from Heaven, because hearing from Heaven produces unity of the faith.*

Our Heavenly Father's plan and desire is to establish His body in unity of the faith. Truthful and hungry believers and followers of Messiah Yahshua will humble themselves, receive change from His Spirit and *OBEY HIM!* Remember, the Holy Scriptures were written by over forty different authors, spanning a period of over fifteen hundred years! Most of them could not possibly have known each other and yet they agree with one another and confirm one another's writings. ***They had to hear from Heaven and so do you!*** They listened and wrote down what the Spirit of

Yahweh instructed as they were moved on by His Spirit. Some believers do not hear Yahshua speak to them. They deny His gifts are available and needed by them today. They are in error and think His power, miracles, and overflowing of His Spirit with the biblical evidence of unknown tongues (prayer language) is not for them. They think these gifts are not needed by them. They have been deceived by false doctrines of devils from the antichrist or religious spirit. Much of the "so-called" church or body of Messiah is just that, "so-called." They are social Christians and think that Christianity is synonymous with American or being "good people." That is why they will be easily deceived when lying wonders are done by the antichrist and will quickly fall away from the faith during the Great Tribulation. They can be likened to the story of the ten virgins in Matthew 25. They have light and they are virgins symbolizing they are followers of Messiah. However they have no source of power or oil to replenish the light. The oil is a symbol of the Holy Spirit and they are lacking in this critical area. They mean well but they cannot walk in the power of Yahshua! They are unable to sustain themselves and are left outside in outer darkness where there is weeping and gnashing of teeth! Now that you have read this far in this book, I know you are hungry for Truth and His oil. ***You are a child of the King of Kings!*** Study and become like small children and receive the Instructions of Yahweh! Let's look again at Yahshua's Instructions paraphrased in Matthew 18:3-4, "Unless you become converted (born again) and as a small child (humble), you will in no way enter the Kingdom of Heaven." We must become born again and humble like a small child, to even think we need and can receive more of His power and Spirit. An example of denying His power would be to reject praying in the spirit in unknown tongues, or laying hands on the sick personally and seeing them recover. Our mindset has to be focused on *His* abilities. A Scriptural example of this is found in Isaiah

59:19b, "When the enemy shall come in like a flood- *comma and pause*-the Spirit of Yahweh shall raise a standard against him." Consider this pause in the translation, "When the enemy comes in- *comma and pause*-like a flood the Spirit of Yahweh raises a standard against him." The Creator is the one with the overwhelming power NOT Satan! The flood is uncontrollable and cannot be contained- this sounds a lot like our Creator-certainly not the enemy of our souls! Remember, to deny the vast power and greatness of Yahweh and to show our Creator with less power than Satan, is a working or act of the antichrist or religious spirit. We must study and show ourselves approved to Yahweh, **rightly dividing** the Word of Truth, that we may be able to stand at Yahshua's appearing according to 2 Timothy 2:15. There is the need for, and duration of, the five ministry gifts from Yahweh, to bring us to a unity in the faith as stated in Ephesians 4:13, "Until we all come to the unity of the faith and to the knowledge of the Son of Yahweh and become as mature men in the fullness of Yahshua the Messiah."

When will these and other ministry gifts for building up the body of Messiah pass away? When we all come to a unity of the faith, and that happens when we see Him face to face as recorded in 1 Corinthians 13:12! There is a Scripture that talks about the rejoining of the twelve tribes represented by Judah (Jews) and Ephraim who are the ten scattered tribes who are mostly known as Christians, and are grafted in to Israel. The Scripture is Psalm 133:1, "Behold. How good and pleasant it is for brothers to dwell together in unity." This unity of born again believers is the purest form of brotherhood. Yahshua told the religious leaders of His day that their father was the devil! They studied much and were definitely religious, but they did not have a relationship with Yahweh, and did not *hear* from Him! Born again people really cannot be brothers or sisters of those who haven't been born again. We must humble ourselves, receive His Spirit and then we can become the unity of the faith. As we grow in

Him by yielding our spirits to His Spirit we become the unity of the faith. Then we will say, "How good it is, that we brothers and sisters dwell together in unity!"

Chapter Fourteen:
Power to Overcome

How do we become what Yahshua's (God's) definition is of a mature believer?

Simply put, we humble ourselves to the Word and obey as He teaches us and corrects us from our own ways and traditions of men that have been taught us as doctrines of Yahweh. "We put aside all evil, and all deceit and hypocrisies, and envies, and all evil speaking, and desire the sincere milk of the Word, that we may grow (spiritually) thereby." (1 Peter 2:1-2)

We must become as small children concerning our belief in the Scriptures. Small children trust and obey. At least, until they find that not everyone is truthful and trustworthy. Remember, Yahshua (the Word), is the Truth. He is trustworthy, and He said in Luke 18:17, "Verily (truthfully), I say to you, whoever shall not receive the Kingdom of Yahweh as a little child, shall in no wise enter there." In Luke 6:46, Yahshua asks His disciples who are the disciplined ones, "Why do you call Me Lord, Lord, and not do the things I say?" It seemed incredible to Him that some would call Him King and Lord but not obey Him. Why is humbling ourselves to obedience so important in receiving His power to overcome? Acts 5:32 shows us, "And we are witnesses to these things (miraculous); and so is the Holy Spirit, Whom Yahweh has given to those that *obey* Him." Remember, He said in John that whoever says they love Him but will not obey Him is a liar. We, too, must continually alert ourselves to submit and learn of Him, so that we won't be those He defines as liars.

Do we call Him King and Lord and not obey Him?

In John 8:31-32, Yahweh promises: "(31) If you <u>continue</u> in My Word, then you are My disciples indeed; (32) and you shall know the Truth, and the Truth shall make you free." How do we continue in His Word? Again, we become as small children: hearing, understanding, and obeying in trust, we become His disciples, His disciplined ones.

I asked the Lord one time about this scripture, *"Lord, what does continue in Your Word mean? Does it mean to keep reading?"* I thought I heard a chuckle and the reply, *"Yes son, you must continue reading and hearing My Word. But you must also believe My Word like a small child would. A small child will not doubt, they will only believe what they are told. You must believe like that, doubting nothing."*

One critical area Satan has fought and stolen power from most believers is the area of the baptism of the Holy Spirit. He has supplied the doctrine of devils that tricks believers into erroneously believing they have all the Holy Spirit they will ever need once they are born again. *They can't understand why they seemingly have no power to resist the devil or their own flesh nature.* They go to churches that teach only salvation and the born again experience. That is good, but certainly there is more. It is not enough to get born again and not receive the power and armor to overcome the enemy of your soul. Especially when Yahshua promised it in John 14 and John 16:17 "Even the Spirit of Truth Whom the world (unborn again) cannot receive, because it sees Him not, neither knows Him, but you know Him, for He dwells in you and shall be in you." John 16:13-14 "(13) However, when the Spirit of Truth is come, He will guide you into all Truth: He shall not speak of His own, but whatever He shall hear, that shall He speak: and He will show you things to come. (14) And He shall glorify Me; for He shall receive from Me and show it to you."

The Scriptures give us insight in Isaiah 12:2-4 about once we are born again we are a well of salvation to others; "(2) Behold, Yahweh is my salvation; I will trust and not be afraid: For Yahweh is my strength and my song; He also is become my salvation. (3) Therefore with joy shall you draw water out of the *wells of salvation.* (4) And in that day, shall you say, Praise Yahweh, call on His Name, declare His doings among the people, make mention that His Name is exalted." This is scripturally showing that when we get born again we become a life source to help others come into the Kingdom. We are a well of salvation and deliverance. Everyone knows most wells will not sustain everyone. They are usually enough to water a family or a small village, but they are usually limited in their resource of water supply. However, one who receives the overflowing of the Holy Spirit has become a river of life to others around them. Think of it like this with me: a river can go downstream and produces life wherever it goes, whereas a well is stationery and produces life only where it is dug.

In John 7:37-39, Yahshua stood and cried out on the Great Day of the Feast, the last day of the Feast of Tabernacles, "(37) If any man *thirst,* let him come to Me and drink. (38) He that believes in Me, as the Scripture has said, out of his belly shall flow *rivers of living water.* (39) But this He spoke of the Spirit, which they that believe on Him shall receive: for the Holy Spirit was not yet given, because that Yahshua had not yet been glorified." So we know that Yahshua told His disciples when He arose to go up into heaven in Luke 24:49, "And behold, I send you the promise of My Father upon you: but tarry in the city of Jerusalem until you are endued with *power* from on high." They waited in Jerusalem until Shavuot or the counting of the omer from Passover. This period or Feast is called Pentecost by many today. *Pente* is the root word in Greek for five or five tens in this case. It is the day after seven periods of seven days from the day following First Fruits or the Wave Offering., which is a Set Apart Day and a *called* Sabbath, three days after the Passover meal and during the week of the Feast of Unleavened Bread. The year Yahshua became the Passover lamb, First Fruits or the Wave Offering fell on a Sunday, but most of the time it does not. We know these dates now, based on computer astronomical calculations. This Shavuot period equates to forty-nine days plus one, or fifty days.

We can see from this statement by Yahshua in John seven, that it is imperative that *we get thirsty for Him and His Spirit.* If we don't already have that thirst or a hunger for more of Him and His power, then we should ask Him. The Scriptures tell us, "Ask and you shall receive, seek and you shall find, knock and the door shall be opened for you." So ask Him for thirst so that *rivers of living water may flow from your belly!* None of us have any reason to boast in ourselves, because anything good we have is because we have received it from the Father Whom the Scripture declares in James 1:17, "Every good and perfect gift is from above, and comes down from the Father of Lights, with Whom there is no changing or shadow of turning." Our Heavenly Father never changes. So, if anyone thirsts, let him come to Yahshua and drink freely of the rivers of life!

> **What is the physical manifestation or evidence of having received the Baptism of the Holy Spirit or the overflowing of His Spirit?**

Let's look at what the Scriptures say. When the disciples were waiting on Solomon's Portico, the upper room, here's what happened as recorded in Acts 2:1-4, "(1) And when the day of Shavuot (Pentecost) was fully come, they were all (one hundred and twenty of them were obedient) in one place. (2) And suddenly there came a sound from heaven as of a rushing mighty wind, and it filled the entire place where they were sitting. (3) And there appeared to them cloven tongues as of fire and it came over hovering on each of them, (4) and *they were filled with the Holy Ghost, and began to speak with unknown tongues as the Spirit gave utterance.*" The evidence we must go by of the filling to overflowing by His Holy Spirit has to be from Scripture, not on your church's', your friends, your family or even your own experience. See from the Scripture that the *Holy Spirit gave the utterance and the believers did the speaking.*

You must open your mouth and move your tongue to speak. Sometimes believers will expect to pray in unknown tongues, but will not open their mouths to receive what is flowing from Heaven into their spirit, and would flow out of their mouths, if they would just open them. Note also, that not *some* of them spoke with unknown tongues but *all* of them did. He is no respecter of persons and be assured He is the same, yesterday, today and forever! Some would have you believe that this evidence is no longer helpful or is from the devil. I would caution those who speak that unknown tongues is of the devil to study the following warning Yahshua gave to the religious leaders of His day, that any gift from the Father that was assigned to the works of the devil, would grieve the Holy Spirit and would not be forgiven. Not in this age or in the one to come. That is the unpardonable sin mentioned in Matthew 12:24-32. You should read this for yourself.

Why is the power to speak in other tongues so important? We are told in Romans 8:26-28, "(26) Likewise, the Spirit also helps our weaknesses, for we do not know what we should pray for as we ought: but the Spirit Himself makes intercession for us by *groanings* which cannot be uttered in our own or known languages. (27) And He that searches our hearts knows the mind of the Spirit, because He makes intercession for us according to the will of Yahweh (28) *And we know the will of Yahweh is to work all things good for those who love Him and are called according to His purpose.*" Sadly, many take Romans 8:28 out of context and apply it to mean every damned or condemned thing, such as sickness, poverty, disease, death, that the evil one does to us, is done by Yahweh to help us work it for good. They must assume that our Creator wants to use them to grow us somehow. When in actuality, Yahshua paid the price for all these areas of curses, so we would not have to. Romans 8:28 is really teaching that although we don't always understand what we are speaking in unknown tongues, we can know and trust Yahweh is working it for our benefit. That is not to say that Father doesn't even work evil things that Satan has done to us for our benefit, because He does. If Satan really had any brains he would leave us alone, because we only run to our Heavenly Father for help when he attacks us. Realize that when you don't know how or what to pray for, you can pray in unknown tongues because the Holy Spirit does know what to pray for. Jude twenty Commands us as believers, "But you beloved, build up yourselves in your most holy faith, praying in the Holy Ghost."

> **I submit for your consideration, that until we surrender our tongues, we have not completely surrendered at all.**

Why would I make such a statement? The Scriptures tell us in James 3:3-8 that the tongue is compared to a rudder for ships or a bridle for a horse. In other words it steers our direction. It further states that the tongue is set on fire from hell and no man can tame it. It is apparent from these Scriptures that only Yahweh can tame the tongue for <u>all things</u> are possible for those that believe in Him. As we surrender our tongue, we also can pray in the Spirit for those things we don't understand or don't even know we have a need for. Raise your hands to heaven and ask Him to give you utterance, then get your mind out of the way and utter whatever comes out of your belly. Do not judge what you utter and don't despise small beginnings. Do not pray in your known language! Just close your eyes and free your mind from distractions. It may be helpful to put on some good worship music. Think and concentrate on His goodness and His love for you and start moving your tongue and speaking as the Holy Spirit gives you utterance. Pray this prayer:

Say, "Yahshua, John the Baptist said that he baptized with water for repentance, but there was one coming after him Whose sandals he was not worthy to unloose that would baptize with the Holy Spirit and fire, and I believe you are the One who baptizes with the Spirit and fire. I ask you to baptize me in your Spirit and fire and I now believe I will also have a prayer language to pray in unknown tongues! I promise to do the speaking as you give me the utterance."

It may be helpful for you to have someone who you know has a prayer language to lay hands on you as this power is transferable, but if there is no one available to do that it is not imperative. Go ahead and receive for yourself His wonderful gift! Now that you are already born again you are certainly good enough to enter heaven. So you are also good enough to receive more of heaven here on the earth! Close your eyes, raise your hands, ***open your mouth*** and start uttering what He gives you. Do not judge what it sounds like, just let it flow from your belly! You will be given more and more as you practice praying in the Spirit so do not worry if you get one word, a few words or many words! Remember, a baby doesn't start speaking fluently immediately. Exercise your faith in this area often and your prayer vocabulary will grow!

When I first received a prayer language, I was concerned that I was speaking the same thing over and over. As that is what it sounded like to me. Shortly thereafter, I was watching a television news program and a Chinese government official was speaking in his native Chinese. The Holy Spirit spoke to me and asked what the man said. I replied, "Lord, I have no idea what he spoke. You know I don't understand Chinese, but it sounded like he said the same thing over and over." The Lord spoke again, "Just like you *thought* your praying in unknown tongues was saying the same thing over and over, he was speaking his language. Just continue praying in tongues because you are offering mysteries to Me, and indeed, no man understands but I do." In other words, when I was yielding in tongues He understood, even though *my* mind was unfruitful, the Spirit was fruitful and prayed exactly what was needed. Because when I pray in the Spirit and my mind is unfruitful, then I can actually do something else with my mind at the same time as praying in unknown tongues in the Spirit. I might want to read a book, work a crossword puzzle, balance my checkbook, study my Bible or whatever may require my intellect, and I can still pray in the Spirit! This removes all doubt that it is not the person's mind or intellect that is praying, it is you allowing your spirit man inside of you to connect with Yahweh, Who understands!

How can we know that praying in the Holy Ghost is praying in unknown tongues as He gives utterance? 1 Corinthians 14:2, 4, 5, "(2) For he that speaks in an unknown tongue speaks not to men, but to Yahweh:

for no *man* understands him; however *in the Spirit he speaks mysteries.* (4) He that speaks in an unknown tongue edifies (charges his spiritual battery) himself; but he that prophesies edifies the assembly or the body of Messiah. (5) I wish you all spoke in tongues, but even more important that you prophesy; for the one that prophesies is greater than he that speaks in unknown tongues, unless there is interpretation so that the assembly of believers is edified." We continue with instruction in 1 Corinthians 14:13-15, "(13) Therefore, let him who speaks in an unknown tongue pray that he may interpret. (14) For if I pray in an unknown tongue, *my spirit prays* but my mind (understanding) is unfruitful. (15) What should I do then? I will pray with my spirit and pray with my mind also: I will sing with the Spirit and sing with my understanding also."

> ## *How can we know this is an added experience after I am born again?*

Again we must search the Scriptures for Truth. There are two examples that come to mind. First we look at Cornelius, the first believer that was not Hebrew. Peter went to his home and was teaching him and his family about how to receive salvation when the Holy Spirit fell on them. How do we know? What was the evidence they claimed? Acts 10:44-47 explains, "(44) While Peter was still speaking the words, the Holy Ghost fell on them that heard the Word. (45) And they of the circumcision (Jews with Peter) which believed were astonished, as many as came with Peter, because that on the Gentiles (non-Jews) also was poured out the gift of the Holy Ghost. (46) For *they heard them speaking in tongues* and magnify Yahweh, then answered Peter (47) Can any man forbid water that these should not be baptized, which *have received the Holy Ghost just as we have?*"

The second example that comes to mind, is where Paul goes to Ephesus and finds certain disciples, apparently already believers, in Acts 19:2-6: "(2) He said unto them, have you received the Holy Ghost *since* you believed? And they said unto him, we have not even heard that there is a Holy Ghost. (3) And he said unto them, what then were you baptized in? And they said, in John's baptism. (4) Then Paul said, John truly baptized with the baptism of repentance, saying to the people, that they should believe on Him that would come after him, Yahshua, the Messiah. (5) When they heard this, they were baptized in the name of Yahshua the Messiah. (6) And when Paul laid his hands on them, the Holy Ghost came on them; and they *spoke with tongues and prophesied.*"

> *Yahshua told me this analogy, "Someone who can read and does not, has no advantage nor gains any benefit better than the person who cannot read; likewise, the person who can pray in unknown tongues and does not, has no benefit over the person who cannot pray in the spirit."*

Practice praying in the Spirit. Learn to yield your tongue to Him. We are Commanded to pray unceasing and this is the only way this seems to be attainable. The Bible asks the question in 1 Corinthians 12:30 "Do all speak (pray) in tongues?" and leaves the answer implied that certainly they do not. Of course not everyone does, but not everyone is saved and born again either, but it is His will that none would perish. Of course, we know that everyone not born again is perishing. It is His will also that everyone pray in tongues, as He would not give this free and powerful gift only for a select few. He is no respecter of persons and He watches over His Word to perform it. 1 Corinthians 14:39 says, "Forbid them not to speak in tongues." Finally, to remove all doubt on the matter, the Word states in 1 Corinthians 14:5, "I wish you all spoke in tongues...." It is available to everyone who is born again, but you should realize the devil will fight you harder in this area because it is a supernatural weapon that will produce results against his kingdom of darkness. Satan doesn't want you to pray in the Spirit against his plans and schemes. He wants you to remain ignorant, helpless, and without power against him.

Once you are baptized in the Holy Spirit and have received your prayer language in unknown tongues, the rest of the signs that accompany believers in Yahshua's definition of a believer in Mark 16 are almost automatic. You will begin to cast out devils, speak in unknown tongues more regularly, and lay hands on the sick and see them recover! You **do** have the power to use Yahshua's Name and cast out devils, but please listen to Yahshua and do so only when He tells you to. Ask Him for a heart of compassion and wisdom. Yahshua obviously did not pray for every sick person. He also did not cast out devils from every one that He met on the street that had a demon. You do not want to cast out devils from someone who wants to keep them. One time while passing out tracts in Cabo San Lucas Mexico, I kept meeting this old man who would growl at me like a dog. I continued to let it pass, as I knew he was carrying some passengers (demons). Then, some of the children (mine and others) who were there helping pass out tracts were a little frightened and said he had also growled at them. So, I decided to go and find him and ask if he wanted deliverance. I found him, and he was fearful of being confronted in the name of Yahshua. He tried to talk, but could only fearfully motion me away. He didn't want freedom, but he certainly stayed away from us after that. Yahshua always listened to what His Heavenly Father said. We, too, must listen and be attentive to our Heavenly Father. We don't need to go looking for demons in every one. When we come face to face with the demonic, you will know what to do, because the Spirit of Yahweh is in you.

Can a person who is a born again believer and follower of Yahshua be *possessed by a demon*? Not possessed, for sure, because the demon spirit would have to overthrow the Holy Spirit and he cannot. Certainly, through the sin of rebellion, or ignorance of Yahshua's Word, a believer can be *oppressed*. We can be tormented and attacked by demons when we give into our flesh nature and continue to sin. We can certainly open doors for the demonic realm to attack us, gain ground for habitation in our flesh bodies and our minds or soul realm. 1 Peter 5:8 warns us, "Be sober, be diligent; because your adversary the devil, walks about as a roaring lion, seeking whom he <u>may devour</u>." Notice that he is not the roaring lion. The real lion happens to be Yahshua, the Lion of the tribe of Judah! Notice also that he seeks whom he **MAY** devour. *(Comment: permission has been granted by our actions against YHWH's Word)* Satan cannot devour us unless we permit it. We give permission when we sin and disobey our Heavenly Father. I believe the body and bride of Messiah Yahshua has grossly underestimated our enemy! One primary way we allow satanic attack is through unforgiveness. As followers of Messiah Yahshua, we must forgive and walk in obedience in all areas of our lives. If we sin, we can then ask for forgiveness and repent as promised in 1 John 1:9, "If we confess our sins, He is faithful and just to forgive us our sins, and cleanse us of all unrighteousness."

Yahshua taught on the subject of the demonic realm in Matthew 12:28-29, "(28) But if I cast out devils by the Spirit of Yahweh, then the Kingdom of Yahweh is come upon you. (29) Or else how can one enter into a strong man's house and spoil his goods, except he first bind the strong man? And then he may spoil his house." We have to have Yahshua's authority, to have authority over the demonic. Satan cannot have anything over us. This means we cannot allow any sin in our lives if we are to walk in power. Now, He continues the topic at Matthew 12:43-

45, (43) "When the unclean spirit is gone out of the man, he walks about the dry places and seeks rest, but finds none. (44) Then the demon says; I will return to my house where I was cast out; and when he arrives he finds it empty, swept and put in order. (45) Then he goes and finds and brings with him seven more demon spirits more wicked and evil than him, and they all enter in and dwell there in the man; and the end result for that man is worse than before. Even so, shall it be with this wicked generation." Please consider this word of caution about casting out devils, though. Don't cast out devils out of people, unless afterwards, you will witness to them, and have them confess Yahshua as Lord! Also, tell them to go and sin no more, less a worse thing come upon them. The point I want to make is this: If you cast out a devil, teach the person to flee the sin and use his own authority to keep the doors shut. We must shut doors to sin, as sin allows demonic spirits free access to our souls (minds) or bodies, and that leaves the person worse off than before you cast the devil(s) out. I am saddened to say, I know this from first hand experience. That person would have been better off if I had known and paid attention to Yahshua's teaching on the matter.

One time in Jerusalem, I was visiting with a friend who had formerly worked for the NSA (National Security Agency) in America. We were discussing Isaiah 17:1 that says Damascus will be a ruinous heap. I had mentioned that the Scripture had not been accomplished yet. He didn't seem to remember the Scripture, but was very much interested. He said that he had friends in high government places in Israel, who had just that week discussed bombing the "hot seat" for terrorists, *Damascus!* I had fasted many weeks, so when he asked me to go with him and cast out a devil from a lady friend of a companion, I agreed. He had been told by mutual friends that I had the ability to do that. Of course, it was not me, but Yahshua dwelling in me, that could do that. Remember, you, or me, even the least of us born again, are greater than John the Baptist according to

Yahshua. I went with him and met the person who seemed quite demented. She had been a believer before deciding to move in with an unbeliever in Jerusalem. I started commanding the demon out of her. I seemed to have some break through and then she seemed worse. I finally stopped, went in another room, and asked Yahshua, "Why can't I have authority over this devil?" Yahshua replied to my horror, "She has denied me, son" It would have been much wiser to ask Yahshua in the first place, than my allowing so many orthodox Jews that did not believe in Yahshua, to mistakenly confirm the error they already believed. I had no authority where Satan was god. The girl then ran away and that's the last I saw of her. I have cast out many devils and seen people fall in the floor and foam at the mouth, etc., and I have definitely seen people get free! However, His power is best used when we teach and get people to *stay* free! Usually, when I command a devil to go from someone, I remind the person and the demon(s) about the power of the blood of Yahshua! By using The Name above all names, Yahshua of Nazareth, and speaking a steady reminder of the power of the blood of the lamb, Satan's power is absolutely broken!

Many times while sensing the need to pray, but not knowing of any specific needs, I will pray in unknown tongues and let the Holy Spirit pray for what He knows needs prayer and intercession. Once, while passing out gospel tracts in Cabo San Lucas on the Baja peninsula of Mexico, I was praying in unknown tongues softly as I walked. It was sundown and I approached two men who were apparently drunk and fighting in the street. I paused to watch them for a moment, amazed at their conditions and the fighting. I determined that these two definitely needed the Spanish gospel tracts on becoming "born again." They were still fighting as I stretched out my hand to offer them both a tract. The next thing I witnessed was some invisible force knocking them both to the ground about six feet away! Whatever that force was (an angel?), it was extremely sobering to say the least. They both got up appearing somewhat dazed and bewildered as they were wondering who had hit them with such power. They were looking at me, and must have thought I had hit them. They were very attentive, obviously impressed by my strength, and ready to listen to anything I had to say. I handed them the tract on how to receive eternal life by being "born again" and explained that I had not touched them, but the Creator of all things, Yahweh, wanted their attention because of His great love for them. They took the tracts and answered, "Muchas gracias" meaning much thanks. Then I watched them walk away together reading the tracts and talking. Apparently an angel of the Lord wanted their full attention, and I walked away still praying in the Spirit and praising Yahweh for His marvelous works! You too, will be given supernatural help as you determine to do the works of the Lord and produce fruit for His Kingdom. It is His plan that none would perish!

> *Know this truth; a person with a biblical experience is never at the mercy of someone with a biblical theory! Once you have received the Baptism of the Holy Spirit, and have experienced the wonder of praying in the spirit, no person or religious spirit will be able to twist the Scriptures, and convince you that this experience and blessing is "passed away" or from the devil!*

What if we don't trust or have faith in what He promises? Remember, faith comes by hearing and hearing the Word of Yahweh according to Romans 10:17. Romans 3:3-4 says, "(3) For what if some do not believe? Shall their unbelief make the faith of Yahweh (God) of none effect? (4) Yahweh forbid; (Certainly not) let Yahweh be true and every man a liar; as it is written, that you may be justified in your speaking and might overcome when you are judged." So when you disagree with the Word of Truth, Yahshua, you are the one who is lying, not Him! I remember once when Yahshua asked me if I was healed. I answered and said, "I don't feel healed, Lord." He reminded me not to walk according to how I felt. I replied, "Lord, if I say I'm healed and I don't feel like it, I feel like a liar." He answered with a soft question, "Can you lie if you agree with Me son?" I replied, "It sure seems that way." He softly replied again, *"I am the TRUTH,* I cannot lie and when you disagree with Me, *YOU are the liar."* We gain faith by hearing The Truth not by hearing the facts. The facts are temporary or as the Bible call them *temporal* in 2 Corinthians 4:18, "the things which are seen are temporal." What is seen are the facts but realize they are temporary and therefore subject to change! What is unchangeable is the Word of Truth, for it will remain forever! Continue to speak His Holy Word! We are taught that we are a triune being in 1 Thessalonians 5:23, "May the Elohim (God) of peace sanctify you wholly (make you pure), and I pray that your whole *spirit* (born again now), *soul* (mind, will, intellect and emotions), and *body,* (your flesh) be preserved blameless at the coming of Yahshua the Messiah." So now your spirit man, the *hidden man of the heart,* is reborn or recreated in Yahweh's image. *We are spiritual beings with a soul (mind, will, intellect and emotions) and we live in physical bodies.*

1 Peter 3:3-4 states, "(3) Whose adorning let it not be that outward adorning of plaiting the hair, wearing of gold, or putting on fine clothes, but (4) let it be the *hidden man of the heart,* in that which is not corruptible, even the adorning of a meek and quiet spirit, which is in the sight of Yahweh of great price and value." A meek (gentle) and quiet spirit should be our personal goal. *Most of today's cultures put too much emphasis on how good the outsides of us look, and not nearly enough attention to what is put on the inside and stored there.* This reminds me of most marriages today: If they spent nearly the time, money, and effort preparing for living in the marriage as they do preparing for the wedding day, we would know how to live together according to Yahweh's principles. The results would

be far less divorces, after the newness of the marriages have worn off! Now your spirit man is born again, but what about your soul (mind, will, intellect and emotions) and your body? This is where you make decisions about *who will rule your life*, whether or not you will receive **blessings or curses.** There is an ongoing battle for rulership of your life between your flesh and spirit. Galatians 5:16-17 says. "(16) This I say then, walk in the spirit and you shall not fulfill the desires of the flesh. For the flesh wars against the spirit and the spirit wars against the flesh; and these are contrary the one to the other; so that you cannot do the things you would."

> *It is of great importance to you, as a follower of your Creator, to make sure you allow your recreated spirit man to rule your life, and allow Yahweh's protection, provision, and blessings to empower your life and fulfill your destiny. That destiny will produce fruit that will remain long after your life in this body of flesh. It will produce life everlasting!*

Romans 12:1-2 tells us, "(1) I beseech (urge) you therefore, by the mercies of Yahweh, that you present your body a living sacrifice, holy, acceptable to Yahweh, which is your reasonable service. (2) And be not conformed to this world: **but be transformed** by the renewing of your mind, that you may prove the good, acceptable, *perfect will of Yahweh*." This Scripture certainly shows us that we can (our spirits) rule over our flesh nature and conform to His plan, His word, by renewing our minds (souls) with His Words of Instruction. We can, by choice, know and obey the perfect will of Yahweh. This will produce fruit that is eternal. In John 15:4, Yahshua states, "Abide in Me, and I in you. As the branch cannot bear fruit of itself, except it abides in the vine, no more can you, except you abide in Me." What is the reward of remaining in Him? In John 15:7, He promises: "If you remain in Me, and My Word remains in you, ask what you wish and it will be done for you by My Father which is in Heaven."

Remember, your flesh doesn't want to obey, study, and grow up spiritually. It wants to do what brings pleasure only. When you present your body as a living sacrifice, you are making it obey. When you study to show yourself approved and a workman that will not be ashamed at Messiah Yahshua's appearing, you are not conforming to the world, the natural pathway of your flesh nature. You are being transformed by the renewing of your mind when you choose to read and obey the Scriptures. You are actually submitting yourself to Yahweh (God) and resisting the devil (the enemy of your soul) according to James 4:7 and he (Satan) will flee from you. Ephesians 1:17-23 gives the following prayer for you: "(17) I pray Yahweh, the Father of glory, give you the Spirit of wisdom and revelation in the knowledge of Him, (18) the eyes of your understanding being enlightened, that you may know the hope of His calling *(your destiny)*, and what the riches of the glory (His mercy and goodness revealed) of His inheritance in the believers (19) and what is the *exceeding greatness of His power to us who believe*, according to the working of His mighty power, (20) which He wrought in Yahshua the Messiah, when He raised Him from the dead, and set Him at His Own right hand in heavenly places (21) far above all principality, and power, and might, and dominion, and every name that is named, not only in this world, but also in the world to come; (22) and has put all things under His feet, and gave Him to be the Head (of the body of believers) over all things to the assembly (believers). (23) Which is His body, the fullness of Him who fits all in all." Note that there is great power and wisdom available to those of us who believe and we can know our destiny and calling.

Ephesians 2:1-8 states, "(1) And you has He made alive (quickened-born again) who were dead in trespasses and sins; (2) wherein in times past you walked according to the course of this world, according to the prince of the power of the air, (Satan), the spirit that now works in the children of disobedience; (3) among whom we also had our conversation in times past, in the lusts (passions and desires) of our flesh and of the mind (unrenewed) and were by nature the children of (Yahweh's) wrath, even as the others. (4) But Yahweh, who is rich in mercy, for His great love with which He loves us (5) even when we were dead in our sins (transgressions against His Word) He has made us alive together with Messiah, (by grace, an unmerited gift are you saved) (6) and has raised us up together, and made us sit together in heavenly places in Yahshua the Messiah. (7) That in the ages to come, He might show the exceeding riches of His grace in His kindness toward us in Yahshua. (8) For by grace are you saved (delivered from all the plan of hell's attack) through faith (belief), and that not of yourselves, it is the gift of Yahweh." In Hosea 4:6, Yahweh states "My people are destroyed for lack of knowledge." We must desire the understanding of the Word and grow from it. We cannot stay spiritual babies and stay protected. You are on the right path so study and desire Truth. Rightly divide the Word of Truth by growing in your relationship with your Creator. He loves us and promises; He stands at the door (our spirit, soul, and body) and knocks, whoever opens the door, He will come in and fellowship with us and we with Him. We can have an intimate relationship with our Creator. It is worth our effort and we will receive His peace, His joy, His righteousness, and His victory over death, Satan, and the works of the flesh nature.

Author's Note on Power to Overcome: As the Holy Spirit Early Rain Outpouring was given at the conclusion of the Spring Feasts of the Lord; (Feast of Weeks or Shavuot called by many Pentecost) it stands to reason that the Latter Rain Outpouring of the Holy Spirit will be the conclusion of the Fall Feasts of the Lord. (I expect The Last Great Day or 8th day of the Feast of Tabernacles in 2010?)

Chapter Fifteen:
Heaven or Hell

nderstand there is a place created and reserved for the devil and his followers called hell and a place reserved for Yahweh (God) and His followers called Heaven. Here are some Scriptures that give us a glimpse of hell: Matthew 10:28 "Don't be afraid of him who can destroy your body but cannot kill the soul. Rather, be afraid of the One Who can destroy both your body and your soul in hell." Mark 9:43 "If your hand causes you to sin, cut it off, It is better for you to enter into life maimed than with two hands to go into hell, where the fire never goes out and the worm dies not." Luke 16:23 "In hell, where he was in torment..." Matthew 25:41 "Then shall He (Yahshua) say to them on His left hand, Depart from Me you cursed, into everlasting fire, prepared for the devil and his angels."

When you take your last breath on the earth, your spirit man, the inner person of the heart, (the real you- the eternal spirit) will stand before Yahshua, the righteous judge of the earth, and give account for the life you lived here according to 1 Peter 1:17. Your body of flesh was made from the dirt and back to the dirt it will go. Your spirit came from Yahweh's spirit and back to Him you will go and give account. You can obey and follow Yahshua and receive eternal life or you can start practicing now by screaming and gnashing your teeth at the same time. This will prepare you for your eternal torture in hell with Satan and his angels. Try it once and I'm sure you'll agree that is not an option! Since the Bible clearly states that we all have sinned by transgressing His Commands, all have fallen short, we must have received Yahshua's righteousness by being born again and following and obeying Him at that time.

> *Yahshua, the Word made flesh, does not say that everyone that **knows about Him** will be with Him in heaven.*

Only those that love Him and *love is synonymous with obedience.* Remember in John 14:21 Yahshua says, "Whoever **_has_** My Commands and **_obeys_** them, that's the one that loves me..." There are two requirements here, **have** His Commands which means you must read, understand, and receive them, and secondly, humble yourself and **obey** them. Most people are deceived. They think that by being "normal" and good in their own eyes they will go to heaven. They are dead wrong! How can I make such a statement? Yahshua said it in Matthew 7:13-14, "Enter in by the narrow gate; for wide is the gate that leads to **_destruction_** and many (most) enter in thereby, (14) but straight is the gate and narrow is the way, which leads to life, and **_very few_** find it." Romans 3:23 explains our dilemma, "For *all* have sinned (transgressed His Instructions) and come short of His perfection and glory (mercy and truth)." Since we *all* come up short, we must receive His righteousness and He received our sin and the punishment for our sin. Most are entering into hell and that surprises many people. You don't have to do anything to enter into hell, just be as "good" as you can without receiving His righteousness and that is the wide gate and the road most traveled.

You can be popular and fit in naturally with this world system, but remember, Satan is the god of this world. At least until his lease runs out at the end of six days, or six thousand years. The Scriptures tell us in 2 Peter 3:8-9, "(8) Be not ignorant of this one thing, that *one day with Yahshua is as a thousand years and one thousand years as one day.* (9)

Yahshua is not slack concerning His promise; but He is patient toward us, not willing that any would perish, but that everyone would come to repentance." Biblically, recorded time is only about six thousand years. A biblically and astronomically corrected Jewish calendar is somewhere just under or near that number. You may have been taught that the earth is billions of years old. Many have been deceived by the faulty premise made in carbon dating. That faulty premise assumes that the harmful rays of the sun have always bombarded the earth at the same level of intensity. You may want to study the sites at www.creationevidence.org or www.creationresearch.org again. I will condense the story quickly for your consideration. Prior to Noah's flood, there was a canopy of vapor covering the Earth. Scientists believe this probably blocked much of the harmful and deteriorating radiation. We know that even now, more and more harmful rays are penetrating the atmosphere due to the loss of ozone. Prior to the flood, the Scriptures express that the earth was watered by a mist from the earth in Genesis 1:6. Apparently, up to the time of the flood, there had never been rain. Scientists believe that the source of the waters of the flood was the bursting of the protective vapor ring around the earth. Additionally, during the eruption of Mt. St. Helens in America, scientists made a startling observation. The lava flows created a stratus of earth that was previously believed to take millions of years! Only problem with that theory was, we all watched it happen on television in a few days.

Adam was given *dominion* for mankind in the Garden of Eden but lost it when Eve was deceived and he willingly disobeyed Yahweh. Yahweh promised Adam that *the day* he disobeyed, Adam would surely die in Genesis 2:17. This won't come as a surprise to you, but Adam did die within the time frame of *the day*, before one thousand years completed, at the age of 930. We may not always understand, but His Word is infallible. A *day* with the Lord is as a thousand years, and a thousand years as one *day*. They lost their intimacy and fellowship with their Creator,

Yahweh. 1 John 2:15 tells us that anyone who loves this world system does not have the love of the Father in them and is an enemy of Yahweh!

Chapter Sixteen:
Warnings: Return to the Roots of Our Faith And The End of the Age

W hy would we want to return to the Hebrew roots of our faith? <u>The promise made concerning the covenant and it's promises are first marked by keeping the Sabbath</u>, which is the first of all the Feasts and Commanded Appointments (Moedim) of the Lord. Not by keeping *any* Sabbath you decide on but keeping His Sabbath. Exodus 31:17 YHVH (Yahweh) speaks through Moses, "**It is a sign between Me and the children of Israel forever** for in six days YHVH made heaven and earth, and on the seventh day He rested and was refreshed." Secondly, understand the Scriptures were written by Hebrews in the Hebrew tongue. We have been removed from what was originally taught by Yahshua by nearly seventeen hundred years. Nearly anything left to man long enough will be compromised and changed. I have a good friend, Gilbert Vincent, who is a believer that was shown that we are to Keep the Feasts of YHWH or *BE A FEAST!* A valid point is made by Gilbert based on the Scriptures because we are told to keep His Commands and Feasts forever. Then at the end of the Book of Revelation in the Bible we are told about the Messiah destroying His enemies or those that won't obey Him and keep

His Feasts and Commands. Remember, He considers us to hate Him if we will not obey Him and to love Him if we have and obey His Commands according to John 14:21. Yahshua destroys His enemies and calls for the fowls to come and eat their carcasses in Revelation 19:17, 18 & 21, "(17) And I saw an angel standing in the Sun; and he cried with a loud voice, saying to all the fowls that fly in the air, come and gather yourselves together for the supper of the Great Elohim (God); (18) that you may eat the flesh of kings, and the flesh of captains, and the flesh of mighty men, and the flesh of horses and their riders, and the flesh of all men both free and slave, both small and great. (21) And the remnant was slain by the sword of Him that sat upon the horse, for the sword proceeded out of His mouth, and the *fowls were filled with their flesh.*" Remember, in 325 A.D. Constantine changed all the holidays or Holy Days and the Sabbath which are the festivals called the Feasts of the Lord Commanded by Yahweh. Additionally, we are told by Hebrew, Aramaic and Greek scholars such as Dr. James Trimm who translated the entire Bible from Hebrew and Aramaic text, that the Hebrew language has idioms or ideas that are specifically understood by the Hebrew culture and those keeping the festivals of the Torah, and the Commands of Yahweh. I would recommend this new translation, which is the Hebraic-Roots Version or the HRV published in 2004 and can be purchased at www.isr-messianic.org.

I will mention a few of these idioms to give you the idea. When Yahshua said concerning His return and the end of the age that *no man knows the day or the hour* that He would return, every Hebrew there understood what He was saying. There were at least twelve days (new moons) that no one could pre-determine on the Hebrew calendar. Biblically, you could never have a 28 day or 31 day month as Pope Gregory's calendar known as the Gregorian calendar in use today has. The moon cycles the earth mathematically every 29.54 days, so Biblically and astronomically the month will always be either 29 or 30 days. Twenty nine days if you could atmospherically (no clouds etc.) visibly see it that day and automatically deferred to the thirtieth day if it was not spotted. The first month started when the new moon was seen over Jerusalem on either the twenty-ninth or thirtieth day of the month after the twelfth new moon, and the second witness being the barley *abib* or at a stage of fruitfulness that it could be ready within a few weeks for First Fruits or the Wave Offering. First Fruits was the thanksgiving to Yahweh for the harvest three days after the Passover supper. If the barley was not *abib* then an additional month was added to the past year called Adar Bet. They would test the barley grain by fire to see if it was abib/ready, that is at a stage of fruitfulness and not burn up when fire was put to it. The analogy is simple, when we have the fiery trials of tribulation put to us, will we produce fruit that will remain, or burn up and escape through the flames only?

Because of these variables of the new moon sighted over Jerusalem and the barley being *Abib*, you could never prefigure the first day that started the year. Only after the year started, and even then you would have to wait for each month to be determined, and see when the new moon could be seen over Jerusalem on either the 29th or 30th day of the month. Then you would have to wait until the seventh new moon was sighted because that is when the Feast of Trumpets is according to the Scripture Command, and the Scriptures declare that the trump will sound, and the dead in Messiah will rise first. So what Messiah Yahshua was actually saying was, "I will return on the Feast of Trumpets!" Every Hebrew there understood what He was saying, because they kept the Feasts and understood they are Holy Convocations or *rehearsals that show us what is to come*. Which Feast of Trumpets you ask? When you see all these things begin to come to pass. The generation that sees these things coming to pass mentioned in Matthew 24, Mark 13, and Luke 21. Take some time and study these chapters yourself. The recent Bible Code findings discussed in chapter eighteen will give us tremendous insight as to the timing of this massive chain of events. Also, it would be wise to study and pray over the visions and dreams found at these sites: www.visionsofthelastdays.com, www.americaslastdays.com, and www.etpv.org. Another site for studying the signs in the heavens is www.biblicalastronomy.com.

Another Hebrew idiom would be *"in that day." "In that day"* nearly always refers to the Sabbath rest day or the seventh millennium and is synonymous with The Day of the Lord. Remember the Scriptures say that a thousand years is as a day and a day is as a thousand years.

Another idiom is *"under the fig tree."* Why would Nathaniel who was without deceit or guile respond that Yahshua was Messiah after Yahshua told him He saw him *"under the fig tree?"* Because *"under the fig tree"* was a time of rest, provision, and study, specifically referring to the last, or Sabbath millennium. It was the Sabbath rest time as mentioned in 1 Kings 4:24b and 25, "(24b) he had peace on all sides round about him. (25) And Judah and Israel dwelt safely, every man under his vine and under his fig tree." He was referring to the Seventh millennium when Messiah dwells and rules on the earth. Since Nathaniel knew about his own lifestyle and how he was without deceit or guile, he knew he would be with Messiah during that time. When Yahshua spoke that He saw Nathaniel *"under the fig tree,"* it witnessed to Nathaniel that Yahshua really was the Messiah!

The Greek mindset is just the opposite of the Hebrew mindset. For example, the Greek thought magnifies human strength and power. Therefore, the antiquities contain Greek statues of men of great strength, beauty, and intellect. Whereas, the Hebrew thought is based on intuitive and heavenly thought and every young Jew was taught the Holy Scriptures by Torah observant and obedient parents. Every Pharisee, such as Sha'ul,

(Hebrew name for Paul) had to memorize verbatim the Torah, the first five books of the Bible, by the time they were twelve and before they turned thirteen! This is when they became a man or bar mitzvah, *a son of the Commandments!* The Greek thought is to magnify man whereas the Hebrew thought is to magnify God or Yahweh. The Greek method is to have one man be the great one and many underlings. This might be as a Pastor or teacher, etc. One man will have the attention and the high esteem of all and somehow is expected to do all the thinking and work for all the believers. I have been to Israel and seen the ancient synagogues for the assembling of the believers. They were all round and had the raised type of seating much like you would think of a miniature coliseum. This type of seating arrangement allowed for ministry of the body to itself.

Since one person is not designed to fulfill the works of all the believers, and one person cannot receive that much adoration and esteem, this puts the church leader or pastor in an extremely dangerous position! Besides, a true pastor is called of Yahweh, has a servants' heart and wants to serve the others, not be the head and receive honor. Hebrew thought would be we are all servants and have One Master, Yahshua the Messiah. Under Hebrew thought one would give a song, another give a word, another a prophecy and we are all part of the body and all minister to each other. Greek thought is how the Doctrine of the Nicolaitans works as the thing Yahweh hates as recorded in Revelation two. *Nico* means to conquer and *laity* is the people. So Nicolaitan mean to conquer the people. Similar to many religious systems of church denominations today, which glorify men with titles. Many of those with titles, authority, and honor from men are the very first in line to attack and persecute true believers who walk in the obedience and power of the gospels. The religious Pharisees are alive and well in the church system today. Like their counterparts of biblical days, they will not give their positions of authority up easily!

How can returning to the Hebraic roots of our faith help us understand the Scriptures you may ask? I will answer that question first with a short study done by my good friend Brad Scott of www.wildbranchministries.com. Brad's study defines the meanings in Hebrew of the first 10 names in the Bible that declare the plan of salvation!

Keep in mind the names only have this meaning in Hebrew.

Hebrew meaning of 10 Names –Adam through Noah (Removed- Cain and Able)

YHWH'S Plan through the Ages: Salvation

Adam-	Man
Seth-	Is Appointed
Enosh-	Mortal
Caanan-	Sorrow
Mahal'el-	But the blessed El
Yared-	Shall come
Enoch-	Teaching that
Metushelach-	His death shall bring
Lamech-	The desperate
Noah-	Comfort and rest

Understand that I am not suggesting that we get justified by keeping the Law or the Torah! Here is a letter sent to me recently of his account of recent questioning along these lines:

Clay Mitchell, a dear friend, wrote me about the following conversation concerning the Torah:

I was asked once about keeping Torah and was told, "No one is justified by the Law." Next, they continued saying that keeping "the Law" is unnecessary because it is not the means of our justification, implying that I was obeying "the Law" to be justified. And you declared that no one is justified (declared righteous) by keeping the Law. On this point we agree. We are, in fact, declared righteous by the merit of Yahshua, Who kept "the Law" perfectly. It was Yahshua who was "in all points tempted like as we are, yet without sin" (Hebrews 4:15).

Let us remember that the Bible defines sin as "the transgression of the Law" (1 John 3:4). By faith, we become members of the body of Messiah, and, as such, Messiah's righteousness has been imputed to all who believe. Thus, we are justified or declared righteous by Yahshua's deeds, not our own. If our ultimate goal is that of salvation, He would define salvation as "going to heaven."

However; my goal is to become a citizen in the Kingdom of YHWH. Having been genuinely touched by the love of YHWH as displayed in the life, death, and resurrection of Yahshua the Messiah, I embraced the cross to become a member of the body of Messiah. I, like Yahshua, seek to demonstrate love for YHWH by putting my old, selfish man to death and submitting to the Word of YHWH, living as an obedient "Law"-abiding citizen of the Kingdom. I also, realize that salvation is not the goal but the starting point of this faith and walk. If the head (Yahshua) kept the Law perfectly, we should expect no less from the body! To be a good citizen of the Kingdom means to keep the Laws of our King! I agree with you that our justification to enter the Kingdom is to be found in the merits of Yeshua.

The heresy of antinomianism (anti=against, nomos=law) teaches that "the Law" has been done away with. However, the Scriptures define sin as the transgression or violation of the Law.

1 John 3:4 *"Whosoever committeth sin transgresseth also the Law: for sin is the transgression of the Law."* (KJV)

Without the Torah defining sin, we would not know what is and what is not an offense to YHWH. Shaul (Paul) understood this very point when addressing the Romans.

Romans 7:7 *"What shall we say then? Is the Law sin? Elohim forbid. Nay, I had not known sin, but by the Law: for I had not known lust, except the Law had said, Thou shalt not covet."* (KJV)

To do away with the Torah is to do away with the very revelation of YHWH which distinguishes between sin and righteousness. If the Law has been done away with, there is no sin. If there is no sin, there is no need for faith, righteousness, or Yeshua. No one can be judged, and nothing will be restored. Antinomianism allows sin to continue to reign, ultimately leading to death.

"No one is justified by the Law." Obedience to the Torah is not, nor has it ever been, a means for justification. It declares our need for the Messiah.

Galatians 2:21 *"I do not frustrate the grace of Elohim: for if righteousness comes by the Law, then Messiah is dead in vain."* (KJV)

Galatians 3:11 *"But that no man is justified by the Law in the sight of Elohim, it is evident: for, the just shall live by faith."* (KJV)

Paul (Shaul) taught in his letters that we are not justified by our ability to keep the Torah. He taught, rather, that we are justified by grace through faith.

Galatians 2:16 *"Knowing that a man is not justified by the works of the Law, but by the faith of Yeshua Messiah, even we have believed in Yeshua Messiah, that we might be justified by the faith of Messiah, and not by the works of the Law: for by the works of the Law shall no flesh be justified."* (KJV)

Romans 5:9 *"Much more then, being now justified by His blood, we shall be saved from wrath through Him."* (KJV)

Hebrews 7:19 *"For the Law made nothing perfect, but the bringing in of a better hope did; by the which we draw nigh unto Elohim."* (KJV)

The High Priest also understood that justification did not come by his ability to keep the Torah, as you suggest. He too offered a sacrifice - not just for the people but for himself as well.

Leviticus 9:7-8 *"(7) And Moses said unto Aaron, Go unto the altar, and offer thy sin offering, and thy burnt offering, and make atonement for thyself, and for the people: and offer the offering of the people, and make atonement for them; as YHWH Commanded. (8) Aaron therefore went unto the altar, and slew the calf of the sin offering, which was for himself."* (KJV)

Hebrews 9:7 *"But into the second went the high priest alone once every year, not without blood, which he offered for himself, and for the errors of the people."* (KJV)

Yeshua, our High Priest, conquered the "sting of death," which is sin (1 Corinthians 15:56). Therefore, He alone is worthy to be our High Priest after the order of Melchizedek, justifying through His blood all those who believe.

Romans 5:18 *"Therefore as by the offence of one judgment came upon all men to condemnation; even so by the righteousness of one the free gift came upon all men unto justification of life."* (KJV)

Hebrews 9:22 *"And almost all things are by the Law purged with blood; and without shedding of blood is no remission."* (KJV)

Hebrews 13:12 *"Wherefore Yeshua also, that He might sanctify the people with His own blood, suffered without the gate."* (KJV)

Isaiah 53:6 *"All we like sheep have gone astray; we have turned everyone to his own way; and YHWH has laid on Him the iniquity of us all."* (KJV)

Your assumption that I was obeying "the Law" to be justified creates several problems. First, justification or being declared righteous is not a new concept derived and promoted only in the Renewed Covenant. Salvation has always been by faith in the provision of YHWH. In chapter eleven of Hebrews, the author lists those of old who heard their calling and responded by faith. Those listed lived long before the birth of Messiah or the writing of the Scriptures, yet we are assured that they too will be in the Kingdom, showing all who would come after them that justification does indeed come by faith!

Let us now address the erroneous concept that keeping "the Law" is unnecessary, as implied by you. Earlier, I shared a few thoughts that I could point out to my friend, all of which should cause you to retreat from your position that it is unnecessary to keep "the Law." That said, let us put on the whole armor of Elohim and give Me the ammunition necessary to defend myself and give you the Scriptural reasons for obeying the Torah.

The children of Israel received YHWH'S Law corporately after they were redeemed, delivered, and saved from Egypt. While we may rightly say that Israel's faith in YHWH'S provision of the lamb saved them, it is clearly understood that the "saving work" was an act of "grace" on YHWH'S part. It was Elohim Who redeemed and delivered Israel from the bondage of Egypt with an outstretched arm and with great judgments.

Exodus 6:6 *"Wherefore say unto the children of Israel, I am YHWH, and I will bring you out from under the burdens of the Egyptians, and I will rid you out of their bondage, and I will redeem you with a stretched out arm, and with great judgments."* (KJV)

YHWH went on to say:

Exodus 19:4-5 *"(4) Ye have seen what I did unto the Egyptians, and how I bare you on eagles' wings, and brought you unto Myself. (5) Now therefore, if ye will obey My voice indeed, and keep My Covenant, then ye shall be a peculiar treasure unto Me above all people: for all the earth is Mine."* (KJV)

The people responded:

Exodus 19:8 *"All that YHWH has spoken we will do."* (KJV)

The Renewed Covenant affirms this blueprint.

John 14:15 *"If ye love Me, keep My Commandments."* (KJV)

Romans 7:22 *"For I delight in the Law of Elohim after the inward man."* (KJV)

1 Corinthians 6:20 *"For ye are bought with a price: therefore glorify Elohim in your body, and in your spirit, which are Elohim's."* (KJV)

Through studying and obeying the Torah, we receive divine revelation, insight, and understanding of our relationship with YHWH. The Feast Days and the care of the poor, the widows, and the orphans are but a few examples of the selfless instructions written in the Torah. However, to gain an understanding of the Almighty, these Laws must not just remain written instructions; they must become living words brought to life by those who obey them from the heart.

Psalm 119:97 *"Oh how I love Your Law! It is my meditation all the day."* (KJV)

Psalm 49:3 *"My mouth shall speak of wisdom; and the meditation of my heart shall be of understanding."* (KJV)

Psalm 111:10 *"The fear of YHWH is the beginning of wisdom: a good understanding have all they that do His Commandments: His praise endures for ever."* (KJV)

By obeying the Laws of YHWH, we become a light to others. We are to be a light to the world. By our obedience to the Torah, we illuminate the very character of YHWH to the world.

Matthew 5:16 *"Let your light so shine before men, that they may see your good works, and glorify your Father which is in heaven."* (KJV)

Matthew 5:14 *"Ye are the light of the world. A city that is set on a hill cannot be hid."* (KJV)

Matthew 5:15 *"Neither do men light a candle, and put it under a bushel, but on a candlestick; and it giveth light unto all that are in the house."* (KJV)

Deuteronomy 4:5 *"Behold, I have taught you statutes and judgments, even as YHWH my Elohim Commanded me, that ye should do so in the land whither ye go to possess it."* (KJV)

Deuteronomy 4:6 *"Keep therefore and do them; for this is your wisdom and your understanding in the sight of the nations, which shall hear all these statutes, and say, Surely this great nation is a wise and understanding people."* (KJV)

In conclusion, you should clearly understand that both my motivation and our own for obedience to the Torah is not for justification; rather, it is out of love for the One Who redeemed, delivered, and saved us! As John said:

1 John 4:19 *"We love Him, because He first loved us."* (KJV)

I never claimed that my salvation or justification came through my obedience to the Torah. You falsely assumed I am seeking salvation by obedience. You do not understand the Renewed Covenant or the purpose of the Holy Spirit. "A Rood Awakening"

Next I will answer Five Questions of why we should return to Hebraic roots of the faith with a short study.

Five Questions Answered;
Why return to the Hebraic Roots of our Faith

Jeremiah 16:19-21 "(19) O יהוה, my strength and my stronghold and my refuge, in **the day of distress** the gentiles shall come to You from the ends

175

of the earth and say, **Our fathers have inherited only falsehood, futility, and there is no value in them**. [See Psalm 147:19, Isaiah 2:3, Isaiah 60:2-3, John 4:22, Romans 2:20; 3:2; 9:4.] (20) Would a man make mighty ones for himself, which are not mighty ones? (21) Therefore see, I am causing them to know, this time I cause them to know My hand and My might. And they shall know that My Name is יהוה!" (Pronounced: Yahweh- YHWH)

Zechariah 8:23 "Thus says YHWH of hosts; In those days *it shall come to pass*, that ten men shall take hold out of all languages of the nations, even shall take hold of **the skirt** *(Comment: tzi tzis, wings, appendages of Tallit or prayer garment/closet)* of him that is a Jew, saying, We will go with you: for we have heard *that* YHWH *is* with you."

> **Today is the day of our deliverance- in our hearing Him and repenting!**

First Question: Who was the WORD on Mt. Sinai?

John 1:1-15 "(1) In the beginning was the Word, and the Word was with YHWH, and the Word was YHWH. (2) The same was in the beginning with YHWH. (3) All things were made by Him; and without Him was not anything made that was made. (4) In Him was Life; and the Life was the Light of men. (5) And the Light shines in darkness; and the darkness comprehended it not. (6) There was a man sent from YHWH, whose name *was* John. (7) The same came for a witness, to bear witness of the Light that all *men* through Him might believe. (8) He was not that Light, but *was sent* to bear witness of that Light. (9) *That* was the true Light, which lights every man that cometh into the world. (10) He was in the world, and the world was made by Him, and the world knew Him not. (11) He came unto His own, and His own received Him not. (12) But as many as received Him, to them He gave power to become the sons of YHWH, *even* to them that believe on His Name: (13) which were born, not of blood, nor of the will of the flesh, nor of the will of man, but of YHWH. (14) And the Word was made flesh, and dwelt among us, (and we beheld His glory, the glory as of the only begotten of the Father,) full of grace and truth. (15) John bare witness of Him, and cried, saying, this was He of Whom I spake, He that comes after me is preferred before me: for He was before me.

Common misunderstanding: Graceless Father- even angry, mean, full of wrath; but merciful and graceful Son. Grace is not some new thing for the New or ReNEWed Covenant- Noah found grace in His eyes.

Second Question: Who is the NEW COVENANT made to? Renewed?

Let's look at WHO the New Covenant is made to:

Jeremiah 31:31-37 "(31) See, the days are coming, declares יהוה, when I shall make a new Covenant with the **house of Yisra'ĕl and with the house of Yehud'ah**, [See Hebrews 8:8-12; 10:16-17.] (32) not like the Covenant I made with their fathers in the day when I took them by the hand to bring them out of the land of Mitsrayim (Egypt), My Covenant which they broke, though I was a husband to them," declares יהוה. (33) For this is the Covenant I shall make with the house of Yisra'ĕl after those days, declares יהוה: I shall put My Torah in their inward parts, and write it on their hearts. And I shall be their Elohim, and they shall be My people. (34) And no longer shall they teach, each one his neighbor, and each one his brother, saying, 'Know יהוה,' for they shall all know Me, from the least of them to the greatest of them, declares יהוה. For I shall forgive their crookedness, and remember their sin no more. (35) Thus said יהוה, who gives the sun for a light by day, and the laws of the moon and the stars for a light by night, Who stirs up the sea, and its waves roar – יהוה of hosts is His Name: (36) If these Laws vanish from before Me, declares יהוה, then the seed of Yisra'ĕl shall also cease from being a nation before Me forever. (37) Thus said יהוה, If the heavens above could be measured, and the foundations of the earth searched out beneath, I would also cast off all the seed of Yisra'ĕl for all that they have done, declares יהוה.''

Third Question: What is sin?

1 John 3:4-9 "(4) Whosoever committeth sin transgresseth also the Law: **for sin is the transgression of the <u>Law</u>. (Translated "Law" in Greek but in original Hebrew is Torah or Instructions)** (5) And you know that He was manifested to take away our sins; and in Him is no sin. (6) Whosoever abideth in Him sins not: whosoever sins hath not seen Him, neither known him. (7) Little children, let no man deceive you: he that does righteousness is righteous, even as He is righteous. (8) He that commits sin is of the devil; for the devil sinned from the beginning. For this purpose the Son of YHWH was manifested, that He might destroy the works of the devil. (9) Whosoever is born of YHWH does not commit sin; for His seed remains in him: and He cannot sin, because He is born of YHWH.

> *Is it important to discern what <u>Laws</u> last days believers in the following verse were breaking?*

Matthew 7:21-23 "(21) Not everyone who says to Me, Lord, Lord, will enter the kingdom of heaven, but he who does the will of My Father Who is in heaven *will enter.* (22) Many will say to Me on that day, Lord, Lord, did we not prophesy in Your Name, and in Your Name cast out demons, and in Your Name perform many miracles? (23) And then I will declare to them, I never knew you; DEPART FROM ME, **YOU WHO PRACTICE LAWLESSNESS**."

> *Will you and I repent and obey or will we too erroneously assume the Law and its Commandments are done away?*

Matthew 5:17-19 "(17) Do not think that I came to abolish the Law or the Prophets; I did not come to abolish but to fulfill. (18) For truly I say to you, until heaven and earth pass away, not the smallest letter or stroke shall pass from the Law until all is accomplished. (19) Whoever then annuls one of the least of these Commandments, and teaches others *to do* the same, shall be called least in the Kingdom of Heaven; but whoever keeps and teaches *them,* he shall be called great in the Kingdom of Heaven." (Lawlessness is Torahlessness and these wrongfully believed the Law was done away with and ALL fulfilled)

Fourth Question: What was the last letter added to the English alphabet?   When?

History

The letter "**J**" was originally used as a swash character to end some Roman numerals in place of the "*i.*" There was an emerging distinctive use in Middle High German. Gian Giorgio Trissino (1478-1550) was the first to explicitly distinguish "I" and "J" as representing separate sounds, in his

Epistola del Trissino de le lettere nuωvamente aggiunte ne la lingua italiana ("Trissino's epistle about the letters recently added in the italian language") of 1524. Originally, both "I" and "J" represented "i," "i:," and "j;" but Romance languages developed new sounds (from former "j" and "g") that came to be represented as "I" and "J;" therefore, English J (from

French J) has a sound value quite different from "j" (which represents the sound in the English word "yet") **Use in English**.

The first English-language book to make a clear distinction between "I" and "J" was published in 1634. In loanwords such as *raj*, "J" may be pronounced "ʒ" by some, but not all, speakers. In some such cases, including *raj*, *Taj Mahal* and others, the regular "dʒ" is actually closer to the original sound of the foreign language, making this realization a hyperforeignism. Occasionally *"J"* represents other sounds, as in Hallelujah which is pronounced the same as "Halleluyah" (See the Hebrew yud for more details).

Comment: Several quick examples of misunderstanding and loss of meaning due the addition of the letter "J".

1. HaleluYAH- **Praise is to YHWH** in the shortened form- YAH.

2. Jesus, which can literally be translated to Ha-Zeus or hail Zeus whom the Greeks actually considered deity or correctly **Yahshua** which means **YHWH's salvation**.

3. John from Yochanan was actually Hebrew- **Yah**-chanan or **Yah's mercy**.

4. Jerusalem from **Yah's** shalom or **His city of peace**.

5. Jeremiah from Hebrew Yere mi **Yah** hu meaning YHWH will set free and rise up.

Fifth Question: What are idioms?

Idiom From Wikipedia, the free encyclopedia:

An **idiom** (Latin: *idioma*, "special property," f. Greek: *idiōma*, "special phrasing," f. Greek: *idios*, "one's own") is an expression, word, or phrase whose meaning is figurative — its implication comprehended only through common use; whereas the literal definition of the idiom, itself, does not communicate its meaning as a figurative usage.

In linguistics, idioms are usually presumed to be figures of speech contradicting the principle of compositionality; yet the matter remains debated. Collocation — words commonly used in a group — redefines each component word in the word-group and become an *idiomatic expression*. The words develop a specialized meaning as an entity, as an *idiom*. Moreover, an idiom is an expression, word, or phrase whose sense means something different to what the words literally imply. **When a speaker uses an idiom, the listener might mistake its actual meaning, if he or she has not heard this figure of speech before**. Idioms usually do not translate well; in some cases, when an idiom is translated into another language, either its meaning is changed or it is meaningless. Idioms might be the most difficult language for a learner of a new language.

Background

In the English expression *to kick the bucket*, a listener knowing only the meanings of *kick* and *bucket* would be unable to deduce the expression's true meaning: *to die*. Although this idiomatic phrase can refer to kicking a bucket, native speakers of English rarely use it so. It cannot be translated to other languages – the same expression in Polish is *kopnąć w kalendarz* ("to kick the calendar"), with "calendar" detached from its usual meaning, just like "bucket" in the English phrase. In Dutch the phrase is *het loodje leggen* ("to lay the piece of lead").

Idioms tend to confuse those unfamiliar with them; students of a new language must learn its idiomatic expressions as vocabulary. Many natural language words have *idiomatic origins*, but are assimilated, so losing their figurative senses.

Idioms and culture

An idiom is generally a colloquial metaphor — a term requiring some foundational knowledge, information, or experience, to use only within a culture, where conversational parties must possess common cultural references. Therefore, idioms are not considered part of the language, but part of the culture. As culture typically is localized, idioms often are useless beyond their local context; nevertheless, some idioms can be more universal than others, can be easily translated, and the metaphoric meaning can be deduced.

> **One of the most misunderstood Hebrew idioms is "But of that day and hour no one knows**, not even the angels of heaven, nor the Son, but the Father alone. **(Feast of Trumpets idiom)** For the coming of the Son of Man will be just like the days of Noah."

Matthew 24:33-39 "(33) ...so, you too, **when you see all these things**, recognize that He is near, *right* at the door. (34) Truly I say to you, this generation will not pass away until all these things take place. (35) Heaven and earth will pass away, but My Words will not pass away. (36) **But of that day and hour no one knows**, not even the angels of heaven, nor the Son, but the Father alone. **(Feast of Trumpets idiom)** (37) For the coming of the Son of Man will be just like the days of Noah. (38) For as in those days before the flood they were eating and drinking, marrying and giving in marriage, until the day that Noah entered the ark, (39) and they did not understand until the flood came and took them all away; so will the coming of the Son of Man be."

1 Thessalonians 5:1-6 "(1) Now as to the times and the seasons, brethren, you have no need of anything to be written to you. (2)

For you know full well that The Day of YHWH will come just like a thief in the night. (3) While **they** are saying, Peace and safety; then destruction will come upon **them** suddenly like labor pains upon a woman with child, and **they** will not escape. (4) But you, brethren, are not in darkness, that The Day would overtake you like a thief; (5) for you are all sons of Light and sons of day. We are neither of night nor of darkness; (6) so then let us not sleep as others do, but **let us be alert and sober**.

The DAY: Hebrews 10:23-25 "(23) Let us hold fast the confession of our hope without wavering, for He who promised is faithful; (24) and let us consider how to stimulate one another to love and good deeds, (25) not forsaking our own assembling together, as is the habit of some, but encouraging *one another;* and all the more as you see **The Day** drawing near (approaching)." THE DAY is a Hebrew idiom for the Day of the Lord (Judgment Day), the Sabbath, and the millennium reign of Messiah. The assembling was always about the various Feast Days (Feasts of YHWH) beginning with the weekly Sabbath and includes the Day of Atonement (Judgment Day and Yom Kippur).

The Day of Affliction means literally when one is under attack but the idiom represents the time approaching Sabbath Millennial Reign of Messiah Yahshua and is the time also known as **JACOB'S TROUBLE!** *(Comment: NOT Judah's trouble only- it's all 12 tribes of believers who are grafted in; read the Book of Joel and see it is a time of great distress)*

Now I will give a small portion of an excellent study done by my friend Monte Judah in the following article in his magazine: Yavoh, He is

Coming! Lastly, I will follow with three of my own weekly Bible Study Newsletters: SHABBAT SHALOM LOVED ONE!

YAHVOH HE IS COMING!

The Stolen Book of Revelation ... and seven other amazing facts,
by Monte Judah.

Many years ago, I attended a seminar hosted by a local synagogue for the benefit of church pastors in the city. It was my first opportunity to hear a Rabbi share their view on Jesus and the New Testament. The seminar was entitled, "What Jews think about Jesus and the New Testament." In the question and answer period, we were afforded the opportunity to ask questions. My question was about the Book of Revelation. The Rabbi's answer stunned me. "It's a stolen book. There is nothing new in the book. All the symbols and distinct prophecies originate from Moses and the Prophets of Israel."

He was right! In a sense, the book of Revelation is stolen. All of the relevant prophecies are spoken of or introduced first by the prophets. Students of the Bible are taught many key methods to interpret the Scriptures. One of them is to let the Bible interpret the Bible. When you find another passage of Scripture discussing the same element or theme of your study, you must reconcile and consider all passages from the Old Testament, and in the specific study of Revelation, the comparisons to the Old Testament is extensive. If you have a cross reference system in your Bible, just scan it as you skim through the pages of Revelation. Most cross reference systems will lead you to many passages for further consideration. To illustrate my point more specifically, consider the topic list and the supporting parallel passages from Moses and the Prophets. Rev Chapter One Yahshua's reference to being the Alpha and Omega is what most English Bibles say translating from the Greek. However, this is a Hebrew

Messiah from the Tribe of Judah, talking to a Hebrew Prophet. More likely He spoke Hebrew and said He was the Aleph and the Tav. The Aleph and the Tav is a deeper teaching of Yahweh originating in Genesis 1:1. It is the fourth word in the text, which is not translated to English. John's gospel speaks to this directly in John 1:1.

> *In the beginning (Bereshit) was the Word (the Aleph and the Tav word is Et) and the Word (Et) was with Yahweh Elohim, and the Word (Et) was Yahweh Elohim. He was in the beginning (Bereshit) with Yahweh. John 1:1-2*

Knowing what Moses said in Genesis 1:1 is critical to understanding what Yahshua said in Revelation 1:8 and John 1:1.

<u>Rev Chapter One</u> The Lord's Day referenced in Revelation 1:10 is not about Sunday worship. The Messiah's Day is the last day- the Sabbath Day. According to Moses and the Prophets, Sabbath is a picture of the Messiah's coming Kingdom, when He will rest from His labors of dealing with His enemies. Yahshua emphatically stated that He was Lord of the Sabbath; therefore the Lord's Day is Sabbath. Yahshua also explained that the Sabbath was made for man, not man for the Sabbath. The same can be said for the Kingdom. The Kingdom was made for man, the bride of the Messiah, not man for the Kingdom.

<u>Rev Chapter Two</u> Revelation 2:17 speaks to hidden Manna, a white stone, and new names written on stone. The story of the manna in the wilderness is critical to understanding this statement. The white stone is reference to the Urim and the Thummin. (a subject virtually unknown to believers) The name written on stone is a vintage Messianic Kingdom prophecy in Zechariah. *"(8) Now listen, Joshua the high priest, you and your friends who are sitting in front of you-indeed they are men who are a symbol, (9) for behold, I am going to bring in My servant the Branch. For behold, the*

185

stone that I have set before Joshua; on one stone are seven eyes. Behold, I will engrave an inscription on it, declares the Lord of hosts, and I will remove the iniquity of that land in one day. (10) In that day, declares the Lord of hosts, every one of you will invite his neighbor to sit under his vine and under his fig tree." Zechariah 3:8-10

The promises to the overcomers (the letter to the seven churches) such as this one make no sense without the understanding of Moses and the Prophets.

<u>Rev Chapter Two</u> Revelation 2:14 warns the church at Pergamum that there are those who hold to the teaching of Baalam. Baalam was a prophet who was paid to curse but could only bless. But he offered something else to Balak (the enemy king who wanted to destroy Israel) that was even more powerful than a curse. It is called the teaching of Baalam and you must understand Moses and the Prophets to even know what the teaching is. The teaching of Baalam is to not listen to the teaching of Moses nor follow the customs of Moses.

<u>Rev Chapter Seven</u> The 144,000 sons of Israel sealed for the Great Tribulation begs for proper interpretation originating from Moses and the Prophets. Ezekiel 9 speaks to sealing and explains it in conjunction with the first judgment of God- the judgment that comes on the household of God. The tribulation saints are waiting with Palm branches. Zechariah says the first celebration in Messiah's Kingdom will be the Feast of Tabernacles. Palm branches are essential to building a proper tabernacle or booth.

<u>Rev Chapter Eight</u> The angel that hurls his censor to the earth (Revelation 8:3-5) replicates the actions of Aaron when he took his censor into the people to stop God's judgment upon Israel in Numbers chapter 16. They had approached God's altar in contempt. This is also the starting event of

the Great Tribulation- the contemptuous act of stopping the daily sacrifice on the altar.

<u>Rev Chapter Nine</u> The fifth trumpet angel foretells of a time of darkness when demons appear on the earth harassing mankind. The description of the demons and how they are organized is addressed by the prophet Joel in Chapter 2. There really is a reason to blow a trumpet in Zion and sound an alarm on my Holy Mountain.

Hopefully, this small portion of Monte's teaching will give you a taste for the need to understand the Bible from a Hebrew root perspective. Again, you may find this teaching and others in their entirety at his website: www.lionlamb.net

We are approaching the end of the sixth day or the end of the sixth millennium of recorded time. At the writing of this book (October 2009), the current Biblical Hebrew year is 5769 (Not Rabbinic calendar.), which in our Gregorian calendar given by Pope Gregory, is 2009 A.D. If the Hebrew calendar were correct, we would be starting the seventh millennium, year 6001, in 235 years! However, Bible chronologists can prove that the Jews in captivity left off about 240 years. Apparently, when they had evil kings or just wanted to blot out the memory they didn't count the years. If that information is correct, then we would be approximately 6 years into the seventh millennium, somewhere around 6006. The current Muslim uprising and terrorism started in Israel on the Feast of Trumpets at the Temple Mount as Ariel Sharon, the current Israeli Prime Minister, surrounded with thousands of police, entered the Temple Mount in Jerusalem. This was the celebration of the harvest year in the Gregorian year of 2001 A.D., and the Jewish scholars and Rabbis declared that it was the start of the seven years of "Jacob's Troubles." Personally, I do not believe the last seven years was the time of Jacob's trouble, I expect it is coming starting at the Feast of Trumpets 2010. I do know we are closer to it than any other time in mankind's history. I am hopeful concerning the Scripture promise that says of Messiah Yahshua, "After two days, He will revive us." That means that after two thousand years have passed, He will revive us. Revive us means resurrect us if we are dead and change our bodies from mortal to immortal or corruptible to incorruptible if we are still alive at His coming. Question though, "Does the counting start at His death and resurrection or at His birth?" I think it starts at His birth. If the counting begins at His death, then we could have until around 2029-2030 since He was born in approximately two B.C. and lived to just over age thirty-one (not 33). If the counting starts at His birth, then we are arrived at the end of the age and things prophesied concerning Jacob's troubles should begin to happen in a visible way about 2010. If this information is correct, then it is possible that the 42 months of great tribulation could start as early as Passover 2014. We will look closer at the Bible Code in-depth in Chapter 18.

You may want to research these ideas for yourself at: www.aroodawakening.tv where you can even order an underwater video of the Red Sea Crossing site showing many relics found there. Additionally, you can just search the web for Bible chronologists. Another great study site is Monte Judah's teaching website at www.Lionlamb.net. Other great sites for you study would be www.yourarmstoIsrael.org and Eddie Chumney's Hebraic Roots of Christianity at www.hebroots.org. Another great site for your study is Mike Clayton's site at www.joinedtohashem.org.

Following are the three weeks promised of our weekly study **SHABBAT SHALOM LOVED ONE!** This weekly newsletter is my weekly Bible Torah Study. If you would like to actually receive this weekly Bible Torah study which may help you understand the Scriptures from a

Hebraic perspective, you may email me at tbmccut@seedtime2harvest.com and I will gladly add you to our weekly email list free of charge.

July 4, 2009
<u>Shabbat Shalom Loved One</u>!

Today we start our study by remembering who we are and that we are scattered around the planet. Deuteronomy 4:27-29 "(27) **YHWH will scatter you among the peoples and you will be left few in number among the nations where YHWH drives you**. (28) There you will serve YHWH's the work of man's hands, wood and stone, which neither see nor hear nor eat nor smell. (29) <u>From there you will seek YHWH your Elohim, and you will find Him if you search for *Him* with all your heart and all your soul</u>."

> ***When these things happen is the latter days (NOW!) Only by His mighty outstretched hand will He direct and protect us!***

Deuteronomy4:30 "<u>When you are in distress and all these things have come upon you, in the latter days you will return to YHWH your Elohim and listen to His voice</u>." Deuteronomy 4:31-35 "(31) YHWH your Elohim is a compassionate Elohim; He will not fail you nor destroy you nor forget the covenant with your fathers which He swore to them. (32) Indeed, ask now concerning the former days which were before you, since the day that YHWH created man on the earth, and *inquire* from one end of the heavens to the other. Has *anything* been done like this great thing, or has *anything* been heard like it? (33) Have any people heard the voice of YHWH speaking from the midst of the fire, as you have heard *it*, and survived? (34) Or has a Elohim tried to go to take for himself a nation from within *another* nation by trials, **by signs and wonders and by war and by a**

mighty hand and by an outstretched arm and by great terrors, as **YHWH your Elohim did for you in Egypt before your eyes?** (35) To you it was shown that you might know that YHWH, He is YHWH; there is no other besides Him."

> **Trouble's coming but obedience brings YHWH's deliverance!**

Deuteronomy 30:1-8 "(1) So it shall be when all of these things have come upon you, the blessing and the curse which I have set before you, and you call *them* to mind in all nations where YHWH your Elohim has banished you, (2) and you return to YHWH your Elohim and obey Him with all your heart and soul according to all that I command you today, you and your sons, (3) then YHWH your Elohim will restore you from captivity, and have compassion on you, and will gather you again from all the peoples where YHWH your Elohim has scattered you. (4) If your outcasts are at the ends of the earth, from there YHWH your Elohim will gather you, and **from there He will bring you back**. (5) YHWH your Elohim will bring you into the land which your fathers possessed, and you shall possess it; and He will prosper you and multiply you more than your fathers. (6) Moreover YHWH your Elohim will circumcise your heart and the heart of your descendants, to love YHWH your Elohim with all your heart and with all your soul, so that you may live. (7) YHWH your Elohim will inflict all these curses on your enemies and on those who hate you, who persecuted you. (8) And you shall again obey YHWH, and observe all His Commandments which I Command you today."

In the USA the date of July 4th (This Shabbat) has always stood for **INDEPENDENCE!** (At least since 1776) We were **not depending** on other men and countries to sustain us, but dependent on YHWH and His directions for our blessings. Many of our founding fathers wrote about their beliefs and following of the Scriptures as our sole reason for our freedoms and blessings. I give a few examples as my summary of the signers of our Constitution and will list several pages of quotes as an attachment for why we should expect our liberties to soon vanish and tyranny to prevail, because without absolute repentance and turning our stubborn hearts as a country and society we must unravel and be ruled by other than YHWH and His principles.

Apparently, we can have <u>wicked</u> (<u>twisted</u> from Torah instructions) men and countries rule us or we can follow and obey our Creator as King. Last week's study was about our ancestors of the faith demanding a king rather than YHWH. So what's different with us today? We in the USA and other countries have kicked out YHWH from our Courts, from our schools and from our families, yet we have bumper stickers that say "YHWH Bless our country!" With that ridiculous thought in place, (sadly humorous) let's take a quick look of what the Founding Fathers say has brought the many blessings to our country:

Thomas Jefferson:
3rd U.S. President, Drafter and Signer of the Declaration of Independence: "YHWH who gave us life gave us liberty. And can the liberties of a nation be thought secure when we have removed their only firm basis, a conviction in the minds of the people that these liberties are of the Gift of YHWH? That they are not to be violated but with His wrath? Indeed, I tremble for my country when I reflect that YHWH is just; that His justice cannot sleep forever; that a revolution of the wheel of fortune, a change of situation, is among possible events; that it may become probable by Supernatural influence! The Almighty has no attribute which can take side with us in that event."

John Adams and John Hancock:
We Recognize No Sovereign but YHWH, and no King but *Jesus!* [April 18, 1775]

John Adams:
John Adams in a letter written to Abigail on the day the Declaration was approved by Congress "We have no government armed with power capable of contending with human passions unbridled by morality and religion. Avarice, ambition, revenge, or gallantry, would break the strongest cords of our Constitution as a whale goes through a net. **Our Constitution was made only for a moral and religious people. It is wholly inadequate to the government of any other**." -- *October 11, 1798.*

John Quincy Adams:
"The Law given from Sinai [The Ten Commandments] was a civil and municipal as well as a moral and religious code." John Quincy Adams. *Letters to his son.* p. 61

Charles Carroll:
Signer of Declaration of Independence -- **Portrait of Charles Carroll "Without morals a republic cannot subsist any length of time**; they therefore who are decrying the Christian religion, whose morality is so sublime and pure...are undermining the solid foundation of morals, the best security for the duration of free governments." [Source: To James McHenry on November 4, 1800.]

Benjamin Franklin: Portrait of Ben Franklin
"YHWH governs in the affairs of man. And if a sparrow cannot fall to the ground without His notice, is it probable that an empire can rise without His aid? We have been assured in the Sacred

Writings that except the YHWH build the house, they labor in vain that build it. I firmly believe this. I also believe that, without His concurring aid, we shall succeed in this political building no better than the builders of Babel"–*Constitutional Convention of 1787 | original manuscript of this speech* "In the beginning of the contest with Britain, when we were sensible of danger, we had daily prayers in this room for Divine protection. Our prayers, Sir, were heard, and they were graciously answered... do we imagine we no longer need His assistance?" [Constitutional Convention, Thursday June 28, 1787]

Alexander Hamilton:
"For my own part, I sincerely esteem it [the Constitution] a system which without the finger of YHWH, never could have been suggested and agreed upon by such a diversity of interests." [1787 after the Constitutional Convention]

James Madison:
"**We've staked our future on our ability to follow the Ten Commandments with all of our heart**." "We have staked the whole future of American civilization, not upon the power of government, far from it. We've staked the future of all our political institutions upon our capacity...**to sustain ourselves according to the Ten Commandments of YHWH**." [1778 to the General Assembly of the State of Virginia]

It appears from these writings that the Founding Fathers of our country (USA) recognized that if a country (any country) ever moved away from obeying the Bible and the 10 Commandments as its constitution, that country would not be sustainable! This brings us to today's study of the Torah: YHWH's Constitution! **The Torah (Bible) is the Constitution, Preamble, and Bill of Rights we now have, and will still operate under**

in our coming King's KINGDOM! Knowing these things, how then shall we live? This then is how we should (Will/must) live. These are the days left of our preparation times. The fire is kindled as we read today!

Here are this week's Torah Bible Scriptures

Chukat *"Statute"*

Numbers 19:1- 25:9; Judges 11:1-33; Micah 5:6- 6:8; 2 Thessalonians Chapters 1, 2, and 3; and 1 Timothy Chapters 1-6

Please note:
The First sign of inconvenience or trouble the people murmured and complained! These are for our warnings and teaching.

Numbers 20:1-5 "(1) Then the sons of Israel, the whole congregation, came to the wilderness of Zin in the first month; and the people stayed at Kadesh. Now Miriam died there and was buried there. (2) There was no water for the congregation, and they assembled themselves against Moses and Aaron. (3) The people thus contended with Moses and spoke, saying, If only we had perished when our brothers perished before YHWH! (4) Why then have you brought YHWH'S assembly into this wilderness, for us and our beasts to die here? (5) Why have you made us come up from Egypt, to bring us in to this wretched place? It is not a place of grain or figs or vines or pomegranates, nor is there water to drink."

> *Here we are to learn that speaking what*
> *YHWH says is the FIGHT OF FAITH!*

Numbers 20:6-11 "(6) Then Moses and Aaron came in from the presence of the assembly to the doorway of the tent of meeting and fell on their faces. Then the glory of YHWH appeared to them; (7) and YHWH spoke to Moses, saying, (8) Take the rod; and you and your brother Aaron assemble the congregation and **speak to the rock** before their eyes, that it may yield its water. You shall thus bring forth water for them out of the rock and let the congregation and their beasts drink. (9) So Moses took the rod from before YHWH, just as He had Commanded him; (10) and Moses and Aaron gathered the assembly before the rock. And he said to them, Listen now, you rebels; shall we bring forth water for you out of this rock? (11) Then Moses lifted up his hand and **struck the rock** twice with his rod; and water came forth abundantly, and the congregation and their beasts drank."

Disobedience has a price: Lost Blessings!

Numbers 20:12-17 "(12) But YHWH said to Moses and Aaron, Because you have not believed Me, to treat Me as Holy in the sight of the sons of Israel, therefore you shall not bring this assembly into the land which I have given them. (13) Those *were* the waters of Meribah, because the sons of Israel contended with YHWH, and He proved Himself Holy among them. (14) From Kadesh Moses then sent messengers to the king of Edom: Thus your brother Israel has said, you know all the hardship that has befallen us; (15) that our fathers went down to Egypt, and we stayed in Egypt a long time, and the Egyptians treated us and our fathers badly. (16) But when we cried out to YHWH, He heard our voice and sent a Messenger and brought us out from Egypt; now behold, we are at Kadesh, a town on the edge of your territory. (17) Please let us pass through your land. We will not pass through field or through vineyard; we will not even drink water from a well. We will go along the king's highway, not turning to the right or left, until we pass through your territory."

> **This is why the Scriptures declare Edom will be destroyed in the last days: for their shedding of innocent blood. HAMAS (An acronym) means Terror in Modern Hebrew.**

Genesis 36:15-16 "(15) These are the chiefs of the sons of Esau. The sons of Eliphaz, the firstborn of Esau, are chief Teman, chief Omar, chief Zepho, chief Kenaz, (16) chief Korah, chief Gatam, chief Amalek. These are the chiefs descended from Eliphaz in the land of Edom; these are the sons of Adah."

We studied last week about rebellion and Korah, note that Korah, Amalek, and Esau are EDOM! Today these are mostly Muslim extremist nations. Let's quickly look at one prophesy about YHWH's ***LAST DAYS PLAN*** *of judgment for rebellion and terror against His people.*

Numbers 24:18-23 "(18) **Edom shall be a possession**, Seir, its enemies, also will be a possession, while Israel performs valiantly. (19) One from Jacob shall have dominion, and will destroy the remnant from the city. (20) And he looked at **Amalek** and took up his discourse and said, Amalek was the first of the nations, **but his end *shall be* destruction**. (21) And he looked at the Kenite, and took up his discourse and said, Your dwelling place is enduring, and your nest is set in the cliff. (22) Nevertheless **Kain** will be consumed; how long will Asshur keep you captive? (23) Then he took up his discourse and said, Alas, who can live except YHWH has ordained it?"

Psalm 83:2-8 "(2) For behold, your enemies make uproar, and those who hate you have exalted themselves. (3) They make shrewd plans against your people, and conspire together against your treasured ones. (4) **They have said, Come, and let us wipe them out as a nation, that the name**

of Israel be remembered no more. (5) For they have conspired together with one mind; against you they make a covenant: (6) **The tents of Edom** and the Ishmaelites, Moab and the Hagrites; (7) Gebal and Ammon and **Amalek, Philistia** with the inhabitants of Tyre; (8) **Assyria** also has joined with them; They have become a help to the children of Lot. Selah."

Isaiah 34:1-8 "(1) Draw near, O nations, to hear; and listen, O peoples! Let the earth and all it contains hear, and the world and all that springs from it. (2) For YHWH's indignation is against all the nations, and *His* wrath against all their armies; He has utterly destroyed them; He has given them over to slaughter. (3) So their slain will be thrown out, and their corpses will give off their stench, and the mountains will be drenched with their blood. (4) And all the host of heaven will wear away, and the sky will be rolled up like a scroll; all their hosts will also wither away as a leaf withers from the vine, Or as *one* withers from the fig tree. (5) **For my sword is satiated in heaven, Behold it shall descend for judgment upon Edom And upon the people whom I have devoted to destruction.** (6) The sword of YHWH is filled with blood; it is sated with fat, with the blood of lambs and goats, with the fat of the kidneys of rams. For YHWH has a sacrifice in Bozrah and a great slaughter in the land of Edom. (7) Wild oxen will also fall with them and young bulls with strong ones; **thus their land will be soaked with blood,** And their dust become greasy with fat. (8) For YHWH has a day of vengeance, a year of recompense for the cause of Zion."

> *We have just read about what the following rebellion against YHWH and His treasure will cost the Muslim nations shortly.*

Numbers 20:18-22 "(18) Edom, however, said to him, **You shall not pass through us, or I will come out with the sword against you.** (19) Again, the sons of Israel said to him, We will go up by the highway, and if I and my livestock do drink any of your water, then I will pay its price. Let me only pass through on my feet, nothing *else*. (20) But he said, You shall not pass through. And Edom came out against him with a heavy force and with a strong hand. (21) Thus **Edom refused to allow Israel to pass through** his territory; so Israel turned away from him. (22) Now when they set out from Kadesh, the sons of Israel, the whole congregation, came to Mount Hor."

Disobedience brings death!

Numbers 20:23-29 "(23) Then YHWH spoke to Moses and Aaron at Mount Hor by the border of the land of Edom, saying, (24) Aaron will be gathered to his people; for he shall not enter the land which I have given to the sons of Israel, **because you rebelled against My Command at the waters of Meribah**. (25) Take Aaron and his son Eleazar and bring them up to Mount Hor; (26) and strip Aaron of his garments and put them on his son Eleazar. So Aaron will be gathered *to his people*, and will die there. (27) So Moses did just as YHWH had commanded, and they went up to Mount Hor in the sight of the entire congregation. (28) After Moses had stripped Aaron of his garments and put them on his son Eleazar, Aaron died there on the mountain top. Then Moses and Eleazar came down from the mountain. (29) When the entire congregation saw that Aaron had died, all the house of Israel wept for Aaron thirty days."

We can all be used by YHWH; we only need to humble ourselves and willingly obey- even if we are stubborn donkeys!

Remember that Moab and Edom are from the same (Today Muslim) people groups.

Exodus 15:15-18 "(15) **Then the chiefs of Edom were dismayed; the leaders of Moab**, trembling grips them; all the inhabitants of Canaan have melted away. (16) Terror and dread fall upon them; by the greatness of your arm they are motionless as stone; Until Your people pass over, O YHWH, until the people pass over whom You have purchased. (17) You will bring them and plant them in the mountain of your inheritance, the place, O YHWH, which you have made for your dwelling, the sanctuary, O YHWH, which your hands have established. (18) YHWH shall reign forever and ever."

It is not possible to bless what YHWH has cursed (Please hear you who bless "food" that YHWH has cursed; it is sanctified only by the WORD and PRAYER) nor can we Curse what YHWH has blessed as we see below! Don't get mad at the messenger, just "read the red" here: Matthew 5:17-19 "(17) Do not think that I came to abolish the Law or the Prophets; I did not come to abolish but to fulfill. (18) For truly I say to you, until heaven and earth pass away, not the smallest letter or stroke shall pass from the Law until all is accomplished. (19) Whoever then annuls one of the least of these Commandments, and teaches others *to do* the same, shall be called least in the Kingdom of Heaven; but whoever keeps and teaches *them*, he shall be called great in the Kingdom of Heaven." ***This is why there will be many Pastor LEASTS in the Kingdom!***

We must guard against listening to prophets for profit! Note that Baalam (Bil'am) had a price even though he heard from Heaven; he certainly was disobedient and sought reward.

Numbers 22:4-27 "(4) And **Mo'ab** said to the elders of Midyan, Now this company is licking up all that is around us, as an ox licks up the grass of the field. Now Balaq son of Tsippor was sovereign of the Mo'abites at that time, (5) and he sent Angels to Bil'am son of Be'or at Pethor, which is near the River in the land of the sons of his people, to call him, saying, See, a people has come from Mitsrayim (Egypt). See, they have covered the surface of the land, and are settling next to me! (6) And now, please come at once, curse this people for me, for they are too strong for me. It might be that I smite them and drive them out of the land, for I know that he whom you bless is blessed, and he whom you curse is cursed. (7) And the elders of Mo'ab and the elders of Midyan left with *the fees for* divination in their hand, and they came to Bil'am and spoke the words of Balaq to him. (8) And he said to them, Spend the night here and I shall bring back word to you, as יהוה speaks to me. So the heads of Mo'ab stayed with Bil'am. (9) And Elohim came to Bil'am and said, Who are these men with you? (10) And Bil'am said to Elohim, Balaq, son of Tsippor, sovereign of Mo'ab, has sent to me, saying, (11) See, a people has come out of Mitsrayim (Egypt) and covers the surface of the land. Come now, curse them for me. It might be that I am able to fight against them and drive them out. (12) And Elohim said to Bil'am, **Do not go with them. You do not curse the people, for they are blessed**. (13) And Bil'am rose in the morning and said to the heads of Balaq, Go back to your land, for יהוה has refused to allow me to go with you. (14) And the heads of Mo'ab arose and went to Balaq, and said, Bil'am refuses to come with us. (15) Then Balaq again sent heads, more numerous and more esteemed than they. (16) And they came to Bil'am and said to him, This is what Balaq son of Tsippor said: Do not be withheld from coming to me, please, (17) for I esteem you very greatly, and whatever you say to me, I do. Therefore please come, curse this people for me. (18) And Bil'am answered and said to the servants of Balaq, Though Balaq were to give me his house filled with silver and gold, I am unable to go beyond the word of יהוה my Elohim, to do less or more. (19) And now, please, you also stay here tonight, and let me find out what more יהוה says to me. (20) And Elohim came to Bil'am at night and said to him, If the men come to call you, rise and go with them, but only the word which I speak to you that you do. (21) And Bil'am rose in the morning and saddled his donkey, and went with the heads of Mo'ab. (22) But the displeasure of Elohim burned because he went, and the Angel of יהוה stationed Himself in the way as an adversary against him. And he was riding on his donkey, and his two servants were with him. (23) And the donkey saw the Angel of יהוה standing in the way with His drawn sword in His hand, and the donkey turned aside out of the way and went into the field. So Bil'am beat the donkey to turn her back onto the way. (24) Then the Angel of יהוה stood in a narrow passage between the vineyards, with a wall on this side and a wall on that side. (25) And when the donkey saw the Angel of יהוה, she pushed herself against the wall and crushed Bil'am's foot against the wall, so he beat her again. (26) And the Angel of יהוה went further, and stood in a narrow place where there was no way to turn aside, right or left. (27) And when the donkey saw the Angel of יהוה, she lay down under Bil'am. So Bil'am's displeasure burned, and he beat the donkey with his staff."

> **Supernatural power from YHWH accompanies
> the goals of YHWH- it should be our life's
> desire to find out what YHWH says and DO it!**

Numbers 22:28-41 "(28) Then יהוה opened the mouth of the donkey, and she said to Bil'am, What have I done to you, that you have beaten me these three times? (29) And Bil'am said to the donkey, Because you have mocked me. I wish there were a sword in my hand, for I would have killed you by now! (30) And the donkey said to Bil'am, Am I not your donkey on which you have ridden, ever since I became yours, to this day? Was I ever known to do so to you? And he said, No. (31) Then יהוה opened

Bil'am's eyes, and he saw the Angel of יהוה standing in the way with His drawn sword in His hand. And he bowed his head and fell on his face. (32) And the Angel of יהוה said to him, Why have you beaten your donkey these three times? See, I have come out to stand against you, because your way is reckless before Me. (33) And the donkey saw Me and turned aside from Me these three times. If she had not turned aside from Me, I certainly would have killed you by now, and let her live. (34) And Bil'am said to the Angel of יהוה, I have sinned, for I did not know you stood in the way against me. And now, if evil is in your eyes, let me turn back. (35) And the Angel of יהוה said to Bil'am, Go with the men, but only the word that I speak to you, that you speak. Bil'am then went with the heads of Balaq. (36) And when Balaq heard that Bil'am was coming, he went out to meet him at the city of Mo'ab, which is on the border at the Arnon, which was in the extremity of the border. (37) And Balaq said to Bil'am, Did I not urgently send to you, calling for you? Why did you not come to me? Am I not able to esteem you? (38) And Bil'am said to Balaq, See, I have come to you! Now, am I at all able to say somewhat? **The word that Elohim puts in my mouth that I speak**. (39) And Bil'am went with Balaq, and they came to Qiryath-hutsoth. (40) And Balaq slaughtered cattle and sheep, and he sent some to Bil'am and to the heads who were with him. (41) And it came to be the next day that Balaq took Bil'am and brought him up to the high places of Ba'al, and from there he saw the extremity of the camp."

Numbers 23:1-30 "(1) Then Balaam said to Balak, Build seven altars for me here, and prepare seven bulls and seven rams for me here. (2) Balak did just as Balaam had spoken, and Balak and Balaam offered up a bull and a ram on each altar. (3) Then Balaam said to Balak, Stand beside your burnt offering, and I will go; perhaps YHWH will come to meet me, and whatever He shows me I will tell you. So he went to a bare hill. (4) Now YHWH met Balaam, and he said to Him, I have set up the seven altars, and I have offered up a bull and a ram on each altar. (5) Then YHWH put a word in Balaam's mouth and said, Return to Balak, and you shall speak thus. (6) So he returned to him, and behold, he was standing beside his burnt offering, he and all the leaders of Moab. (7) He took up his discourse and said, From Aram Balak has brought me, Moab's king from the mountains of the East, Come curse Jacob for me, and come, denounce Israel! (8) **How shall I curse whom YHWH has not cursed? And how can I denounce whom YHWH has not denounced?** (9) As I see him from the top of the rocks, and I look at him from the hills; Behold, a people *who* dwell apart, and will not be reckoned among the nations. (10) Who can count the dust of Jacob, or number the fourth part of Israel? Let me die the death of the upright, and let my end be like his! (11) Then Balak said to Balaam, What have you done to me? I took you to curse my enemies, but behold, you have actually blessed them! (12) He replied, Must I not be careful to speak what YHWH puts in my mouth? (13) Then Balak said to him, Please come with me to another place from where you may see them, although you will only see the extreme end of them and will not see all of them; and curse them for me from there. (14) So he took him to the field of Zophim, to the top of Pisgah, and built seven altars and offered a bull and a ram on *each* altar. (15) And he said to Balak, Stand here beside your burnt offering while I myself meet *the YHWH* over there. (16) **Then YHWH met Balaam and put a word in his mouth and said, Return to Balak, and thus you shall speak**. (17) He came to him, and behold, he was standing beside his burnt offering, and the leaders of Moab with him. And Balak said to him, What has YHWH spoken? (18) Then he took up his discourse and said, Arise, O Balak, and hear; Give ear to me, O son of Zippor! (19) **YHWH is not a man, that He should lie, nor a son of man**

that He should repent; has He said, and will He not do it? Or has He spoken, and will He not make it good? (20) Behold, I have received *a command* to bless; When He has blessed, then I cannot revoke it. (21) He has not observed misfortune in Jacob; nor has He seen trouble in Israel; YHWH his Elohim is with him, and the shout of a king is among them. (22) YHWH brings them out of Egypt; He is for them like the horns of the wild ox. (23) For there is no omen against Jacob, nor is there any divination against Israel; At the proper time it shall be said to Jacob And to Israel, what YHWH has done! (24) Behold, a people rises like a lioness, and as a lion it lifts itself; it will not lie down until it devours the prey, And drinks the blood of the slain. (25) Then Balak said to Balaam, Do not curse them at all nor bless them at all! (26) But Balaam replied to Balak, Did I not tell you, Whatever YHWH speaks, that I must do? (27) Then Balak said to Balaam, Please come, I will take you to another place; perhaps it will be agreeable with YHWH that you curse them for me from there. (28) So Balak took Balaam to the top of Peor which overlooks the wasteland. (29) Balaam said to Balak, Build seven altars for me here and prepare seven bulls and seven rams for me here. (30) Balak did just as Balaam had said, and offered up a bull and a ram on *each* altar."

Numbers 24:1-14 "(1) When Balaam saw that it pleased YHWH to bless Israel, he did not go as at other times to seek omens but he set his face toward the wilderness. (2) And Balaam lifted up his eyes and saw Israel camping tribe by tribe; and the Spirit of YHWH came upon him. (3) He took up his discourse and said, The oracle of Balaam the son of Beor, and the oracle of the man whose eye is opened; (4) the oracle of him who hears the words of YHWH, Who sees the vision of the Almighty, Falling down, yet having his eyes uncovered, (5) How fair are your tents, O Jacob, Your dwellings, O Israel! (6) Like valleys that stretch out, Like gardens beside the river, like aloes planted by YHWH, like cedars beside the waters. (7)

Water will flow from his buckets, and his seed *will be* by many waters, and his king shall be higher than Agag, and his kingdom shall be exalted. (8) YHWH brings him out of Egypt; He is for him like the horns of the wild ox. He will devour the nations *who are* his adversaries, and will crush their bones in pieces, and shatter *them* with his arrows. (9) He couches, he lies down as a lion, And as a lion, who dares rouse him? Blessed is everyone who blesses you, and cursed is everyone who curses you. (10) Then Balak's anger burned against Balaam, and he struck his hands together; and Balak said to Balaam, I called you to curse my enemies, but behold, you have persisted in blessing them these three times! (11) Therefore, flee to your place now. I said I would honor you greatly, but behold, YHWH has held you back from honor. (12) Balaam said to Balak, Did I not tell your messengers whom you had sent to me, saying, (13) Though Balak were to give me his house full of silver and gold, I could not do anything contrary to the command of YHWH, either good or bad, of my own accord. What YHWH speaks, that I will speak? (14) And now, behold, I am going to my people; come, *and* **I will advise you what this people will do to your people in the days to come**."

What advice did the prophet Balaam (Bi'lam) give that would bring YHWH's judgment on this blessed people? Disobey and bring in pagan worship practices! (**Numbers 25:1 below**)

Numbers 24:15-25 "(15) He took up his discourse and said, The oracle of Balaam the son of Beor, and the oracle of the man whose eye is opened, (16) the oracle of him who hears the words of YHWH, and knows the knowledge of the Most High, Who sees the vision of the Almighty, Falling down, yet having his eyes uncovered. (17) I see him, but not now; I behold him, but not near; A star shall come forth from Jacob, <u>A scepter shall rise from Israel, and shall</u> **crush through the forehead of Moab, And tear down all the sons of Sheth. (18) Edom shall be a possession, Seir, its** enemies, **also will be a possession, while Israel performs valiantly**. (19) One from Jacob shall have dominion, and will destroy the remnant from the city. (20) And he looked at Amalek and took up his discourse and said, **Amalek was the first of the nations, but his end *shall be* destruction**. (21) And he looked at the Kenite, and took up his discourse and said, Your dwelling place is enduring, and your nest is set in the cliff. (22) Nevertheless Kain will be consumed; how long will Asshur keep you captive? (23) Then he took up his discourse and said, Alas, who can live except YHWH has ordained it? (24) But ships *shall come* from the coast of Kittim, and they shall afflict Asshur and will afflict Eber; so they also *will come* to destruction. (25) Then Balaam arose and departed and returned to his place, and Balak also went his way."

Numbers 25:1-9 "(1) **While Israel remained at Shittim, the people began to play the harlot with the daughters of Moab**. (2) **They invited the people to the sacrifices of their gods, and the people ate and bowed down to their gods**. (3) So Israel joined them to Baal of Peor, and YHWH was angry against Israel. (4) The YHWH said to Moses, Take all the leaders of the people and execute them in broad daylight before the YHWH, so that the fierce anger of YHWH may turn away from Israel. (5) So Moses said to the judges of Israel, **Each of you slay his men who have joined themselves to Baal of Peor**. (6) Then behold, one of the sons of Israel came and brought to his relatives a Midianite woman, in the sight of Moses and in the sight of all the congregation of the sons of Israel, while they were weeping at the doorway of the tent of meeting. (7) When Phinehas the son of Eleazar, the son of Aaron the priest, saw it, he arose from the midst of the congregation and took a spear in his hand, (8) and he went after the man of Israel into the tent and **pierced both of them through, the man of Israel and the woman, through the body. So the**

plague on the sons of Israel was checked. (9) <u>Those who died by the plague were 24,000</u>."

May YHWH bless you and keep you, lift up His countenance on you, make His face to shine on you and your loved ones and give you His peace. May YHWH provide for you, direct you and protect you and your loved ones as we come apart from all pagan traditions that He says "Learn not the ways of the heathen" and say you are worshipping me. He still desires obedience above sacrifice and wide is the gate of disobedience and narrow is the path that leads to life, and very FEW find it! May this few be you and your loved ones! Know that your prayers are heard and answered without your SEEING them answered! Give Him thanks and act as though you have the thing you asked for! He is worthy of thanks and praise!

Blessings and Shalom,

Thurston

Thanks for your continued prayers for us loved one, you are a blessing!

Here is the second display of three of our weekly Torah Bible Study:

SHABBAT SHALOM LOVED ONE!

July 11, 2009

Shabbat Shalom Loved One!

Most of us want our King and Messiah to come- just not now. We tend to indulge ourselves in movies, sports, business deals, daily news, entertainment, etc. and we can stick our heads in the sand and hope the world's problems (and ours) go away and leave us alone. Sometimes we think watching the news and sharing our indignation and perplexity about the world, our country and the political nonsense going on will help. The trap is being set for us. All of this to share about what makes us **zealous for the word of YHWH** as our story in Torah tells today. How do we become zealous? <u>I believe it has to do with having been tried by fire and KNOW that YHWH and His Word and instructions will alone be our salvation and deliverer!</u> We can become renewed daily in the Word and become doers of the Word by renewing our minds in His Instructions and draw near to Him. Then our problems are not ours- they belong to Him and our peace comes from HIM! Each of us is making a decision whether we are aware of it or not. The fiery trials are coming whether we are prepared or not. Let's make ourselves ready for Yahshua is coming for a bride without spot or blemish! So many loved ones, including myself are being tested. So many in the Valley of Decision! So much fire does require decisions of each of us. What is it you and I really believe? You and I will be tested. Now is the time to sort out and make our decisions and determine what will stand the tests ahead about what we believe. I am certain the solid foundation of the Torah is all that will remain, but do you and I understand and trust YHWH no matter what fiery trials may come our way? Is YHWH preparing us? Will we murmur and complain, even separating ourselves from those in trials? Let's look at a few Scriptures that may help us to understand how important following the Word through the trials will be to us:

> **Let's become like putty and moldable by our KING!**

Hebrews 4:7, 9-11 "(7) He again fixes a certain day, Today, saying through David after so long a time just as has been said before, **TODAY IF YOU HEAR HIS VOICE, DO NOT HARDEN YOUR HEARTS**. (9) So there remains a Sabbath rest for the people of YHWH. (10) For the one who has entered His rest has himself also rested from his works, as YHWH did from His. (11) Therefore let us be diligent to enter that rest, so that no one will fall, through *following* the same example of disobedience."

> **Remember through every fiery trial and test YHWH is reading us while we read Him!**

Hebrews 4:12 "For the Word of YHWH is living and active and sharper than any two-edged sword, and piercing as far as the division of soul and spirit, of both joints and marrow, and able to judge the thoughts and intentions of the heart." *(Comment: He is discerning/reading us while we read and obey or choose to disobey!)*

> **One of the products of fiery trials is trust or faith**

Hebrews 11:24-40 "(24) By faith Moses, when he was come to years, refused to be called the son of Pharaoh's daughter; (25) Choosing rather to suffer affliction with the people of YHWH, than to enjoy the pleasures of sin for a season; (26) Esteeming the reproach of Messiah greater riches than the treasures in Egypt: for he had respect unto the recompense of the reward. (27) By faith he forsook Egypt, not fearing the wrath of the king: for he endured, as seeing Him Who is invisible. (28) Through faith he kept the Passover, and the sprinkling of blood, lest He that destroyed the firstborn should touch them. (29) By faith they passed through the Red sea as by dry *land*: which the Egyptians assaying to do were drowned. (30) By faith the walls of Yericho fell down, after they were compassed about seven days. (31) By faith the harlot Rahab perished not with them that believed not, when she had received the spies with peace. (32) And what shall I more say? for the time would fail me to tell of Gideon, and *of* Barak, and *of* Samson, and *of* Yephthae; *of* David also, and Samuel, and *of* the prophets: (33) Who through faith subdued kingdoms, wrought righteousness, obtained promises, stopped the mouths of lions, (34) Quenched the violence of fire, escaped the edge of the sword, out of weakness were made strong, waxed valiant in fight, turned to flight the armies of the aliens. (35) Women received their dead raised to life again: and others were tortured, not accepting deliverance; that they might obtain a better resurrection: (36) And others had trial of *cruel* mockings and scourgings, yea, moreover of bonds and imprisonment: (37) They were stoned, they were sawn asunder, were tempted, were slain with the sword: they wandered about in sheepskins and goatskins; being destitute, afflicted, tormented; (38) (Of whom the world was not worthy:) they wandered in deserts, and *in* mountains, and in dens and caves of the earth. (39) And these all, having obtained a good report through faith, received not the promise: (40) YHWH having provided some better thing for us, that they without us should not be made perfect."

> **Will you and I rejoice and give no place for ha'satan to enter and destroy? Faith will lead to the salvation (deliverance) of our souls.**

We must remember we are born again spirits and members of the Kingdom if we are Messiah Yahshua's; however, our souls are still subject to torment and attacks (Our flesh also) and must follow Romans 12:1-2 instruction for deliverance! Lastly, our flesh bodies get delivered only at the Resurrection at the Last Trump!

Let's quickly look:

Romans 12:1-2 "(1) Therefore I urge you, brethren, by the mercies of YHWH, to present your <u>bodies</u> a living and holy sacrifice, acceptable to YHWH, *which is* your <u>spiritual service of worship</u>. (2) And do not be conformed to this world, but be **transformed by the renewing of your mind**, *(Comment: renewing our mind in the Word of YHWH!)* so that you may prove what the will of YHWH is, that which is good and acceptable and perfect."

Our faith (trusting) YHWH through fiery trials will alone purify us like gold in a refiner's fire!

1 Peter 1:6-25 "(6) **In this you greatly <u>rejoice</u>**, even though now for a little while, if necessary, <u>you have been distressed by various trials,</u> (7) so that the proof of your faith, *being* more precious than gold which is perishable, even though **<u>tested by fire</u>**, may be found to result in praise and glory and honor at the revelation of Messiah Yahshua; (8) and though you have not seen Him, you love Him, and though you do not see Him now, but believe in Him, you greatly rejoice with joy inexpressible and full of glory, (9) obtaining as the outcome of your faith the <u>salvation of your souls</u>. (10) As to this salvation, the prophets who prophesied of the grace that *would come* to you made careful searches and inquiries, (11) seeking to know what person or time the Spirit of Messiah within them was indicating as He predicted the sufferings of Messiah and the glories to follow. (12) It was revealed to them that they were not serving themselves, but you, in these things which now have been announced to you through those who preached the gospel to you by the Holy Spirit sent from heaven--things into which angels long to look. (13) Therefore, prepare your minds for action, keep sober *in spirit,* and fix your hope completely on the grace to be brought to you at the revelation of Messiah Yahshua. (14) As obedient children, do not be conformed to the former lusts *which were yours* in your ignorance, (15) but like the Holy One Who called you, be holy yourselves also in all *your* behavior; (16) because it is written, YOU SHALL BE HOLY, FOR I AM HOLY. (17) If you address as Father the One who impartially judges according to each one's work, conduct yourselves in fear during the time of your stay *on earth;* (18) knowing that you were not redeemed with perishable things like silver or gold from your futile way of life inherited from your forefathers, (19) but with precious blood, as of a Lamb unblemished and spotless, *the blood* of Messiah. (20)

For He was foreknown before the foundation of the world, but has appeared in these last times for the sake of you (21) who through Him are believers in YHWH, who raised Him from the dead and gave Him glory, so that your faith and hope are in YHWH. (22) Since you have **in obedience to the truth purified your souls** for a sincere love of the brethren, fervently love one another from the heart, (23) for you have been born again not of seed which is perishable but imperishable, *that is,* **through the living and enduring Word of YHWH**. (24) For, ALL FLESH IS LIKE GRASS, AND ALL ITS GLORY LIKE THE FLOWER OF GRASS. THE GRASS WITHERS, AND THE FLOWER FALLS OFF, (25) **BUT THE WORD OF YHWH ENDURES FOREVER**. And this is the Word which was preached to you." 1 Peter 4:12-14 "(12) Beloved, **do not be surprised at the fiery ordeal among you, which comes upon you for your testing**, as though some strange thing were happening to you; (13) but to the degree that you share the sufferings of Messiah, keep on rejoicing, so that also at the revelation of His glory you may **rejoice** with exultation. (14) If you are reviled for the name of Messiah, you are blessed, because the Spirit of glory and of YHWH rests on you."

> *YHWH will judge His people but if we add patience to our faith great reward is guaranteed by YHWH!*

Remember this is about the deliverance (Salvation) of our souls from the robber of our peace! Will we separate ourselves from the hardship and trials of others who are under great trials? Only if you desire the same or greater trial!

Hebrews 10:30-39 "(30) For we know Him that has said, Vengeance *belongs* to Me, I will recompense, says YHWH. And again, YHWH shall judge His people. (31) *It is* a fearful thing to fall into the hands of the living

Elohim. (32) But call to remembrance the former days, in which, after you were illuminated, **you endured a great fight of afflictions**; (33) partly, while you were made a **gazing stock** both by reproaches and afflictions; and partly, while you became companions of them that were so used. (34) For you had compassion of me in my bonds, and took joyfully the spoiling of your goods, knowing in yourselves that you have in heaven a better and an enduring substance. (35) Cast not **away therefore your confidence, which has great recompense of reward**. (36) For you have need of patience, that, after you have done the will of YHWH, you might receive the promise. (37) For yet a little while, and He that shall come will come, and will not tarry. (38) **Now the just shall live by faith**: but if *any man* draws back, My soul shall have no pleasure in him. (39) But we are not of them who draw back unto perdition; but of them that believe to the **saving of the soul**."

Here are the Torah Scriptures for this week

Numbers 25:1-30:1; 1 Kings 18:46-19:21; 2 Timothy Chapters 1, 2, 3, and 4; Titus Chapters 1, 2, and 3; Philemon

Let's look at Scriptures about zeal; it is said of Yahshua: (Isaiah 9:7) "Of the increase of *His* government and peace *there shall be* no end, upon the throne of David, and upon His Kingdom, to order it, and to establish it with judgment and with justice from henceforth even forever. The zeal of YHWH of hosts will perform this."

> *Let's see again the zeal of Phineas when he heard YHWH's instructions in last week's reading! This is likened to the having the mind of Messiah!*

Numbers 25:3-6 "(3) And Israel joined himself unto Baalpeor: and the anger of YHWH was kindled against Israel. (4) And YHWH said unto

Moses, Take all the heads of the people, and hang them up before YHWH against the sun, that the **fierce anger of YHWH** may be turned away from Israel. (5) And Moses said to the judges of Israel, Slay every one of his men that were joined to Baalpeor. (6) And, behold, one of the children of Israel came and brought unto his brethren a Midianitish woman in the sight of Moses, and in the sight of all the congregation of the children of Israel, who *were* weeping *before* the door of the Tabernacle of the congregation."

> **Zeal is turned to action as we too must be doers of the Word and not hearers only being deceived!**

Numbers 25:7-11 "(7) And when Phinehas, the son of Eleazar, the son of Aaron the priest, saw *it*, he rose up from among the congregation, and took a javelin in his hand; (8) And he went after the man of Israel into the tent, and thrust both of them through, the man of Israel, and the woman through her belly. So the plague was stayed from the children of Israel. (9) And those that died in the plague were twenty and four thousand. (10) And YHWH spoke to Moses, saying, (11) **Phinehas, the son of Eleazar, the son of Aaron the priest, hath turned My wrath away from the children of Israel, while <u>he was zealous</u>** for My sake among them, that I consumed not the children of Israel in My jealousy."

> **Obedience with zeal brings the plan of YHWH- An everlasting covenant of PEACE!**

Numbers 25:12-18 "(12) Wherefore say, Behold, <u>**I give to him My Covenant of peace**</u>: (13) and he shall have it, <u>and his seed after him, *even* the Covenant of an everlasting priesthood; because he was zealous for his Elohim, and made atonement for the children of Israel.</u> (14) Now the name of the Israelite that was slain, *even* that was slain with the Midianitish woman, *was* Zimri, the son of Salu, a prince of a chief house among the Simeonites. (15) And the name of the Midianitish woman that was slain *was* Cozbi, the daughter of Zur; he *was* head over a people, *and* of a chief house in Midian. (16) And YHWH spoke unto Moses, saying, (17) Vex the Midianites, and smite them: (18) For they vex you with their wiles, wherewith <u>they have beguiled you in the matter of Peor</u>, and in the matter of Cozbi, the daughter of a prince of Midian, their sister, which was slain in the day of the plague for Peor's sake."

This is why there is protocol in approaching our KING!

Numbers 26:60-61 "(60) And to Aaron was born Nadab, and Abihu, Eleazar, and Ithamar. (61) And <u>Nadab and Abihu died</u>, when they **offered strange fire before YHWH**."

Do what He says and live!

Numbers 27:12-14 "(12) And יהוה said to Mosheh, Go up into this Mount Abarim, and see the land which I have given to the children of Yisra'ěl. (13) And when you have seen it, **you also shall be gathered to your people as Aharon your brother was gathered**, (14) **because you rebelled against My mouth** in the Wilderness of Tsin, in the strife of the congregation, to set Me apart at the waters before their eyes. These were the waters of Meribah, at Qaděsh in the Wilderness of Tsin."

Doctrine of "laying on of hands"

Numbers 27:15-23 "(15) And Mosheh spoke to יהוה, saying, (16) Let יהוה, the Elohim of the spirits of all flesh, appoint a man over the congregation, (17) who goes out before them and comes in before them, who leads them out and brings them in, so that the congregation of יהוה be not like sheep without a shepherd. (18) And יהוה said to Mosheh, Take

215

Yehoshua son of Nun with you, a man in whom is the Spirit. **And you shall lay your hand on him**, (19) and shall set him before El'azar the priest and before all the congregation, and give him charge before their eyes, (20) and shall put some of your esteem upon him, so that all the congregation of the children of Yisra'ĕl <u>obey</u> *him.* (21) And he is to stand before El'azar the priest, who shall inquire before יהוה for him by the right-ruling of the Urim. At his word they go out, and at his word they come in, both he and all the children of Yisra'ĕl with him, all the congregation. (22) And Mosheh did as יהוה commanded him, and took Yehoshua and set him before El'azar the priest and before the entire congregation, (23) and laid his hands on him and commissioned him, as יהוה commanded by the hand of Mosheh."

Some of the Feasts of YHWH (We thought they were just Jewish) but they are FEASTS OF THE LORD! These are the appointed times our King has scheduled already.

Numbers 29:39 "These you prepare to יהוה at your **appointed times**, besides your vowed offerings and your voluntary offerings, as your burnt offerings and your grain offerings, as your drink offerings and your peace offerings."

> *Remember the Spring Feasts have been fulfilled but the Fall Feasts are near future! Why is that import to you and me? Note carefully below when the Law or Torah/Instructions are done away with according to Yahshua (Jesus)*

Matthew 5:17-18 "(17) Do not think that I came to abolish the Law or the Prophets; I did not come to abolish but to **fulfill**. (18) For truly I say to you, until heaven and earth pass away, not the smallest letter or stroke shall pass from the Law **until all is accomplished**." *(Comment: accomplished=fulfilled)*

Matthew 5:19 "Whoever then annuls one of the least of these Commandments, and teaches others *to do* the same, **shall be called least in the Kingdom of Heaven**; but whoever keeps and teaches *them*, he shall be called great in the Kingdom of Heaven." *(Comment: this is why many Pastors sadly will be called Pastor least in the Kingdom and then to add to horrors Yahshua warns again about those who are "lawless" as these below who do wonderful works in His name are not likely murderers and bank robbers, etc)*

Matthew 7:21-27 "(21) Not everyone who says to Me, Lord, Lord, will enter the Kingdom of Heaven, but he who does the will of My Father who is in heaven *will enter*. (22) Many will say to Me on that day, Lord, Lord, did we not prophesy in Your name, and in Your name cast out demons, and in Your name perform many miracles? (23) And then I will declare to them, I never knew you; DEPART FROM ME, **YOU** WHO PRACTICE LAWLESSNESS. *(YIKES! Shouldn't we each ask the question what is lawless? In the Hebrew it is **TORAH-lessness**- they mistakenly thought the Law was done away with and **nailed** to the cross- that nailing was the punishment-not the Law!)* (24) Therefore everyone who hears these Words of Mine and acts on them may be compared to a wise man who built his house on the rock. (25) And the rain fell, and the floods came, and the winds blew and slammed against that house; and *yet* it did not fall, for it had been founded on the Rock. (26) Everyone who hears these Words of Mine and does not act on them will be like a foolish man who built his house on the sand. (27) The rain fell, and the floods came, and the winds blew and slammed against that house; and it fell--and great was its fall."

Passover *(**fulfilled** as Yahshua-Jesus was and is the Passover Lamb)*

Numbers 28:16-18, 25 "(16) And in the first month, on the fourteenth day, is the Passover of יהוה, (17) and on the fifteenth day of this month is a Festival. For seven days unleavened bread is eaten. (18) On the first day is a Set-Apart gathering, you do no servile work. (25) And on the seventh day you have a Set-Apart gathering, you do no servile work."

First fruits *(Yahshua **fulfilled** when the graves opened!)*

Numbers 28:26 "And on the day of the First-Fruits, when you bring a new grain offering to יהוה at your Festival of Weeks, you have a Set-Apart gathering, you do no servile work."

Feast of Trumpets *(The Hebrew idiom is the day that no man knows the day or hour- the last trump is when this gets fulfilled as we meet Messiah in the air- **not fulfilled yet**)*

Numbers 29:1 "And in the seventh month, on the first day of the month, you have a Set-Apart gathering, you do no servile work, it is a day of blowing the trumpets for you."

Judgment Day *(Yom Kippur or _Day of Atonement_ **not fulfilled yet**)*

Numbers 29:7 "And on the tenth day of this seventh month you have a Set-Apart gathering, and you shall afflict your beings, you do not work."

Feast of Tabernacles *(When Yahshua (Jesus) tabernacles with us on the Earth 1000 years in the millennium- **not fulfilled yet**)*

Numbers 29:12 "And on the fifteenth day of the seventh month you have a Set-Apart gathering, you do no servile work. And you shall observe a Festival to יהוה seven days…"

> **We all should avoid pity parties but when the fire comes….it is not always easy!**

1 Kings 19:1-6 "(1) And when Aḥab reported to Yizebel all that Ĕliyahu had done, also how he slew all the prophets with the sword, (2) Yizebel (Jezebel) sent a messenger to Ĕliyahu, saying, So let the mighty ones do to me, and more also, if I do not make your life as the life of one of them by tomorrow about this time. (3) And he feared, and rose up and ran for his life, and he went to Be'ĕrsheba, which belongs to Yehudah, and left his servant there. (4) But he himself went a day's journey into the wilderness, and came and sat down under a broom tree, and prayed that he might die, and said, It is enough! Now, יהוה, take my life, for I am no better than my fathers! (5) And he lay and slept under a broom tree, and see, an angel touched him, and said to him, Rise, eat. (6) And he looked and saw by his head a cake baked on coals, and a jar of water. So he ate and drank, and turned and lay down."

Angelic help is nice and if we are obedient we can expect the same!

1 Kings 19:7-10 "(7) And the angel of יהוה came back the second time, and touched him, and said, Rise, eat, for the journey is too much for you. (8) And he rose up and ate and drank, and went <u>in the strength of that food forty days and forty nights</u> as far as Ḥorĕb, the mountain of Elohim. (9) And there he went into a cave and spent the night there. And see, the Word of יהוה came to him, and said to him, What are you doing here, Ĕliyahu? (10) And he said, I **have been very zealous for יהוה** Elohim of hosts, for the children of Yisra'ĕl have forsaken Your Covenant. They have thrown down Your altars, and they have slain Your prophets with the sword, and I am left, I alone, and they seek my life, to take it."

Listen for a still small voice from YHWH!

1 Kings 19:11-21 "(11) And He said, Go out, and stand on the mountain before יהוה. And see, יהוה passed by, and a great and strong wind tearing

the mountains and breaking the rocks in pieces before יהוה – יהוה was not in the wind. And after the wind an earthquake – יהוה was not in the earthquake, (12) and after the earthquake a fire – יהוה was not in the fire, and after the fire **a still small voice**. (13) And it came to be, when Ĕliyahu heard it, that he wrapped his face in his robe and went out and stood at the cave opening. And see, a voice came to him, and said, What are you doing here, Ĕliyahu? (14) And he said, I have been very jealous for יהוה Elohim of hosts, for the children of Yisra'ĕl have forsaken Your Covenant. They have thrown down Your altars, and they have slain Your prophets with the sword, and I am left, I alone, and they seek my life, to take it. (15) And יהוה said to him, Go, and return on your way to the Wilderness of Damascus. And you shall go in and anoint Ḥaza'ĕl as sovereign over Aram. (16) And anoint Yĕhu son of Nimshi as sovereign over Yisra'ĕl. And anoint Elisha son of Shaphat of Abĕl Meḥolah as prophet in your place. (17) And it shall be that whoever escapes the sword of Ḥaza'ĕl, Yĕhu does kill. And whoever escapes from the sword of Yĕhu, Elisha does kill. (18) **And I shall leave seven thousand in Yisra'ĕl, all whose knees have not bowed to Ba'al**, and every mouth that has not kissed him. *(Comment: He still has a remnant today also!)* (19) And he went from there, and found Elisha son of Shaphat, who was plowing with twelve yoke *of oxen* before him, and he was with the twelfth. And Ĕliyahu passed by him and threw his robe on him. (20) And he left the oxen and ran after Ĕliyahu, and said, Please let me kiss my father and my mother, and then I follow you. And he said to him, Go and turn back, I have done nothing to you! (21) And he turned back from him, and took a yoke of oxen and slaughtered them and cooked their flesh, using the implements of the oxen, and gave it to the people, and they ate. Then he <u>rose up and followed Ĕliyahu</u>, and became his servant."

Blessings to you Loved One! May YHWH bless you and keep you, make His face to shine on you, lift up His countenance on you and give you PEACE! May He provide for you and your loved ones protect and even direct you with His mighty angels as He did for Elijah in our study today! May He draw you and your loved ones close as we obey and become ZEALOUS for His Instructions as Elijah did!

Thanks again for your intercession and great timely and on target prayers for us. You really are the greatest brothers and sisters on the planet! Thank you, thank you and thank you!
Thurston

Here is the last of the three displays of our weekly study:

SHABBAT SHALOM LOVED ONE!

May 29, 2009

Shabbat Shalom Loved One! *(This is a heavy message only for Truth Searchers!* **Never** *fear as YHWH will guide, provide, and protect us.)*

This is indeed a special Shabbat! They are all special but this Saturday at sundown according to YHWH's biblical Commands of His calendar and counting times and events- it is **Shavuot**! (Pentecost to some) This Shabbat I will address why I believe we MUST come out of **her** *(Comment: Come out of what? "Her" is the whore church system, the whore culture, and the whore country or countries- as it is spirit, soul and body!)* my people or partake of her plaques very shortly! This Set-Apart Day (Shavuot) was the conclusion of the Spring Feasts that **Yahshua fulfilled** at His first coming. The early rain spoken by Ya'akov (James) 5:7-10 "(7) so, brothers, be patient until the coming of the Master. See, the farmer waits for the precious fruit of the earth, waiting patiently for it until it receives the **early and latter rain**. (8) You too, be patient. Establish your

221

hearts, for the coming of the Master has drawn near. (9) Do not grumble against each other, brothers, lest you be judged. See, the Judge is standing at the door! (10) My brothers, as an example of suffering and patience, take the prophets, who spoke in the Name of יהוה."

The early rain was the outpouring of the Ruach HaKodesh (Holy Spirit) after the counting of 7- sevens after First-Fruits as the graves opened and Yahshua fulfilled the High Priest's duty of presenting the wave offering of thanksgiving to the Father YHWH for the precious fruit of the Earth. We will have just finished the counting of seven -7's on Shabbat. This is where we are empowered to become witnesses to produce fruit for the KINGDOM that will remain!

Acts 1:8 "But you shall receive power, after that the Holy Ghost is come upon you: and you **shall be witnesses** to Me both in Jerusalem, and in all Judaea, and in Samaria, and unto the uttermost part of the earth."

Acts 2:1-4 "(1) And when the day of Shavuot (Pentecost) was fully come, they were all with one accord in one place. (2) And suddenly there came a sound from heaven as of a rushing mighty wind, and it filled the entire house where they were sitting. (3) And there appeared unto them cloven tongues like as of fire, and it sat upon each of them. (4) And they were all filled with the Holy Ghost, and began to speak with other tongues, as the Spirit gave them utterance."

I believe the biblical calendar has been discovered and is accurate based on the knowledge that is increased as NASA has calculated the astronomical calendar to 1 ten millionth of a day! We know now that the prophecy by Isaiah that questions "Can a nation be born in a day?" (Paraphrased)

Isaiah 66:8 "Who hath heard such a thing? Who hath seen such things? Shall the earth be made to bring forth in one day? *Or* shall a nation be born at once? For as soon as Zion travailed, she brought forth her children."

This happened on **May 14th, 1948 when Israel was created by the U.N.** in one day. However, this appeared for 60 years to be a *nowhere date also*. It meant nothing special on Pope Gregory's calendar (Gregorian) and meant nothing on the Jewish calendar made up by Hillel II prior to the dispersion. Recently, my friend Michael Rood asked the question also and then used NASA's astronomical calendar programming and noted it was the seventh seven of the counting toward Shavuot which is identical to this Shabbat! **This should prove to us that YHWH still runs His Universe and His Creation according to His calendar!**

Yahshua fulfilled the Spring Feasts down to the day and hour as we now have the capability of rolling back the celestial time clock since NASA has calculated the calendar (Previously known as the Junius/Julian) down to 1 ten millionth of a day! But are they **ALL fulfilled**? No, the Fall Feasts are not yet fulfilled; therefore the Torah (Law-Instructions) is NOT done away with. Not to mention that even the casual observer can still see a heaven and earth.

Matthew 5:17-19 "(17) Think not that I am come to destroy the Law, or the prophets: I am not come to destroy, but to fulfill. (18) For verily I say unto you, till heaven and earth pass, one jot or one tittle shall in no wise pass from the Law, **till all be fulfilled**. *(Comment question. Is all fulfilled biblically? NO!)* (19) Whosoever therefore shall break one of these least Commandments, and shall teach men so, he shall be called the least in the Kingdom of Heaven: but whosoever shall do and teach them, the same shall be called great in the Kingdom of Heaven." *(Comment: Praise YHWH those who refuse to obey His Commands and say the Law is done* *away with may still enter the Kingdom! Now that's mercy even if they are the LEAST in the Kingdom!)*

I believe the time they start fulfillment is the <u>Fall of 2010 at the Feast of Trumpets</u>. The latter rain outpouring for the Fall Feasts would be on the Last Great Day which would be the end of the 2010 Fall Feasts. This is the Sabbath day <u>after</u> the seven day Feast of Tabernacles known as the Season of our rejoicing! This outpouring will be greater than the first outpouring as we will need to walk in power and do exploits in His name. Of course for the sleepy and drunk Christian who is not sober and alert as Yahshua Commanded us, they will be dead and dying as rockets fly at the Feast of Trumpets 2010 which is 15 days prior to the Feast of Tabernacles and the outpouring of the **latter rain empowering** of the sober and humble servants of YHWH.

WHY NOW (Fall of 2010)?

My First Witness

Please note that I realize these traditions today do not mean sun god and fertility Easter worship to Christians and those of the faith. **BUT**, we must understand this is what He says it means to Him in the Scriptures. So our question should likely be what do they mean to **Him**?

In 724 BCE the 10 Northern Tribes of Israel also known as Ephraim were carried away captive for their whoredoms of sun god worship, Easter worship (Fertility goddess where eggs were dipped into the blood of sacrificed babies after Easter priests impregnated virgins on the Easter sunrise altar the prior year for a prosperous and fertile year), Christmas tree (Sun god Phallic symbols with silver and gold balls or testicles).

Remember YHWH Commanded us: Jeremiah 10:2-4 "(2) thus says YHWH, **Learn not** the way of the heathen, and be not dismayed at the

224

signs of heaven; for the heathen are dismayed at them. (3) For the customs of the people *are* vain: for *one* cuts a tree out of the forest, the work of the hands of the workman, with the axe. (4) They deck it with silver and with gold; they fasten it with nails and with hammers that it move not."

Remember Ezekiel laid on his side 390 days (1 day for a year) for 390 years of judgment on Ephraim (Israel not Judah). **Ezekiel 4:4-5** "(4) Lie also upon your left side, and lay the iniquity of the **house of Israel** upon it: *according* to the number of the days that thou shall lie upon it thou shall bear their iniquity. (5) For I have lain upon thee the years of their iniquity, according to the number of the days, **three hundred and ninety days**: so shall thou bear the iniquity of the house of Israel."

Since there was no repentance this judgment was multiplied seven times!

Leviticus 26:18-19 "(18) And if ye will not yet for all this hearken unto me, then I **will punish you seven times more** for your sins. (19) And I will break the pride of your power; and I will make your heaven as iron, and your earth as brass:"

Seven times 390 years equals 2730 years! Many Bible chronologists pinpoint this date to be Aviv 1- 2010. This is the biblical start of 2010, which is sometime in the March April time frame.

I believe this is when the scales come off of **ALL Israel** and not just the Jews as we were once taught. Then, we Christians who were scattered all over the Earth (The lost sheep of Israel that Yahshua came for) will wake up and have the opportunity to come apart from pagan sun god-easter fertility worship traditions and practices we have inherited!

Jeremiah 16:19 "O YHWH, my strength, and my fortress, and my refuge in the day of affliction, the Gentiles *(Comment: Pagans, heathen and added scattered tribes of Israel involved in the same practices and traditions)* shall come unto thee from the ends of the earth, and shall say, surely **our fathers have inherited lies**, vanity, and *things* wherein *there is* no profit."

Therefore we are given seven months to repent once our scales are removed and our eyes are opened. **Remember YHWH judges His people <u>first</u>!**

Hebrews 10:29-31 "(29) Of how much sorer punishment, suppose you, shall he be thought worthy, who hath trodden underfoot the Son of YHWH, and has counted the blood of the Covenant, wherewith He was sanctified, an unholy thing, and has done despite unto the Spirit of grace? (30) For we know Him that has said, Vengeance *belongs* to Me, I will recompense, says YHWH. And again, **<u>YHWH shall judge His people</u>**. (31) *It is* a fearful thing to fall into the hands of the living Elohim."

<u>My Second Witness</u>

Here is my second witness as all things are confirmed by 2 or 3 witnesses.

Deuteronomy 19:15 "One witness shall not rise up against a man for any iniquity, or for any sin, in any sin that he sins: <u>at the mouth of two witnesses, or at the mouth of three witnesses, shall the matter be established</u>."

I recently (June of 2008) finished a 40 day fast concerning these matters. I was told on the 40th day to get a pen and write, which I did. I will now be happy to forward that account to all who want to have it. Here is the jest of it; starting October 1 (2008) the US economy will unravel and the entire world will quickly join. They (The entire world) will try and repair this for 2 years and they will not be able to. We in the USA will suffer civil unrest and even martial law prior to the Feast of Trumpets 2010 (The day that no man knows the day or hour which is a Hebrew idiom for this Feast) – Then <u>ROCKETS FLY</u>! Why Then? Rockets fly to those who claim to know Him after they have been given ample time to repent. Assuming the scales come off sleeping and drunk Ephraim (Christians who are really born again by His Spirit) on Aviv one 2010 (March-April timeframe) and they will still not repent and come apart from sun god and Easter fertility pagan traditions then judgment first falls on His own household 7 months later at the Feast of Trumpets 2010 (September-October time frame).

> 1 Peter 4:17 "For the time *is come* that judgment <u>must begin at the house of God</u>: and if *it* first *begin* at us, what shall the end *be* of them that obey not the gospel of God?"

> *(Comment: During June of 2008 I had no idea October 1, 2008 would be the biblical day for the Feast of Trumpets or the first sliver of the seventh new moon. This is exactly 2 biblical years as He told me- remember it's the day no man knows the day or hour).*

My Third Witness

Next I felt I understood: I will return at the Feast of Trumpets 2017. I also felt that He showed this to be the year of release or a Jubilee. (Many may not agree with me on this and that is okay.) I questioned and stated, "Lord- if this is something critical about jubilee and Jerusalem (50 year sets), then there should be some record of events every 50 years prior to 2017 and there is NOT!" What I thought I heard next was, "**LOOK IT UP!**" **LOOK IT UP? I questioned in my thoughts**. The next thought I had was: GOOGLE IT! This is what I did, although I **actually used Yahoo search**. I typed Jerusalem 1967 (50 years prior to 2017) and that was the year Jerusalem was captured for the first time in thousands of years by the Jews. I was mildly surprised. Next I typed in Jerusalem 1917 and thought,

I know nothing happened then. To my surprise 1917 was the year that Jerusalem was captured by General Allenby of the British forces from the Ottoman Empire. Still not convinced by these happenstances, I typed Jerusalem 1867 into the Yahoo search and **2 events** popped up. First, this is when the American pen name writer Mark Twain visited Jerusalem and *declared this is a desolate place. Exactly what the Scriptures declared it would be when Israel was scattered over the earth for her abominations. Next, in 1867 also, Lieutenant (later Captain) Warren of the British Royal Engineering Corps surveyed the Temple Mount in Jerusalem!*

This was my third witness and concluded the matter for me. Yes, it is okay if you do not agree with me! I don't always agree with myself as we are given ***progressive revelation*** based on our hunger and thirst for more TRUTH! We will never be given more that we hunger and thirst for! Truly, I believe we believers should pray for more and more truth and hunger and thirst for truth and righteousness.

Matthew 5:6 "Blessed *are* they which do hunger and thirst after righteousness: for they shall be **filled**."

Remember, Daniel was told (Paraphrased) "Seal up the book Daniel- it is for the latter days when knowledge increases and men move to and fro upon the earth- you will go sleep with your fathers- it is not for you to understand!"

Caution! *Never rely solely on another's personal revelation! Study these matters out for yourself! We must be like the Berean's and study the Scriptures and search how these things might be true! YOU will be judged based on your actions!* ***Caution!***

Here are our Torah Scriptures for this week

Leviticus 23:15-21; Deuteronomy 14:22-16:17; Numbers 28:26-31; Habakkuk 3:1-19; Acts 2:1-13

Leviticus 23:15-21 "(15) And you shall count unto you from the morrow after the Sabbath, from the day that you brought the sheaf of the wave offering; seven Sabbaths shall be complete: (16) Even unto the morrow after the seventh Sabbath shall you number fifty days; and you shall offer a new meat offering to YHWH. (17) You shall bring out of your habitations two wave loaves of two tenth deals: they shall be of fine flour; they shall be baked with leaven; *they are* the **First Fruits** unto YHWH. (18) And you shall offer with the bread seven lambs without blemish of the first year, and one young bullock, and two rams: they shall be *for* a burnt offering to YHWH, with their meat offering, and their drink offerings, *even* an offering made by fire, of sweet savor to YHWH. (19) Then you shall sacrifice one kid of the goats for a sin offering, and two lambs of the first year for a sacrifice of peace offerings. (20) And the priest shall wave them with the bread of the First Fruits *for* a wave offering before YHWH, with the two lambs: they shall be Holy to YHWH for the priest. (21) And you shall proclaim on the selfsame day, *that* it may be a **Holy Convocation** unto you: you shall do no servile work *therein: it shall be* a statute forever in all your dwellings **throughout your generations**." *(Comment: these "Holy" or Set-Apart Convocations are rehearsals and pictures of things to come)*

Deuteronomy 14:22-28 "(22) You shall tithe without fail all the yield of your grain that the field brings forth year by year. (23) And you shall eat before יהוה your Elohim, in the place where He chooses to make His Name dwell, the tithe of your grain and your new wine and your oil, and of the firstlings of your herds and your sheep, so that you learn to fear יהוה your Elohim always. (24) But when the way is too long for you, so that you are not able to bring the tithe, or when the place where יהוה your Elohim chooses to put His Name is too far from you, when יהוה your Elohim is blessing you, (25) then you shall give it in silver, and shall take the silver in your hand and go to the place which יהוה your Elohim chooses. (26) And you shall use the silver for whatever your being desires: for cattle or sheep, for wine or strong drink, for whatever your being desires. And you shall eat there before יהוה your Elohim, and you shall rejoice you and your household. (27) And do not forsake the Lĕwite [Levite] who is within your gates, for he has no part nor inheritance with you. (28) At the end of every third year you bring out all the tithe of your increase of that year and store it up within your gates."

> *Here is where you and I owe our tithe! Sounds familiar—the widow, orphan and the priest, who is not given himself over to stuff and things of ownership- not some Nico-laitan church system that rules the peons. We are all equal under Messiah!*

Deuteronomy 14:29 "And the **Lĕwite (Levite), because he has no portion nor inheritance with you, and the sojourner and the fatherless and the widow** who are within your gates, shall come and eat and be satisfied, so that יהוה your Elohim does bless you in all the work of your hands which you do."

Blessings to you and your loved ones! May YHWH give us revelation and power to do all He Commands. May your prayers be in agreement with the Word that is established in Heaven! May you receive on behalf of your loved ones the promises of eternal life by faith and trusting Him and not your circumstances! The greatest test we will also soon face is the same picture shown us of Israel not obeying when told to go in to the Promised Land. They were disobedient because they were worried about their wives and children! Result? Their untrusting carcasses were scattered throughout the desert for 40 years and then YHWH safely took the children in! **We must trust Him with our families** *also! May His promises become your Yes and amen! May your prayer to be found worthy, alive and unashamed at His appearing be fulfilled! Make us ready YHWH! Change everything about us you don't like and find offensive in us!*

Shabbat Shalom Loved One,

Thurston

Here are some added thoughts for the hungry for truth:

In 1997 I asked the Lord why the USA was not mentioned in Scripture. I believe He told me "You are- you just don't like the name I give you!" Get your Bible, turn to Revelation 17:1 and read son, you will see your name there. Excited, I ran and got my Bible and opened to find (Paraphrased) "Mystery-Babylon the whore- who rules the nations of the Earth in the last days!" Mystery- because we have only been here about 400 years. Then after Passover in 2000 while camped out in Israel on the Galilee between Bethsaida and Kefar-Nahum (Capernaum) for 11 days and nights I asked another question; "Father, where is a safe place in America to ride out the trouble in the last days with my family?" What I heard next I shared with no one for 1 ½ years! It was such a hard message I could not receive it myself. It literally took a year and a half for the Scriptures He directed me to and the truths He showed me about the USA abominations around the world to soak in where I could understand. Finally, YHWH does nothing without first revealing to us His servants His plans.

Amos 3:7 "Surely YHWH Elohim will do nothing, but he reveals His secret to His servants the prophets." *(Comment: At least those who are not the drunk and asleep shepherds of Ephraim or the USA who rules*

Jerusalem) **NOW YHWH has named the USA! We are officially an OBAMA-NATION!**

Here are Scriptures for your consideration as those that divide Jerusalem (Part His land) will be quickly destroyed and the USA is and has played a key role in forcing this!

Joel 3:2 "I will also gather all nations, and will bring them down into the valley of Jehoshaphat, and will plead with them there for My people and *for* My heritage Israel, <u>whom they have scattered among the nations</u>, and **parted My land**."

Isaiah 28:3-22 "(3) The crown of pride, the drunkards of Ephraim, shall be trodden under feet: (4) And the glorious beauty, which *is* on the head of the fat valley, shall be a fading flower, *and* as the hasty fruit before the summer; which *when* he that looks upon it sees, while it is yet in his hand he eats it up. (5) In that day shall YHWH of hosts be for a crown of glory, and for a diadem of beauty, unto the residue of His people, (6) And for a spirit of judgment to him that sits in judgment, and for strength to them that turn the battle to the gate. (7) But they also have erred through wine, and through strong drink are out of the way; the priest and the prophet have erred through strong drink, they are swallowed up of wine, they are out of the way through strong drink; they err in vision, they stumble *in* judgment. (8) For all tables are full of vomit *and* filthiness, *so that there is* no place *clean. (Comment: traditions inherited of sun god and Easter fertility goddess worship)* (9) Whom shall He teach knowledge? And whom shall He make to understand doctrine? *Them that are* weaned from the milk, *and* drawn from the breasts. (10) For precept *must be* upon precept, precept upon precept; line upon line, line upon line; here a little, *and* there a little: (11) For with stammering lips and another tongue will He speak to this people. (12) To whom He said this *is* the rest *wherewith*

232

you may cause the weary to rest; and this *is* the refreshing: yet they would not hear. (13) But the Word of YHWH was unto them precept upon precept, precept upon precept; line upon line, line upon line; here a little, *and* there a little; that they might go, and fall backward, and be broken, and snared, and taken. (14) Wherefore hear the Word of YHWH, you scornful men, that rule this people which *is* in Jerusalem. (15) Because you have said, we have made a covenant with death, and with hell are we at agreement; when the overflowing scourge shall pass through, it shall not come unto us: for we have made lies our refuge, and under falsehood have we hid ourselves: (16) Therefore thus says YHWH, Behold, I lay in Zion for a foundation a Stone, a tried Stone, a precious corner *Stone*, a sure foundation: he that believes shall not make haste. (17) Judgments also will I lay to the line, and righteousness to the plummet: and the hail shall sweep away the refuge of lies, and the waters shall overflow the hiding place. (18) And your covenant with death *(Comment: Oslo accords and Oslo in Modern Hebrew means toilet seat)* shall be disannulled, and your agreement with hell shall not stand; when the overflowing scourge shall pass through, then you shall be trodden down by it. *(Comment: I believe the overwhelming scourge is rockets flying in the Fall of 2010- first to USA and simultaneously to Israel which YHWH protects! YHWH alone will be Israel's deliverer!)* (19) From the time that it goes forth it shall take you: for morning by morning shall it pass over, by day and by night: and it shall be a vexation only *to* understand the report. (20) For the bed is shorter than that *a man* can stretch himself *on it*: and the covering narrower than that he can wrap himself *in it*. (21) For YHWH shall rise up as *in* mount Perazim, He shall be wroth as *in* the valley of Gibeon, that He may do His work, His strange work; and bring to pass His act, His strange act. (22) Now therefore be you not mockers, lest your bands be made strong: for I have heard from YHWH of host's consumption, **even determined upon the whole earth**."

Remember when the world says **PEACE AND SAFETY**- *sudden destruction comes on **them**! It will come on the world like a thief in the night, but we are children of the light- it will not surprise us! Prepare. Blessings- Thurston*

A question I received from a dear brother in Yahshua was this, "Did I miss where there was a safe place in the USA to have my family when these things happen?" So in fairness I will share now exactly what I heard and you will see why it was so hard for me to receive and understand for 1 ½ years. You will now know exactly why I shared this with no one for that 1 ½ years! My question technically to the Lord was not U.S.A., it was where is a safe place in America? Although, admittedly, I was thinking of the U.S.A. This is what I heard, "Son, there will be nothing left of America. In one hour her destruction will come."

*Here are a few comments and understandings that recently I have added to understanding my thoughts on understanding how these things could be. I also noticed that I had said Israel became a nation in one day on May 24, 1948- that is incorrect as the date was **May 14, 1948**. Next note the lies that are swept away by the overflowing scourge of judgment by war and rockets flying. Understand that the USA is in agreement (Actually the architect and main supporter and enforcer) with Oslo, Roadmap to Peace (More likely the Roadmap to Hell) and the dividing of YHWH's land and the place He has placed His Name, Jerusalem and all Israel- for the promise of peace with the Arabs. These will say peace, peace but there is no peace.*

1 Thessalonians 5:3 "For when they shall say, Peace and safety; then sudden destruction comes upon them, as travail upon a woman with child; and they shall not escape."

Ezekiel 13:16 "*To wit*, the prophets of Israel which prophesy concerning Jerusalem, and which see visions of peace for her, and *there is* no peace, says YHWH Elohim."

The land of the thieves….I considered the matter and remembered a saying my dad had often spoken and warned me, 'If a man will lie to you, he will also steal from you." It seems that thief and liar seem to go hand in hand.

One question I had about Zechariah 5 and the nuclear rockets he saw as most of you already know that in the Hebrew it is not an evil woman but an evil fire offering that consumes wood and stone that goes to the land of the thieves, was where was the land of the thieves? I thought surely that is not the USA. I was wrong as I now see it is the countries that part His land.

Isaiah 28:15, 17-18 "(15) Because you have said, we have made a covenant with death, and with hell are we at agreement; when the overflowing scourge shall pass through, it shall not come unto us: **for we have made <u>lies</u> our refuge**, and **<u>under falsehood</u>** have we hid ourselves. (17) Judgments also will I lay to the line, and righteousness to the plummet: and the hail shall **sweep away the refuge of <u>lies</u>**, and the waters shall overflow the hiding place. (18) And your covenant with death *(Comment: Oslo accords and Oslo in Modern Hebrew means toilet seat)* shall be disannulled, and your agreement with hell shall not stand; when the overflowing scourge shall pass through, then you shall be trodden down by it." *(Comment: I believe the overwhelming scourge is rockets flying in the Fall of 2010- first to USA and simultaneously to Israel which YHWH protects! YHWH alone will be Israel's deliverer!)*

Zechariah 5:1-11 "(1) And I lifted up my eyes again, and looked and saw a **flying scroll**. *(Comment: This is a measured cylinder or rocket he saw which is identical in size to the Scud missiles Iran has used)* (2) And He said to me, What do you see? And I answered, I see a flying scroll, **twenty cubits long and ten cubits wide**. *(Size of a scud missile)* (3) And He said to me, This is the curse that goes forth over the face of all the earth: everyone who is stealing shall go unpunished, on the one side, according to it, and, everyone who has **sworn falsely** *(Comment: **LIARS**)* shall go unpunished, on the other side, according to it. (4) I shall send it out, declares יהוה of hosts, and it shall come into the house of the thief and the house of the one **who shall swear falsely by My Name**. *(Comment: Liars!)* And it shall remain in the midst of his house and shall **consume** it, both its timber and stones. (5) And the Messenger who was speaking with me came out and said to me, Lift up your eyes now, and see what this is that is going forth. (6) And I said, What is it? And He said, It is an ĕphah-measure that is going forth. Again He said, This is their appearance throughout the earth: *(Comment: Missiles flying in the Earth!)* (7) And see, a **lead cover** lifted up, and this: a woman *(Comment: the word for woman is pronounced isha Strong's H802 means woman but spelled almost identically in Hebrew is aysha Strong's H784 which means fire)* sitting inside the ĕphah-measure! (8) And He said, This is wickedness! And He threw her down into the ĕphah-measure, and threw the **lead weight** over its mouth. *(Comment: **lead** blocks radiation of nuclear bomb assembly and handling)* (9) And I lifted up my eyes, and looked and saw **two women**, *(Comment: Again these are evil fire offerings or nuclear missiles as they are flying scrolls or cylinders)* coming with the wind in their wings. And they had wings like the wings of a stork, and they lifted up the ĕphah-measure between earth and the heavens. (10) Then I said to the Messenger who was speaking to me, Where are they taking the ĕphah-measure? (11) And He said to me, To build a house for it in the land of Shin'ar. *(Comment: Shinar is part of Iraq and Iran)* And it shall be established and set there on its own base."

Remember, if you would like our free weekly Torah Bible study, you may email your email address to me at tbmccut@seedtime2harvest.com.

The last forty-two months of the first seven years of the new millennium will start with great troubles for Jacob (Israel) or all those joined to the commonwealth of Israel by being born again.

Jeremiah (Yeremeyahu) 30:7-11 "(7) Alas! For that day is great, so that none is like it: it is even the time of Jacob's (Yaakov's) trouble, but it shall be saved out of it. (8) For it shall come to pass in that day, says Yahweh of Hosts, that I will break this yoke from off your neck, and will destroy your bondage, and strangers shall no more be served of you: (9) But you shall serve Yahweh, your Elohim, and David your King (Yahshua the Messiah), whom I will raise up for you (resurrect). (10) Therefore, do not fear My servant Jacob (Ya'akov or grafted-in Israel); neither be dismayed, O Israel, for I will save you from afar, and your seed (children) from the land of their captivity, and Jacob (grafted-in Israel) shall return, and shall be at rest, and none shall make him afraid. (11) For I am with you declares Yahweh, and will save you, although I make a full end to those nations where you are scattered to, yet, I will not make a full end of you: but I will correct you in measure and will not leave you altogether unpunished."

Serious times like these require a serious relationship with a Mighty Savior! It would be reasonable to suggest that we may have only a few years left before our Messiah will return as King. **Some would have you believe that Jacob's trouble or the tribulation period is only for the Jews. Of course that is ridiculous since Judah is only one of the twelve tribes, which the twelve apostles are to be heads of during the one**

thousand years of Yahshua's reign on the earth, according to the Scriptures in Revelation, and you are hopefully grafted in. (Or there is no gate for your entry)

Remember, all who are truly *born again* are grafted into Israel according to Ephesians 2:12 and Romans 11, and Israel is synonymous with Jacob as it is the same person, having been renamed by Yahweh. Again, the last 42 months of this seven-year time that will start the seventh millennium and is called the Great Tribulation, when the anti-messiah or Satan, makes war against the believers and declares to everyone that he is god. He makes everyone, small and great, rich and poor, to take a mark of allegiance. This is probably a computer chip insert of some kind as it allows no buying or selling without this mark. Remember, the Bible clearly teaches that anyone who takes this mark of allegiance with Satan will receive the full wrath of Yahweh and be cast into the lake of fire that burns forever! The Scriptures tell us that men's hearts will fail them during this time for fear of what's coming on the earth. **Still, do not take the mark!**

Thankfully, Yahshua comes and delivers (saves us) at the *last* trump, a period during the Great Tribulation according to 1 Corinthians 15:52 and Revelation chapters ten and eleven. That day, called the Day of the Lord, will begin the Sabbath rest day of our Creator, when He rules on the earth and Satan is locked away for one thousand years. In Revelation 5:10, the angel speaks of Yahshua and says, "and He has made us unto Yahweh, kings and priests and we shall reign on the earth" We can understand that earth will be restored and those of us who have learned to obey Him will be ruling with Him on the earth during the millennium.

The first time Yahshua (Jesus) came, He came as the willing and obedient sacrifice, to do His Father Yahweh's will. That was to pay for our sins by dying in our place, a Lamb without blemish. He was and is "The Lamb of God Sacrifice." I mention this only because there are other sacrifices that are a pleasing aroma to Yahweh, and this will be important for you to understand and not speak against when the Jews get part of the Temple Mount back and restart the animal sacrifices. They will get part of the Temple Mount back as this must happen to allow Satan to stop the sacrifices and start the Great Tribulation. **DO NOT speak against these sacrifices or this altar.** Your very life may depend on it! It is the antichrist or anti-messiah who STOPS these sacrifices. That is what starts the 42 months of Great Tribulation. That is the abomination that makes desolate written by the prophet Daniel. Our heavenly Father assigns an angel to insure the measuring of His altar, whose altar *YOU* are. Remember out of the heart the mouth will speak according to Mathew 12 and words are spirit. Remember judgment starts with the household of God. Next, Yahshua opens the seals and starts sending the angels with trumpets that usher in the Great Tribulation. Even if you do not understand, **DO NOT speak against this altar** where the sacrifices are taking place. Do not let your voice agree with these so-called animal lovers and the antichrist. You will have made an extremely poor choice of alignment. Many Christian believers will not understand and call this altar the abomination that makes desolate. They will have effectively agreed with Satan. Please do not make this grave mistake. He was and is the Lamb of God sacrifice. The 2300 evening and morning oblations (1150 days worth) are free will offerings and even though they are blood sacrifices, they are not the Lamb of God sacrifices, which died for our sins. The first time He came He was Messiah Ben Joseph the suffering Messiah. The next time He comes, He is Messiah Ben David, the King of Kings. The first time He came they beat Him and killed Him. Next time He comes with a rod and He will do the correcting and ruling with a rod of iron. There is a big difference between a Lamb and a Lion from the tribe of Judah and reigning King in the respect they demand. The end of mankind's lease, which Satan had stolen, will start the seventh day or year 6001, as a day with the Lord is as a thousand years and a thousand years as a day.

The Day of the Lord starts out with great trial and tribulation, a day of great sorrows as Joel chapter two reports. Those that think the coming of the Lord is the first thing that happens in the Day of the Lord should read there. After the starting of the Day of the Lord with great troubles, tribulation, and fiery trials, the god of this world system (Satan) will be dethroned and locked away for one thousand years, and this is *the Sabbath millennium or the Day of the Lord.* This millennium will be Yahshua's reign on the earth to complete the seven-day (7,000 years) plan of Yahweh, before as Revelation states; we then receive a new heaven and a new earth.

The recent *NEW YORK TIMES BESTSELLER*, "**BIBLE CODE II, The Countdown**," by Michael Drosnin is another way your merciful Creator is warning of the times we live in. The author, Michael Drosnin states that he is not a believer in God. An Israeli mathematician, Dr. Eliyahu Rips, has uncovered a secret code hidden in the Hebrew lettering of the first five books of the Bible called the Torah, which were given to Moshe (Moses) at Mount Sinai. Dr. Rips' field of expertise is Math Theory, the field that underlies quantum physics. This code was apparently put in place by some intelligence that could see across time and encoded in such a way that allowed mankind to crack the code using computers at this precise point in time. The code has been confirmed with a senior code breaker at the United States National Security Agency (NSA), the spy agency that breaks codes for American military intelligence. A few samples of what is encoded in the ancient Hebrew are as follows: (1) twin towers, airplane, it knocked down, they saw the smoke burning (2) Bush,

Arafat, Sharon, atomic war, end of days, 5766 (Hebrew year for 2006), terrorism/ birth pangs of the end of days, peace. (3) New York, guided missile, 5764 (2004). The portions of data in the sets cross each other by equal distance lettering, in a text over three thousand years old. Many predictions have been uncovered, even the death of an Israeli Prime Minister and the year he would die, and many have come true. If you would want to search this matter out for yourself I found the book available at Wal-Mart stores. I believe there are other biblical and math scholars who have done even more advanced work and I will cover that in the last chapter, which is concerning the most recent Bible Code findings. Also, many believers agree that it was actually a Messianic believer and Rabbi named Yacov Rambsel who found the original Bible Codes by hand. Yacov is from San Antonio, Texas and his website is www.yacovrambsel.com.

Isaiah 26:9b says, "When your judgments come upon the earth, the people of the world learn righteousness."

This is sadly true, as after the terrorist actions on 911, church attendance went up dramatically, but less than six months later interest in learning about and following God was subsided. These greater judgments could be just ahead, even at the door. So, it is imperative for you to prepare your spirit, soul (mind and emotions), and body (physically) for that which is ahead. Proverbs 22:3 instructs us to prepare, "A prudent man foresees evil and hides, but the simple pass on and are punished."

Every time Israel fell into great sin, Yahweh punished them by allowing their enemies to conquer them and take them into captivity as slaves. Usually, they were taken captive, by those less righteous than they, because Israel *had a Covenant* to be followers of Yahweh. I would not be shocked at all if that same judgment awaits the United States, as we *claim* to be a godly nation also. Many people I know have had dreams and visions showing just that. I'll give you a few examples now, later I will cover an entire chapter on dreams and visions.

First, Linda, my sister, who is a very godly woman, had a dream. I'm pleased to report, by the grace of Yahweh, that all of my sisters are godly. In the dream, she was being forced to march with many women and children. She saw no men and understood the men were either dead or captured. These women and children, who were forced to march, were held captive by Chinese soldiers. She awoke and prayed against this, but reveals it was very realistic.

Second, a friend of mine saw armed paratroopers filling the sky above San Angelo, Texas in a dream.

Third, another believer from Big Spring, Texas had a dream and from her own words, "Everyone was forced on the main street to watch this army, marching down the main street and high stepping in military parade. We were forced to pay allegiance and respect to them, as they had apparently conquered us. It reminded me of the movies of the World War II Nazi troops. I thanked God, on waking, that we have never had a war on American soil!"

Fourth, I had a dream that showed six or seven meteors or fireballs (possibly missiles?) go overhead from Mertzon, a small town in West Texas. It was nighttime and I perceived and thought at the time- those are headed toward Houston or possibly San Antonio, Texas! In the dream, I went to wake up my daughter to get her to come away from that place but she did not yet see the danger. The dream was very vivid and is not something I can forget. I was just thankful in the dream that the fireballs went over us and kept going. Then I heard what sounded like a rumbling and the earth shook, even where I was. It was at this time I thought it may have been missiles.

Lastly, another believer who lived in San Angelo, Texas told that, she too, had a dream. She was in a parked car near the area of Arden, near San Angelo, Texas. She watched, immobilized, as a cruise missile went just overhead, apparently under radar and following closely to the contour of the landscape, moving at a high speed toward San Angelo! She waited a minute and then started to flee when she heard the explosion and saw a wave of fire overtaking her. There are many more dreams and visions people have had, but for now that should suffice to give you the picture of possibility.

Most of these dreams were set in the area where the people lived, but believers all over will be warned. If you have had a recurring or unforgettable dream about these end-times scenarios I would enjoy hearing from you. My email and regular mail address are in the back of the book. Assuming you are walking uprightly with our Creator, if a dream or vision is unforgettable or recurring, it is most likely a message from your Heavenly Father! The prophet Amos said that Yahweh will do (or allow) nothing on the earth, without warning through His prophets. There are several sites that have a number of visions and dreams recorded for your reading if you want to know what may be happening next. Remember Amos 3:7, "Surely Yahweh will do nothing without first revealing it through His servants the prophets."

He wants you to be ready and not like an ostrich with its head stuck in the sand, thinking that will protect you from danger. So when these troubles that are prophesied come to pass, you are not surprised or unprepared. For your preparation, here are the sites again: www.visionsofthelastdays.com, www.etpv.org, www.americaslastdays.com, and the signs in the heavens:

www.biblicalastronomy.com. The Bible is being played out in our day on the evening news, so prepare. You may be used to doing it *your way* as the famous song says, *I did it my way*, but understand this; you cannot do it your way and enter into life everlasting. Loved one, do not be deceived, you must obey and do it His way! Your destiny is to walk with Him in loving obedience. As you obey Him, you will receive His blessings, which include life and that more abundantly. You have chosen life! He sent His Spirit to guide you into all Truth and teach you of things to come.

Am I suggesting that we are just months or a few years away from judgment and the Great Tribulation or Jacob's trouble? I believe *it's certainly possible*. I can only tell you what I believe I know. During a time of fasting about seven years ago, I was told by Yahshua, "When armies surround Israel, make sure you are not in the city and be in the country at least twenty miles by a March time frame as America will be attacked." These are personal revelations and as such are not meant for everyone and should be searched out and judged by the Scriptures. Of course, this is not my reason to tell you this as He has shown me all the corresponding Scriptures to my satisfaction. My reason for telling you is that as you seek Him you will be given personal revelation also, and you too, will need to judge by the Scriptures.

Remember, He draws His own into the wilderness for a time, times, and a half time or three and one half years, where they are cared for during the forty-two months of Great Tribulation. Just like the first exodus out of Egypt, a type of the world system, we will be required to trust Him with everything before moving into the promise land or the promises fulfilled. We will need to especially trust Him with our loved ones. They didn't trust Him with their loved ones and got to roam in the desert for forty years until they all perished, then He took their loved ones in. Let us not make the same mistakes our forefathers of the faith made. Does an attack on the

U.S.A. mean we are in the Great Tribulation? No, it just means we in the U.S.A. are in a tribulation.

How can we know when the Great Tribulation is started? We are reminded by Yahshua's word in 2 Thessalonians 2:1-4 "(1) Concerning the coming again of Yahshua the Messiah and our being gathered to Him, (2) we ask you brothers, not to become alarmed or easily unsettled by some prophecy, report, or letter supposed to have come from us, saying that the Day of the Lord has already come. (3) Don't let anyone deceive you in any way, for that day will not come until the rebellion or **falling away from the faith** occurs, **and** the **man of lawlessness**, *(Torahlessness: the one who breaks Yahweh's Laws and Instructions)*, the anti-messiah or antichrist, **is revealed**, the man doomed for destruction. (4) He will exalt himself and oppose everything that is of Yahweh or is worshipped, so that he sets himself up in Yahweh's Temple (the temple mount in Jerusalem) proclaiming himself to be Yahweh."

Stopping of the sacrifice on Yahweh's Altar on the Temple Mount and the proclaiming he is God from there, is the abomination that makes desolate warned about by the prophet Daniel. Yahshua reminded us to watch for this event in Matthew 24:15. So **before the Great Tribulation starts**, there will be a great falling away from keeping the Torah, which is the Instructions of Yahweh, and the **antichrist will be revealed**. The antichrist will declare himself God, probably on the Temple Mount in Jerusalem, and start to make war with the believers! Also, the Bible declares that they will divide up His land Israel, which would include the holy city Jerusalem, according to Joel 3:2. Amos 3:7 declares, "Yahweh will do nothing except He reveals it (first) to His servants the prophets." Of course, then the prophets will tell those who are sober and alert and being about their Heavenly Father's business, as they are the only ones who will have ears to hear and perceive truth.

What is the *falling away from the faith* mentioned in this Scripture? Could it possibly be the falling away from the Sabbath on the seventh day and the keeping of the Feasts of the Lord mentioned by Command *forever* in Leviticus twenty-three? Could it additionally be the replacement of these Commandments with new holy days or holidays not ascribed by Yahweh, such as Easter, Christmas, Lent, etc.? A great source for more study and understanding the origins of paganism in Christianity are two books available at www.fossilizedcustoms.com. One book is named Fossilized Customs and the other is Come Out Of Her My People. These can also be ordered by mail from the publisher at 2303 Watterson Trail PMB #26, Louisville, Kentucky, 40299. Another good book is Two Babylon's by Alexander Hislop available at Barnes and Noble bookstores. Of course the man of lawlessness is the anti-messiah or antichrist who will declare he is God and will make war against the true believers and followers of Messiah Yahshua. If there is *no Law we are required to obey* as some would report, then there is no sin, since the definition of sin is transgression against the Law. This is recorded in 1 John 3:4, "Whoever commits sin transgresses the Law; for sin is transgression of the Law." Remember Yahshua tells the self-proclaiming believer who was reminding Yahshua of his great service for him on Judgment Day also known as the Day of Atonement or Yom Kippur in Matthew 7:23, "I never knew you, depart from Me you worker of *lawlessness!*"(*Torahlessness*)

Many believers are waiting on a pre-tribulation rapture. They believe that Yahweh would not let them suffer. Some even believe that all that is required of them is to confess Him as Lord once, and then they can live as they wish. They still expect to be raptured and meet the Messiah in the air before any trouble starts. **They believe wrongly**, or else, why would Messiah Yahshua say the following in Revelation 3:10? "Because you kept My commands to endure patiently, I will keep you from the <u>trials that are coming on the whole world to test those that live on the earth.</u>"

There is coming a test for believers. It will require patience and endurance. The Messiah is not coming for a whore; He is coming for a bride without spot or wrinkle. Therefore, there is a need for testing and a refiner's fire. There is a requirement to study, grow spiritually, and keep His Commands with enduring patience. He reminds us over and over to be sober and alert, lest that time come on you unaware. If the pre-tribulation rapture theory was correct, then there would be no need to stay *prayerfully sober and alert* that the time might come on us unaware. Just being *born again* would be sufficient and we'd be "raptured" away without a care in the world! I am afraid the pre-tribulation rapture theory has been quickly believed by itching ears that hear what they want to hear. I have heard believers, some of them even Pastors, say they would not want to live during the Great Tribulation. They are fearfully concerned about their own well being, and not concerned with producing fruit for the Kingdom of Heaven. They say they would rather die than live through that incredibly stressful season. They may get their wish, as there may not be much physical difference between an atomic holocaust and the rapture they so eagerly await. They would definitely be absent from their bodies, and the Scripture declares in 2 Corinthians 5:8, that to be absent from the body is to be present with the Lord. Understand, there will be Great Tribulation, such has never been seen on the earth, but it is about refining us and molding us into trusting and worthy vessels of His Covenant, that we may produce fruit for the Kingdom of Heaven, and accomplish our destiny! If a person is living for pleasure and self-indulgences alone, and if their purpose is not to produce fruit for the Kingdom of Heaven, then perhaps this "thermonuclear rapture" of sorts will suffice. In 1 Thessalonians 5:2-6 we read: "(2) For you yourselves know perfectly well that the Day of the Lord comes like a thief in the night. (3) For when they say peace and safety then sudden destruction shall come on them as birth pains on a woman with child, and **they shall not escape**. (4) But you brothers are not in darkness, that that day should overtake you as a thief. (5) You are children of the light, and the children of the day: we are not of the night, nor of darkness. (6) Therefore let us not sleep as others do, but **let us prayerfully watch and be sober**."

Understand Yahweh's wrath is not laid up for the obedient believer. The seals and the trumps are not Yahweh's wrath, they are basically Satan trying to destroy mankind and take and establish his command. The Greek words are different for the seals, the trumps, and the bowls of wrath. They are all translated the same in the King James Bible as wrath. The words increase as to the depth of seriousness and intensity, with the bowls being angry and intense judgment with vindication. The seals and trumpet blasts are essentially the birth pangs of labor of His bride coming forth without spot or blemish! They are also the judgment of the false gods of this world. Yahweh judged the gods of Egypt (a type of world) when He judged the Egyptians with Moses. The Egyptians worshipped many gods, but did not know the Elohim of the Hebrews, Yahweh who is *I AM!* This is illustrated in Exodus 5:1-2 "(1) And afterward Moses and Aaron went in and told Pharaoh; Yahweh, the God of Israel says, Let My people go, that they may come and hold a Feast and worship Me in the wilderness. (2) Who is Yahweh that I should obey His voice and let Israel go? I do not know Yahweh; neither will I let Israel go."

We know that Pharaoh had many gods and even thought he was god. It makes you wonder how people can be so arrogant and ignorant and still breathe. The reason Yahweh set Israel free, and will also set us free, is *to come and worship Him.* Every judgment He made was to bring down a false god. He will once again judge the gods of this world as the seals, trumps, and bowls bear witness. Many people worship the creation and not the Creator. They idolize and worship things of nature such as trees, the oceans, the rivers, the animals, whales, the moon and stars, sports teams and athletes, movie stars, and even rock musicians and the like, of whom many live very selfish, ungodly and unethical lives! Our loving and merciful Creator will plead with these who do this by judging these false "gods" and idols. He will prove to all that these are not really gods at all, and that there is only one Elohim and true God, and His name is Yahweh. He desires that none perish, but if they will not repent and follow Him, then they will perish. Yahshua takes the Kingdom of the earth back from Satan and that is what the 42 months called the Great Tribulation is about. Satan had stolen mankind's reign from Adam but the six days of mankind's lease are up. The number six is about man. The last day which is day seven, is the Day of the Lord, and the Sabbath rest millennium. Yahshua will reign on the earth one thousand years while Satan is locked away. At the *last* trump we meet Messiah in the air according to 1 Corinthians 15:52. During the time it takes Yahshua to have the bowls of His wrath poured out on the disobedient, the raptured believers that met Yahshua in the air will be with Him, possibly in Heaven. Then at the end of the bowls of wrath, some forty-five days later, we come back with Yahshua with thousands times ten thousands described in Revelation 5:11. Also, Jude verse 14 talks of the believers coming with Yahshua to judge the unrighteous, "And Enoch also, the seventh from Adam, prophesied of these, saying, Behold, Yahshua comes with ten thousands of His obedient followers. To execute judgment upon all, and to convince all that are ungodly that have committed ungodly deeds and of all their evil speech against Yahshua."

It is possible that we will be with Yahshua to be part of His army to judge the disobedient. I suppose that is not so important now though, as we will find out when we meet Him in the air! The *last trump* is after the seven seals and the first six trumps. Notice how the Scripture starts in 1 Corinthians 15:51-52, "(51) Behold, I show you a *mystery*, we shall not all sleep (be dead) but we shall all be changed, (52) in a moment, in the twinkling of an eye, *at the last trump*, for the trumpet shall sound and the dead in Messiah Yahshua shall rise incorruptible, and we shall be changed." Flesh cannot inhabit heaven. We will be changed to incorruptible bodies like Yahshua had when He rose from the dead. He still had a body but could walk through walls, and still had flesh and bone and even ate food according to the biblical accounts. What is the *mystery* discussed in 1 Corinthians 15:51? Let's look at the Scripture that tells about the completion of the sixth trump and just prior to the last trump in Revelation 10:7, "But in the days of the voice of the seventh angel, when he shall sound his trump, the *mystery* of Yahweh shall be finished, as He has declared to His servants the prophets." The mystery is complete when the believers are "raptured." These Scriptures are complementary and confirm to us that the "rapture" of the believers is at the sounding of the last trump. I believe that since Yahshua cuts short the time that instead of the full 42 months of Great Tribulation, it will be cut short 30 days as this is a Hebrew idiom for a shortened year based on the barley being ready early. So it is within the realm of speculation that the trump or Feast of Trumpets will occur near the end of the 41st month, leaving 40 days from the Feast of Trumpets until Yom Kippur or Judgment Day. Then 5 days later, you have the Feast of Tabernacles and we celebrate Sukkoth with the Messiah back on the Earth. So, over the 40 days there is given more mercy by Yahweh for those on the Earth to repent or it is possible that they are still only given 10 days to repent and the bowls of wrath or Yahweh's indignation is poured out on the unbelieving, fearful, sorcerers, liars, disobedient and the like, according to Revelation chapter sixteen. It is within the realm of possibilities also that the bowls of wrath are poured out in one day only, Yom Kippur. Whatever the final scenario, it is best that we are obedient and not subject to His wrath! (Even if these bowls are poured out over the whole 42 months of the Great Tribulation) Remember the Scripture that shows the days allotted for the Great Tribulation shows that the number of days will be 1290 days but blessed is he who survives to 1335 days. I believe that is talking about the 45 days difference of the Feast of Trumpets to the Feast of Tabernacles when we celebrate with Yahshua. This fits why I think the "cutting short" idiom is the 30 day early Feast of Trumpets. This is stated in Daniel 12:11-12, "(11) And from the time that the daily sacrifice is taken away (stopping of the Altar sacrifices on the Temple Mount) and the abomination that makes desolate set up (some sort of statue or image to worship the beast), there shall be a thousand two hundred and ninety days. (12) Blessed is the one that waits and comes to the end of the one thousand three hundred and thirty-five days."(45 days brings us to the Feast of Tabernacles)

Even in chaotic and stressful times you can be an overcomer. We overcome by the blood of the Lamb and the words of our testimony, or what we speak agreement with according to Revelation 12:11. We have been given power to overcome all the power of hell according to Luke 10:19. Remember, the Greater One is in us, so we must speak agreement with Him even in dire circumstances or facts. Isaiah 55:11 says, "So shall My Word go forth from My Mouth, it shall not return to Me void; but shall accomplish that which I please, and prosper in the thing for which it was sent." The Word is established in Heaven according to Psalms 119:89 and we must establish it in our lives on the earth, by speaking it directly to our circumstances. It is life and healing to all our flesh according to Proverbs 4:22. Abraham was named Abram before Yahweh called him Abraham, meaning father of many nations or a great multitude. Yahweh gave him the resource to build his faith by renaming him. As he was called Abraham, he was continually hearing "father of many nations" and building his faith, although he was still childless. Romans 10:17 says, "Faith comes by hearing and hearing the Word of Yahweh." This is the principle taught in Romans 4:17b that says, "And called those things that be not as though they were." He established the Word on the earth by not agreeing with his childless circumstance. You can do the same things by using Yahweh's principle. If your children have rebelled and rejected the gospel, you can call those things that be not as though they are! If you have no resources to be a giver, and have life abundantly, remember He gives seed to the sower (giver). Just be sure you plant in good soil and the best and most fertile soil is where He tells you to plant your tithes and offerings. Remember the widows, orphans and the Levite or the preacher who is not covetous of things and is helping save souls! Be moved to give where you have peace in your heart. With the measure you give, even more will be given back to you. If you are sick, don't speak the sickness or the facts and establish that thing against you! Speak the Word or Scripture promise that overcomes the facts! You can effectively call those things that be not as though they were in every circumstance. Get a Strong's concordance or just look in the back of your Bible for Scriptures on health, healing, miracles, finances, salvation, protection, family, etc. Then speak those promises several times daily. The more serious and urgent the problem, the more dosage of Yahweh's medicine you'll need. Yahweh's medicine can change any fact or circumstance, as it is the most powerful remedy for any problem you could have.

We are in the last days' church or body of believers called the Laodicean assembly of believers. Yahshua describes and gives warning to us in Revelation 3:15-22 "(15) I know your works, you are neither cold nor hot: I wish you were cold or hot. (16) So then because you are neither cold nor hot I will vomit you out of My mouth. (17) Because you say, I am rich and increased with goods, and have need of nothing; and you do not know you are wretched, and miserable, and poor and blind and naked: (18) I counsel you to buy from Me gold tried and refined in the fire, that you really may be rich; and white clothing that you really may be clothed, that the shame of your nakedness would not be made apparent to all; and anoint your eyes with salve, that you really may see. (19) As many as I love, I rebuke and chasten: be zealous therefore and repent! (20) Behold, I stand at the door and knock: if any one hears My voice and opens the door, I will come in and dine and fellowship with them, and they with Me. (21) To them that overcome, I will grant to sit with Me in My throne, even as I also overcame, and am sitting down with My Father in His throne. (22) He that has an ear, let him hear what the Spirit says to the assembly of believers."

> **When we have material wealth like this age does, it is easy to be complacent and spend our funds and efforts on pleasure, but He warns us that we really are poverty stricken because of our lack of faith and trust in Him.**

We think we don't need that intimate relationship with Him when our money will purchase for us everything we could possibly need. He counsels us to increase our faith, which is likened to gold tried by fire. 1 Peter 1:7 confirms this, "That the trial of your faith, being more precious than gold that perishes, though it is tested by fire, might be found bringing praise, honor, and glory at the appearing of Yahshua the Messiah." When our faith is tested we grow up spiritually and know we can count on Him, even when we have no money or our money has become worthless. It *will* become worthless during the Great Tribulation as no person can buy or sell without taking Satan's mark, or the mark of the beast system he puts in place. **Still, do not take the mark of the beast!**

He says we are naked and just because we may own and have many clothes in our closets, we cannot take them with us when we leave this earth. He is talking about the robes of righteousness, or the clothing we receive spiritually when we do righteous acts. Without these obedient acts of righteousness, we will be spiritually naked and ashamed. Lastly, he warns us that we are blind and need salve to see. I believe that the salve is revelation knowledge from heaven. We must spend quality and quantity time with our Savior and *hear from heaven* so we can really see, and know what is really going on in this present age. Remember, His sheep hear His voice. Then He reminds us in verses 19, 20, 21, and 22 of Revelation three, that we should grow up spiritually and to do that will require testing of our faith and spankings; that His desire is to have intimate fellowship with us; and whoever overcomes will gain His reward and throne. Finally, whoever has an ear to spiritually understand will hear from Heaven!

Ezekiel 7:19 confirms that *our wealth will not deliver us in the Day of the Lord,* "They shall cast their silver in the streets, and their gold shall be removed: their silver and their gold shall not be able to deliver them in the Day of the wrath of Yahshua: they shall not satisfy their souls, neither fill their stomachs: because their wealth has been their stumbling block of their iniquities."

Real wealth and life more abundantly, is the ability to have every need met supernaturally by our loving Creator!

I will share a personal revelation Yahshua gave me several years ago concerning the rapture. The priests served in divisions, orders, or courses back in the biblical times. For example, Zechariah, John the Baptist's father, was of the course or division of Abiyah. They would serve under the High Priest or Cohen Gadol, for one week twice during the year. Since there were 24 divisions, this would take care of 48 weeks of the year, then they would all serve during the pilgrimage Feasts. It was their job, among others to keep the fire of the altar burning for the evening and morning sacrifice. This was an oblation or free will offering. It was said that the High Priest would sneak in like a thief in the night to check the fire on the altar. The fire would need to consume the sacrifice so the altar would be ready for the morning oblation also. If he found the fire burning and the offering being consumed, it was said that he would have sweet fellowship with the priest who was sober and alert and doing what he was there to do. However, if he found the fire gone out, he would relight the fire, take part of the fire and go look for the sleeping and drunk priest. When he found him he would set fire to his linen prayer garments, and that sleeping priest would run home naked and ashamed. That is what Yahshua told me most believers will do when the Great Tribulation comes *before* the escape of the rapture they are depending on. You see they are not concerned about being witnesses unto death and producing fruit that will remain eternally for the Kingdom of Yahweh. They are selfishly concerned only about themselves and their escape plan. They are asleep. Revelation 16:15 is where Yahshua warns us, "Behold, I come as a thief. Blessed is he that watches (sober and prayerfully alert), and keeps his garments on, lest he walk naked and they see his shame." Understand He will protect you if you are doing His work on the earth! You will have sweet fellowship with our High Priest, Yahshua the Messiah! "I set before you life and death, blessings and curses. Therefore, choose life, that you and your children may live." Deuteronomy 30:19 Note: *You and your children!*

In the spring of 2000, I was in Scotland and Israel for several months. Prior to this time I had been on an extended fast. I saw many miracles and experienced His protection often. While in Scotland, I had the opportunity to visit with some friends who kept the Feasts of the Lord, and had a Bible College in Stewarton, Scotland. David Loughran, the founder of the Bible College, invited me to stay with his family in their home. They were the most gracious and loving people. We had the Passover Seder (meal) and service above a library there. The libraries there are where you can research family roots, so I was asking the Lord in prayer where our family originated from in Scotland, since we are of Scottish descent. The library was closed but a sweet little lady walked up to me and asked what I wanted. I told her I was just thinking of doing a little research on the family name during the break from the Passover Service, but noted the library was closed. She asked, "What be your name, son?" I told her McCutchen. She answered wide eyed, "McCutchen? That be my name!" She was attending the Passover Seder also! I visited with her quickly during our break but had little time to do any research and I really didn't seem to hear anything else about it from the Lord. Just a prayer whose answer would have to wait for who knows how long, I thought.

Later that week, while traveling to the highlands of Scotland I picked up three young girls who were hitchhiking. I witnessed to them about Yahshua but they seemed oblivious. They were sweet girls from Canada and seemed to be about my daughter's ages. They asked to be taken to a remote campground or hostel on the Island of Skye. Since I was driving in that direction, I told them I would do my best to get them there. When we arrived at their destination it was still closed for the winter. They quickly found another destination on their map, about a one-hour drive away, and asked if I would take them to this even more remote spot on the sea. I told them, "sure" and away we drove. Finally upon arriving at the location, the man who owned it said they could stay there, that he would open up the hostel just for them! They were so grateful and pleased that they now had some accommodations in this remote area on the banks of the ocean on the

Island of Skye. As I dropped off the girls, and went with them to help them unload their travel bags, Yahshua spoke to me, *"this is where your family came in."* "My family came in?" I replied with a question. "Lord, my family was *from* Scotland," I reminded Him. Glancing down at my map, I asked Him, "What does this island and the *Hebrides* mean, anyway?" His answer was revealing, "That's the *Hebrews*, son, the *Hebrews*."

When I arrived in Israel three days later I was met by some friends who minister there. They also had a friend with them who was helping with their ministry. This lady looked at me and asked, "What is your last name again?" I replied, "McCutchen." She replied, "That's my maiden name, in fact that was my father's surname and my mother's surname, just spelled differently!" She continued, "We have done extensive research and found that the McCutchen's were from the Isle of Skye." I replied, "Yes, I've heard that." It was really wonderful for Yahshua to answer my question about our roots so vividly. I didn't really expect to get to meet a long lost cousin. She is a prayer warrior named Pat or Penina in Hebrew, who lives in Israel as often as she possibly can.

A few years ago my wife Bonnie and I had the pleasure of returning to Scotland for the Passover service with David Loughran's family and Bible School. David had passed away, but his family was still just as kind and gracious. We were so blessed by their kindnesses as we got to renew old friendships and meet others in the family, even some from Germany. Barbara, one of David's daughters was there with her delightful husband, Jurgen. They had many family members and believers attending Passover from Germany! Later, when we traveled to Europe to minister, we even had the opportunity to stay with them and meet his brother Norbert, and his loving wife, Ingrid! I tell you all of this to share something I discovered while visiting with them. Back in the year 2000 when I attended the Passover with David, I traveled from there to Israel as I mentioned. I had mailed David a shofar or ram's horn trumpet from Israel along with five smooth stones, for his friendship and kindness toward me. I had picked the stones up in the Valley of Elah, from the same brook where David had picked up five stones to fight Goliath. During this time of fellowshipping and enjoying once again their spectacular hospitality, Barbara mentioned that her dad had given the shofar, in his will, to his best friend. Also, that David had willed one smooth stone to each of his five grandchildren! I was blessed, and saw from this action where David's heart was, and what was of importance and value to him. It was truly a heart following after the heart of the King of all Kings, Messiah Yahshua! What a blessing to have known him and to know his precious family!

I didn't really understand the significance of what the scriptures teach concerning *who* Yahshua came for and why and why judgment awaited the United States. After returning from Israel in the year 2000, and back in the United States for a few months, the Scriptures started coming alive concerning the *two witnesses*. The House of Judah who will accept Messiah Yahshua and who obey the Torah or Yahweh's Instructions represented by Moses and the Law, and the House of Ephraim, which has accepted Messiah Yahshua as Lord and savior and will go back to keeping His Laws, His Feasts, and Sabbath etc. Both Houses will have to repent, and I'm sure it will only be a remnant that will repent and follow Him. When Yahshua came, He said He came for the *lost sheep of Israel*. I remind you again that Judah was not lost. They were already back in the land from their captivity from Babylon, as Yahshua is the Lion of the tribe of Judah. The ten northern tribes were scattered for their rebellion against the Torah and because of their continued rebellion they were scattered all over the Earth, as the curse was multiplied times seven! He even promised them they would not even know who they were until the last days. Please be attentive and study this because 2 Thessalonians 2:10 warns us, "And with all manner of deception of unrighteousness in them that perish, for they would not receive the love of the Truth, that they might be delivered."

The prophet Ezekiel laid down on his left side for 390 days to represent Ephraim's punishment of 390 years for idolatry to Yahweh as recorded in Ezekiel 4:4-5 and Leviticus 26:27-28. Ephraim was the younger son of Yoseph (Joseph) who received Jacob's (Israel) blessings as *the last days' great multitude*. The Torah, the first five books of the Bible given to Moses on Mt. Sinai, Commands that if repentance does not come forth within the judgment period, then the curse is multiplied seven fold! Ephraim represented the ten northern tribes, which had been divided from the tribes of Benjamin and Judah (Yehudah also known as Judah or the Jews). They had been divided by the two Kings who split the kingdom of Israel after King Solomon's death. Since Ephraim, the ten northern tribes, were exiled and scattered in 724 B.C., and the 390 year judgment was multiplied by seven, the total judgment of blindness and captivity with the added punishment of being scattered all over the earth, lasted 2,730 years or until Aviv 1, 2010. Earlier in 1996, I and many others first heard of the teachings by Monte Judah and others, and the insight of the Scriptures from a Jewish or Hebrew perspective!

Judah's punishment, represented by Ezekiel lying on his right side as recorded in Ezekiel 4:6 and Ezekiel 23:31-32, was for 40 years plus the 390 years (430 years). Since Judah was divorced from Yahweh for idolatry also, they were scattered in the year of 596 B.C., but Judah had repented, they were back in the land of Israel on Hanukkah, the Feast of Dedication in 166 B.C., known also as the Feast of Lights exactly 430 years later! This scenario reminds us of the story of the prodigal son. Remember, one son was eating pig slop and abominable things. Much like some Christians eat many unclean foods today because the Scriptures have been twisted and they have believed the lie that the *Law has been done away with.* Of course it is not what you eat that spiritually defiles you, but according to Yahshua, it is the words you speak from your mouth that defile you. Not eating kosher or maintaining Torah observance of the dietary laws will not disqualify you from heaven; it may just have you in heaven sooner. You might miss the blessing of physically long life. Judah was taken into captivity to Babylon for whoredom and unfaithfulness, and Ephraim, which are the ten Northern tribes, were scattered into Assyria, and later the entire world for their unfaithfulness. Understand Yahshua could not stay married to an unfaithful wife and cannot marry a whore according to the Torah. The ten northern tribes that had committed adultery by worshipping idols and not keeping Sabbath were still under Yahweh's judgment, and were not back in the land when Yahshua came to the Earth. Only by dying could Yahshua be released from His own Law concerning marrying an adulterer, or spiritually speaking, idolatry. Also, once the husband was dead, then the wife could remarry. Only then could He come for His bride without spot or wrinkle. Of course, Yahshua came and died for *whosoever* will follow Him, but remember He called us, we didn't call Him.

Yahshua states that He came for the *lost sheep* of Israel in Matthew 15:24, "But He answered and said, I am not sent except to the lost sheep of Israel." Judah was back in the land and not lost; only the ten Northern tribes had been taken into captivity by the Assyrians due to their spiritual rebellion were still lost and *scattered*, for their continued sin. In Sha'ul's (Paul's) letters he addresses the *scattered tribes* often. In Matthew 10:6 Yahshua also sends His disciples, "But go rather to the *lost sheep* of Israel." Some have erroneously taught that because of the rebellion of the Jews (they mean the rebellion of all Israel), Yahshua changed to Plan B. That is ridiculous to even consider that Yahshua was not going to accomplish what He planned and was sent to do! The rebellion had to run its course, and as we will now study the Scriptures that teach us about the rejoining of all the tribes of Israel. We now know that many Bible Chronologists and scholars have determined that on Aviv one (the month of the barley abiv) 2010 A.D., the *curse for disobedience ends* for the ten Northern tribes, the called out ones who are believing Christians (Ephraim) that flee paganism. Ezekiel was commanded by YHWH 390 years of judgment to Ephraim, the ten Northern Tribes by removing them from Israel and scattering them around the world for their pagan ways. Fertility goddess of Easter (aka Ishtar and Astarte) worship and sun god worship was rampant in the land. YHWH warns us to not add or subtract from His Commands, statues, Feasts, etc: Deuteronomy 4:1-2 "(1) Now therefore hearken, O Israel, to the statutes and to the judgments, which I teach you, for to do *them*, that you may live, and go in and possess the land which YHWH the Elohim of your fathers gives you. (2) You **shall not add to the Word** which I Command you, **neither shall you diminish** *ought* **from it**, that you may keep the Commandments of YHWH your Elohim which I Command you."

Now we see the results of Sun-day sun god and Easter fertility worship traditions that we too have inherited: YHWH's Judgment!

Ezekiel 4:3-6 "(3) Then get yourself an iron plate and set it up as an iron wall between you and the city, and set your face toward it so that it is under siege, and besiege it. **This is a sign to the <u>house of Israel</u>**.(4) As for you, lie down on your left side and lay the iniquity of the house of Israel on it; you shall bear their iniquity for the number of days that you lie on it. (5) <u>For I have assigned you a number of days corresponding to the **years of their iniquity, three hundred and ninety days**; thus you shall bear the iniquity of the house of Israel</u>. (6) When you have completed these, you shall lie down a second time, *but* on your right side and bear the iniquity of the house of Judah; I have assigned it to you for forty days, a day for each year."

Why would the curse be over now?

Bible Chronologists say that the Assyrians came and carried Israel away captive in 724 BCE. We know from the Torah (Old Covenant Books of Moses) that YHWH promises that if judgment does not bring the people to repentance, YHWH multiplies the judgment times 7! Those 390 years times 7=2730 means 2,730 years of scattering and exile from Israel for the 10 Northern Tribes! That equates from 724 BCE to Aviv one 2010 (March or April 2010) then we know **the scales come off of ALL ISRAEL (Not just the Jews)** and we recognize our paganism and traditions that YHWH did not give us.

> *NOTE: This is not just about Jews or Judah being blinded like so many misquote. This is about how we all; ALL ISRAEL, has been blinded and needs the blindness removed!*

Here are some verses that help us understand our scattering and gathering: Romans 11:25 "for I would not, brethren that you should be ignorant of this mystery, lest you should be wise in your own conceits; that **blindness** (cont'd after comment) *(Comment: I expect the blindness is removed as the scales were removed from Sha'ul in Act 9:17-18 "(17) And Ananias departed, and entered into the house; and laying his hands on him said, Brother Saul, the Master, even Yahshua, who appeared to you in the way which you came, has sent me, that you may receive your sight, and be filled with the Holy Spirit. (18) And straightway there fell from his eyes as it were scales, and he received his sight; and he arose and was baptized;")* (cont'd) in part is **happened to Israel**, until the fullness of the Gentiles be come in."

Romans 11:26-29 "(26) And so **all Israel shall be saved**: *(Comment: all Israel is Judah and Ephraim-the scattered tribes)* as it is written, There shall come out of Sion the Deliverer, and shall turn away ungodliness from Jacob: (27) For this *is* My Covenant unto them, when I shall take away their sins. (28) As concerning the gospel, *they are* enemies for your sakes: but as touching the election, *they are* beloved for the fathers' sakes. (29) The gifts and calling of YHWH *are* without repentance."

Jeremiah 16:13-21 "(13) So I will hurl you out of this land into the land which you have not known, neither you nor your fathers; and there you will serve other gods day and night, for I will grant you no favor. (14) Therefore behold, days are coming, declares YHWH, when it will no longer be said, As YHWH lives, who brought up the sons of Israel out of the land of Egypt, (15) but, As YHWH lives, who brought up the sons of Israel from the land of the north and from all the countries where He had banished them. **I will restore them to their own land which I gave to their fathers**. (16) Behold, I am going to send for many fishermen, declares YHWH, and they will fish for them; and afterwards I will send for many hunters, and they will hunt them from every mountain and every hill and from the clefts of the rocks. (17) For My eyes are on all their ways; they are not hidden from My face, nor is their iniquity concealed from My eyes. (18) I will first doubly repay their iniquity and their sin, because they have polluted My land; they have filled My inheritance with the carcasses of their detestable idols and with their abominations. (19) O YHWH, my strength and my stronghold, and my refuge in the day of distress, to you the nations will come from the ends of the earth and say, **Our fathers have inherited nothing but falsehood, Futility and things of no profit**. (20) Can man make gods for himself? Yet they are not gods! (21) Therefore behold, I am going to make them know-- This time I will make them know My power **and My might; and they shall know that My name is YHWH.**"

Deuteronomy 4:27-31 "(27) <u>YHWH will scatter you among the people</u> and you will be left few in number among the nations where YHWH drives you. (28) There you will serve Elohims, the work of man's hands, wood and stone, which neither see nor hear nor eat nor smell. (29) <u>From there you will seek YHWH your Elohim, and you will find *Him* if you search for Him with all your heart and all your soul.</u> (30) **When you are in distress** and all these things have come upon you, **in the <u>latter days</u>** you will return to YHWH your Elohim and listen to His voice. (31) For YHWH your Elohim is a compassionate Elohim; He will not fail you nor destroy you nor forget the Covenant with your fathers which He swore to them."

Daniel 9:6-11 "(6) Neither have we hearkened unto Thy servants the prophets, which spake in Thy Name to our kings, our princes, and our fathers, and to all the people of the land. (7) O YHWH, righteousness *belongs* to you, but unto us confusion of faces, as at this day; to the men of Judah, and to the inhabitants of Jerusalem, and to **all Israel**, *that are* near, and *that are* far off, through all the countries whither thou hast driven them, because of their trespass that they have trespassed against you. (8) O YHWH, to us *belong* confusion of face, to our kings, to our princes, and to our fathers, because we have sinned against you. (9) To YHWH our Elohim *belong* mercies and forgivenesses, though we have rebelled against Him; (10) neither have we obeyed the voice of YHWH our Elohim, to walk in His Laws, which He set before us by His servants the prophets. (11) Yea, all Israel have transgressed Thy Law, even by departing, that they might not obey Thy voice; therefore the curse is poured upon us, and the oath that *is* written in the Law of Moses the servant of God, because we have sinned against Him."

The curse pronounced on Judah for 40 years was already over from Babylon and so many Jewish believers in Messiah Yahshua have come to the faith prior to this Aviv one 2010 date and those are they that Ephraim, the scattered tribes, have learned from.

Ezekiel 37 tells about the *gathering or rejoining* that Yahshua came and died for, the joining of the *lost sheep of Israel* with Judah, which occurs in the last days.

Ezekiel 37:16-28 "(16) Moreover, son of man, take one stick (branch of the olive tree as we are all grafted back in by faith in Yahshua–including Judah who was divorced also) and write upon it for Judah and for the children of Israel who are his companions; then take another stick (branch of the olive tree) and write upon it for Yoseph (Joseph) the stick (branch of the olive tree) of Ephraim (Joseph's son, the scattered northern kingdom of the ten lost tribes) and for all those of the house of Israel who are his companions; (17) and join them one to the other into one stick (branch of the olive tree), and they shall become one (unified) in my hand. (18) And when the children of your people shall speak to you asking, Will you show us what these things mean? (19) Say to them, Thus says Yahweh, your Elohim; Behold I will take the stick of Joseph, which is in the hand of Ephraim, and the tribes of Israel who are his friends and companions and put them with him and add them to the stick of Judah and make them one stick in my hand. (20) And the sticks (branches of the olive tree) where you write shall be in your hand in their sight. (21) Then say to them, thus says Yahweh your Elohim, Behold, I will take the children of Israel from being scattered among the heathen, where they have gone, and I will gather them on every side and <u>bring them back into the land of Israel.</u> (22) And I will make them one nation in the land on the mountains of Israel; and they shall no longer be two nations; neither will they be divided into two kingdoms again; (23) Neither shall they defile themselves with their idolatry and paganism and their detestable things, nor with their transgressions (going against the Law, the Torah, and saying it is done away with) but I will save them out of their dwelling places, where they have sinned, and I will cleanse them, so they shall be My people and I will be their Elohim. (24) And David (the bloodline of Judah and of course of Yahshua) My servant shall be king over them, and they shall have One Shepherd over them (Yahshua), and they shall walk in My judgments and observe My Commandments and do them. (25) And they shall live in the land that I have given to Jacob (Israel) My servant, where your forefathers (of the faith) lived, and they shall live there, even them with their children and their children's children forever; and My servant David shall be their Prince forever (Messiah Ben David –son of David who is Yahshua of Nazareth). (26) Moreover, I will make a Covenant of peace; **it shall be an everlasting Covenant with them** and will set My sanctuary in the midst of them forever. (27) My home shall be with them and I will be their Elohim (God), and they shall be My people. (28)And the heathen shall know that I Yahweh, do cleanse Israel (all the obedient followers of Messiah Yahshua), and My dwelling shall be in the midst of them forever."

Just by reading the biblical account you can get a picture of the gathering of the twelve tribes represented by the two witnesses on the earth; Judah represented by the Jews who keep the Commands (Law) and will repent and accept the testimony of Yahshua; and Ephraim, represented mostly by the Christians. These are the scattered ones who have already accepted Yahshua and will repent and keep the Commands (Law). This leaves us with a fire tested and refined bride without spot or blemish, a *remnant!*

Next we see a confirmation in the New Testament (Renewed Covenant): Romans 11:17-27 "(17) But if some of the branches were broken off, and you, being a wild olive, were grafted in among them and became partaker with them of the rich root of the olive tree, (18) do not be arrogant toward the branches; but if you are arrogant, *remember that* it is not you who supports the Root, but the Root *supports* you. (19) You will say then, Branches were broken off so that I might be grafted in. (20) Quite right, they were broken off for their unbelief, but you stand by your faith. Do not be conceited, but fear; (21) for if YHWH did not spare the natural branches, He will not spare you, either. (22) Behold then the kindness and severity of YHWH; to those who fell, severity, but to you, YHWH's kindness, if you continue in His kindness; otherwise you also will be cut off. (23) And they also, if they do not continue in their unbelief, will be grafted in, for YHWH is able to graft them in again. (24) For if you were cut off from what is by nature a wild olive tree, and were grafted contrary to nature into a cultivated olive tree, how much more will these who are the natural *branches* be grafted into their own olive tree? (25) For I do not want you, brethren, to be uninformed of this mystery--so that you will not be wise in your own estimation--that a partial hardening has happened to Israel until the fullness of the Gentiles *(Comment: Again- this is Ephraim-scattered tribes and pagans- Goyim who are obedient-whosoever will)* has come in; (26) and so all Israel will be saved; just as it is written, THE DELIVERER WILL COME FROM ZION, HE WILL REMOVE UNGODLINESS FROM JACOB. (27) THIS IS MY COVENANT WITH THEM, WHEN I TAKE AWAY THEIR SINS."

While in Israel, I camped out on the Sea of Galilee at the foot of the Mount of Beatitudes between Capernaum and Bethsaida eleven days and nights. It was there I asked Yahshua where would be a safe place to "hold up" during the future attack on the United States. I was shocked at what I heard, so much so that I didn't tell anyone for over a year. *I just couldn't really believe it myself.* **"Son, there will be no place left in America."**

Truly 9/11 was horrible but try to understand that it was only the beginning of sorrows. The birth pangs will continue to get closer together and more intense, and parallel the birth pangs of a woman in labor. There is much more to come.

The all out attack on The United States is foretold in the Scriptures, at least to my satisfaction. Some believe that the U.S.A. will be the savior of Israel, but they will not. Only Yahweh, the God of Israel, will be their deliverer. As I studied Ezekiel 38 and 39, I saw that in Ezekiel 38:9-10 where Russia and others, along with many Muslim countries, are preparing to attack Israel and the mountains of Israel.

At the same time (verse ten) the leader of that federation of armies has an evil thought. He goes up to the land of unwalled villages (some think this may be the settlers in the disputed areas of Israel but they seem to all have bars and gates around their communities) where the people are gathered from many nations and dwelling safely without bars or gates. He goes to take a spoil. The spoil is food, the livestock and goods in the midst of the land, which is the heartland of America. There are not many cattle in Israel, maybe thousands, however; in America there are millions of cattle and livestock for food. Also, the midst of the land or the heartland is the breadbasket of America. The only country in the world dwelling safely without bars and gates and gathered from all the nations of the world is the United States of America. This appears to be the only country that fits this Scripture and is a mystery, Babylon the whore.

I have an acquaintance that walks the countries of the world as Yahshua tells him and he repents and remits the blood of the innocent. He never tells anyone except Yahshua his ministry needs. He just listens to the command of where to go and what the mission is. Then the money comes in for him to go. He was told that he was to go to Brussels Belgium, and be an ambassador for Christ to the United Nations. He replied to Yahshua that they would not let him in there. Yahshua's reply was to go and obey. So my friend went to Brussels and arrived at the United Nations Headquarters. Upon arrival, he went to go into the main auditorium. They would not let him in. Just then he looked up and saw a tour going in the gates. The Lord spoke to him and told him that he was to follow the last person on the tour into the building. He did so and followed them into the main auditorium. There, the tour guide received a phone call. He reported that he had an unusual phone call and that he would need to leave the building and go to a distant building for about fifteen minutes, and that this kind of detour had never happened in all the years he had been a guide. He instructed the tour assembly to please leave the main auditorium and wait for him in the hall. As my friend, who was the last in line, arrived at the exit door, Yahshua told him to shut the door behind the person in front of him as that man exited. He did so and the next command he heard was, "Now go to the podium and speak what I tell you to speak!" His reply was, "But Lord, there is no one here to listen." Yahshua's reply was, "Go and speak what I tell you to speak!"

He went to the podium and these are the words that came from his mouth, and his voice was commanding, stern and loud:

> *"These are not REBELS! This is My tribe Judah, and every army that comes against them will die in the mountains of Israel!"*

Then my friend was told that was all and to leave now. My friend replied, "But Lord, there is no one here to hear this." To which Yahshua replied, "The walls will cry out and the beams (of wood) will speak!" as it says in Habakkuk 2:11, "For the stone shall cry out of the wall, and the beam out of the timber shall answer it." Now it has been discovered that wood and stone retain sound waves and recently scientists have successfully played messages recovered from stone and wood.

What does all this mean? I believe that Yahshua will engage Ezekiel 37, 38, 39 and the war recorded there for these last days, and Israel will do something that shows they cannot be controlled by the United Nations. Possibly, they will nuke Damascus and Isaiah 17:1 will be fulfilled, "Behold the burden of Damascus is taken away from being a city, and it is become a ruinous heap." Damascus is still there and this Scripture has not occurred yet. Sounds like the Scripture could be speaking of a nuclear attack. Damascus is known by Israel to be the training ground for much of the Muslim terrorist base. This sort of retaliation is certainly a possibility. It may be that Israel will not allow Jerusalem to be divided or maybe they will not pull out of the so-called "occupied territories." This will be seen as an act of defiance to the U.N. Then, I suspect the U.N. Assembly will call Israel a bunch of rebels and prepare to attack them. Then the walls and the beams will cry out and speak to them in a love-based warning of life and death. They will not be able to cut off the microphone or the sound system to stop their warning from Yahshua that every one they send to fight Judah will die in the mountains of Israel. The world and its system will bow their knee to the God of Israel, Yahweh. If you would like to look more into the ministry of Henry Gruver and the many visions he has had from Yahshua, you may find his ministry website at: www.geocities.com/jsminis/. Remember, Yahshua wants intimate fellowship with you and as you determine in your heart and mind to obey Him, you will also have visions and other miraculous experiences.

Psalm 1:1-6 sums up for you the results of your diligence in study: "(1) Blessed is the man (or woman) who walks not in the counsel of the ungodly, nor stands the way of sinners, nor sits in the seat of mockers (2) but his delight is in the law (instructions, Torah), and on this law he will meditate (think on to the extent of muttering or speaking) day and night. (3) He is like a tree planted by rivers, yielding its fruit in season, whose leaf does not wither. Whatever he does prospers. (4) Not so the wicked! (Twisted from the truth as a wick in a candle is twisted) They are like chaff (trash) that the wind blows away. Therefore, the wicked will not stand in the Day of Judgment, or sinners in the assembly of the righteous. (6) For Yahshua watches over the way of the righteous, but the way of the wicked will perish."

Religion is useless without personal relationship. Religion is produced from *duty*, while relationship with the Messiah Yahshua is produced from *desire*. If you really desire an intimate relationship with our Creator, you will desire to study and lovingly obey His instructions. I encourage you to seek Him and His truth by obeying with all your heart what the Scriptures reveal to you by the Holy Spirit, which has been sent you to help, teach, comfort, and guide you into all truth and show you things to come.

Isaiah 54:17 is a great promise for you: "No weapon that is formed against you will prosper; and every tongue that accuses you in judgment you will condemn. This is the heritage of the servants of YHWH, and their vindication is from Me, declares YHWH."

I also urge you to memorize Psalm ninety-one and personalize it to provide protection for you and your family. Begin searching for His promises that provide protection and get them into your spirit so you can call on them in need. One final reminder that Yahshua is in the process of bringing His two last day witnesses and restoring the two houses of Israel is about Judah and Ephraim. The house of Judah, or the orthodox Jew which is the Jew who now keeps Torah and who will accept Yahshua as Messiah; *and* the House of Ephraim, the believers in Messiah who are now called Christians but will learn to keep His Commands or Torah.

These will walk in His power and do great exploits in His Name. You, too, can be part of this *remnant*! I challenge you to start studying the Torah cycle each Sabbath. The Torah study cycle and great teaching with Hebrew insight can be found at www.lionlamb.net or just type in Messianic Torah cycle in your search field on the Internet. Another really great teaching and Torah cycle site is Mike Clayton's www.joinedtohashem.org as it contains many answers to questions regarding the faith from a Hebraic perspective. www.wildbranchministries.org is also a great site of Brad Scott's for your word study. Why did Yahshua go into the Galilee to find ten of His disciples? Because He came for the lost sheep of Israel and the ten scattered tribes that had gone into captivity by Assyria were from that area. That is why the Apostles will rule with Messiah in His Kingdom. They are the chosen heads of the twelve tribes and Yahshua, who is the Lion of the Tribe of Judah, will reign over all. These were all Hebrews, so it is wise that we to return to our roots, flee all the added paganism we have inherited through generations of compromise, and lovingly follow this Hebrew, specifically Jewish, Messiah!

Jeremiah 16:19 tells of these traditions of paganism passed down to us: "O Lord, my strength, and my fortress, and my refuge in the *day of affliction* (great tribulation time ahead) the scattered ones (gentiles or scattered ten tribes or known today as the called out ones, the Christians) shall come from the ends of the earth. And shall surely say, surely *our fathers have inherited lies and things wherein there is no profit.*"

When you inherit something it is not really your fault but you are still required to repent when you find truth. Our fathers didn't realize they had inherited lies or they would not have passed them down to us. Will we break the chain of religious tradition and return to truth for our children? This Scripture is talking about the end of the age time when men return to the roots of our faith and flee paganism.

Become a *doer* of His Word and not a hearer only. Learn to give to those less fortunate than you. Yahshua said, "Whoever gives the least of these little ones (His children) a cup of water for My sake and the gospel's will by no means lose their reward." Purpose your heart to clothe those that need clothes, feed those that are hungry, cast out devils from the oppressed, lay hands on the sick, visit those in prison, and lead sinners in a prayer of repentance to help them get born again into His Kingdom.

Do these acts of kindness in the name of Yahshua the Messiah! Why are the set apart and holy names so important? Throughout the Scriptures, we are reminded to call on His *Name*. Yahshua tells us three times in John seventeen alone, that He taught the Father's name Yahweh to the disciples. Why would He spend so much emphasis on the name if using it were not important? The Tribe of Judah was very diligent in obeying the Commandments, or at least they obeyed what they interpreted them to mean. The Commandment that says to not use the name of the Lord in vain drove them to fear. They determined it would be better to not even use *The Name* than to use it vainly. Even today, they use for a name, Lord or Adonai, or even HaShem which is just Hebrew for "the name." Ironically, because of fear, they disobeyed all the Commands He gave them to call on His Name! When Yahshua arrived on the earth, the religious Pharisees and Sadducees hated Him because He was using and teaching that Name. They had incorrectly interpreted this Scripture of the Ten Commandments and were not using the name at all, as they considered it blasphemy. Sometimes when the disciples were beaten by the religious leaders they would instruct them after beating them, "Do *not* use that Name!" Let's look at the Scripture accounts in John 17:6 as Yahshua speaks, "I have *revealed Your Name* to the men which You gave Me out of the world: Yours They were, and You gave them to Me; and they have kept Your Word."

He continues in John 17:11-12, "(11) And now I am no longer in the world, but these are still in the world, and I come to You. Holy Father, keep through *Your own Name* those whom You have given Me that they may also be one as We are One. (12) While I was with them in the world, *I kept them in Your Name*; those that You gave Me I have kept, and none of them is lost, except the son of perdition that the Scripture might be fulfilled."

Yahshua gives a third witness in John 17:26, "And I have declared to them *Your Name*, and will declare it; that the love You have shown Me may be in them, and I in them."

As you can see from these few Scriptures, using and declaring the Name of Yahweh is a vital part of the relationship. Call on His Name and listen to His voice and He will guide you and protect you.

He will also show you where to give and plant in His Kingdom. When you do these things, you will be planting and watering and He will produce fruit that will remain, as Yahweh will give the increase. The Scriptures declare in 1 Corinthians 3:6 "I have planted, Apollos watered, but Yahweh gives the increase." *So it is not the one who is planting or watering who is special, it is Yahweh who gives the miraculous increase!*

Genesis 8:22 reminds us, "As long as the earth remains there will be seedtime and harvest..." What you plant is important because it is what you will harvest, whether spiritually or physically. Every seed produces after its own kind according to Genesis 1:11-12. When you plant a smile, you'll get a smile back. When you plant anger, you'll receive anger. When you plant food for the hungry, you will receive food when you need it most. The Scriptures in 2 Corinthians 9:6 warn us to not plant sparingly or we will receive a small harvest, but if we plant in abundance, we will harvest in abundance. Act as though you already have the results you are hoping for as you speak the Word of Yahweh over your circumstances and continually give Him thanks. You would give Him thanks if you really believed you had the thing you've prayed for! As believers, we are required to change and become more like Yahshua Who is the Word made flesh. He is the Truth already, and therefore, cannot change. We change by meditating on His Word, and getting His Truth and promises into our spirits and souls. We *do* His Word. One last witness of promise is found in Galatians 6:7-9, "(7) Be not deceived, Yahweh is not mocked: For whatever a man shall plant, that shall he also harvest. (8) For He that plants to the flesh shall harvest corruption; but he that plants to the Spirit shall from the Spirit harvest life everlasting. (9) And let us not be weary in well doing: for in due season we *shall harvest* if we faint not." **Shall harvest!** Not- might harvest, hopefully harvest, or maybe will harvest! Doing His Word guarantees His harvest and results! We can produce fruit that will remain! We overcome by the blood of the Lamb and the word of our testimony! According to 1 Corinthians 15:57-58 we have the victory and the instructions, "(57) Thanks are due Yahweh, Who gives us the victory through Yahshua our Messiah. (58) Therefore, beloved brothers, be steadfast and unmovable, always doing the works of Yahshua, for you know that your labor is not in vain in Him." Yahshua has given us the victory so we are instructed to be strong and unmovable and do the works of Yahshua by standing on His promises. Our flesh, circumstance, nor Satan can have victory over us.

Your obedience brings His victory, think and engrave this in your mind,

VICTORY IS GUARANTEED!

The poem below is circa mid 1800's and was written by Uriah Smith and even though it only speaks of the tribe of Judah and not all of the twelve tribes, you can still get the humor of the point being made.

It's Jewish

By Uriah Smith

When we present Yahweh's Holy Law,
And arguments from Scripture draw,
Objectors say to pick a flaw,
It's Jewish.

Though at the first the Most High blessed,
And sanctified His day of rest,
The same concern is still confessed,
It's Jewish.

Though with the world this rest began,
And thence through all the Scriptures ran,
And Yahshua said was made for man,
It's Jewish.

Though not with sacrificial rites, which passed,
But with the moral law His Feasts were classed,
Which must exist till time shall last,
It's Jewish.

If from the Bible we present,
The Sabbath's meaning and intent,
This answers every argument,
It's Jewish!

Though the disciples, Luke and Paul,
Continue still this rest to call,
The Sabbath Day, this answers all,
It's Jewish.

The good news teacher's plain expression,
That sin is of the Law's transgression,
Seems not to make the least impression,
It's Jewish.

They love the Sun-day rest of man's invention,
But if Messiah's Day we mention,
This puts an end to all contention,
It's Jewish.

O you who Yahweh's day abuse,
Simply cause 'twas kept by Jews,
Their Savior too, you must refuse,
He's Jewish!

The Scripture, then, we may expect,
For these same reasons you'll reject,
For if you will but recollect,
They're Jewish!

Thus, the Apostles too, must fall,
For Andrew, Peter, James and Paul,
Thomas, Matthew, John and All,
Were Jewish!

So to your helpless state resign,
Yourself in wretchedness to pine,
Salvation, surely you'll decline,
It's Jewish!

We are given a picture of the last days and reminder who overcomes and is with our Creator in Heaven, as the angels prepare to pour out the bowls of wrath on the unbelieving and disobedient.

Revelation 15:1-3 says, "(1) And I saw another sign in heaven, great and marvelous, seven angels having the seven last plagues; for in them is filled up the wrath of Yahweh. (2) And I saw as it were a sea of glass mingled with fire: and them that had gotten the victory over the beast, and over his image, and over his mark, and over the number of his name, standing on the sea of glass and having the harps of Yahweh. (3) And they the servant of Yahweh **and** the saying great and marvelous are Your works, Yahweh Almighty; just and true are Your ways, King of the believers."

Notice that these overcoming believers sing because they keep Torah and are obedient to the Law **AND** because they know Yahshua and are *born again.*

Who is it that Satan (the dragon) makes war against? Revelation 12:17 answers: "And the dragon was angry with the woman, and went to make war with the *remnant* of her seed, which *keep the Commandments* of Yahweh, and have the *testimony of Yahshua the Messiah.*"

So, dear reader, I pray you are the remnant who
has this testimony:

I keep the Commandments of YHWH

And I belong to Messiah Yahshua!

Chapter Seventeen:
Dreams and Visions to Consider

Throughout this book, I have included dreams and visions to help show that our God is still the same yesterday, today, and forever, which is the promise recorded in Hebrews 13:8 and Malachi 3:6. He warned Joseph (Yoseph) <u>in a dream</u> to prepare for famine, as he was second in command of Egypt. He told Ananias in Acts 9:10 in a vision to go pray for Sha'ul (Paul) and lay hands on him that he might see. He warned Noah, a preacher of righteousness, to build an ark for the saving of his household prior to Yahweh's judgment of the earth with water. If He really is the same yesterday, today, and forever, then it is reasonable to believe that He will also show us things to come and He promises to do that. Yahshua reminds us in Matthew 24:37, "As the days of Noah were, so also shall it be at the coming of the Son of Man." Those days and culture were wicked to the degree that Yahweh destroyed all humankind except eight souls. Yahweh promised never to destroy the earth with water or a flood again but promised to reserve the second judgment with fire. He has also judged the cities of Sodom and Gomorrah with fire and has this admonition for us recorded by Peter in 2 Peter 3:3-13, "(3) Know this first, there will come in the last days (Translate: End of Days), mockers and scoffers pursuing their own desires. (4) Saying, where is the promise of

His coming? Since our fathers fell asleep (died), all things continue as they were from the beginning of creation. (5) For this they are *willingly ignorant*, that by the Word of God the heavens were of old, and the earth stands out of the water in the water: (6) The world that was being overflowed with water, perished. (7) But the heavens and the earth, which are now here, by the same Word of God, are kept in store and reserved for fire against the Day of Judgment and perdition of ungodly men. (8) Beloved, do not be ignorant of this one thing, that one day with the Lord is one thousand years and one thousand years as one day. (9) Yahweh is not slack concerning His promise as some men are, but is patient and long-suffering, not willing that any would perish but that all would come to repentance. (10) However, the Day of the Lord will come like a thief in the night (Most will be unprepared and not paying attention) the heavens shall pass away with great noise, and the elements shall melt with great heat, the earth also and the works that are in it shall be burned up. (11) Seeing that these things shall be dissolved, what manner of person should we be in righteous conversations and Godliness, (12) looking for with expectancy, the coming of the Day of the Lord when the heavens will be on fire and dissolve, and the elements shall melt in fervent heat? (13) Nevertheless, we according to His promise expect and anticipate a new heaven and a new earth where only righteousness dwells."

I think it is safe to conclude that He does not want us *willingly* or otherwise ignorant of the End of the Age times. Do not be willingly ignorant. Do not take the ostrich approach and hide your head in the ground hoping these concerns and troubles will disappear. He does not want you willingly ignorant so wake up! He wants you sober and alert walking righteously in your conversation and actions. Study and rightly divide the Word that you will not be ashamed at His appearing. Surely, our merciful Creator would warn us about impending judgment with fire so that we could repent and walk righteously with Him that we might be spared certain catastrophe. Yahshua promises in John 16:13, "When the Holy Spirit has come He will lead you into all Truth, for He shall not speak of Himself, but whatever He hears is what He will speak, and *show you things to come.*"

Of course, you have to repent and follow Him to have the ears to hear or ability to hear His warnings and directions. According to Yahshua in Matthew 7:21 not everyone that calls Him Lord, Lord will be able to enter into the Kingdom, or we might paraphrase and say have the ability to hear, but only those who do the will of Yahweh, the Father. I do not promise that all the following dreams and visions are directly from Yahweh or that they apply to you personally. However, with that caveat in place, I believe they are relevant and timely and should be prayed about as you seek direction concerning your own life and the well-being of your family and loved ones. None of us may have accomplished this, but the Torah (Word of God) Commands us to teach the Word to our children and to think on it when we rise, to meditate on it during the day, when we close our eyes at night, and never let it depart from our lips.

> **Now let us examine the promise of the Scriptures as to _WHEN_ the End of the Age is.**

Studying Luke 21:8-36 we see Yahshua warning us His disciplined ones, "(8) Take heed that you are not deceived, for many shall come in My Name saying I am anointed in Messiah (some translations say I am *the* Christ or Messiah here) and the time draws near, do not follow them. (9) When you hear of wars and uprisings do not be fearful, for these things must come to pass but the end is *NOT YET.* (We can see from this Scripture that wars and uprisings are not the sign we are watching for to mark the end of the age) (10) Then Yahshua said, nation shall rise against nation and kingdom against kingdom (11) and great earthquakes shall be many places, and famines, and diseases (plagues), fearful sights and great signs will be in heaven. (12) But even before these take place, they will lay hands on you, persecute you, and deliver you up to the courts and prisons, being brought before kings and rulers because of My Name. (13) And it will be your opportunity to testify about Me. (14) Settle it in your heart not to think and plan on what you will answer, (15) for I will give you the words and the wisdom which all your enemies will not be able to counter or resist. (16) You will be betrayed by your parents and brothers, and your relatives and friends; and some of you they shall cause to be put to death. (17) You will be hated by all men *because of my name*. (18) However, not one hair of your head shall perish. (19) In your *patience*, possess your souls. (There are about five Greek translations for patience in the New Testament: to endure, long suffering, forbearing, waiting and expecting, and trusting with confidence) (20) When you see Jerusalem surrounded by armies, then know that the desolation of it is near. (21) Then let them that are in Judea flee to the mountains, and let them in Jerusalem get out, and those in the country should not enter there. (22) For these are the Days of Vengeance (Day of the Lord), that all things that are written will be fulfilled. (23) Woe to them that are with child and to them that are nursing babies in those days! There will be great distress in the land and wrath on the people. (24) They shall fall by the edge of the sword, and shall be led away captive to all nations, and the heathen shall trample Jerusalem until their time is fulfilled. (Time of the Great Tribulation is 42 months) (25) There shall be signs in the sun, moon and stars. Upon the earth, there will be distress of nations with perplexity and the sea and *waves shall roar!* (Sounds like tsunamis will be a regular event) (26) Men's hearts will fail them due to great fear of looking at the things that are coming on the earth because the powers of heaven will be shaken. (27) Then you will see the Son of Man coming in a cloud with power and great glory. (28) When these things begin to come to pass, look up, for your redemption draws near. (29) Continuing, Yahshua said, pay attention to the fig tree and all the trees. (30) When they grow out you know that Summer is near. (31) Likewise, when you see these things come to pass, know that the Kingdom of Yahweh (God) is near. (32) Truly, I say to you, that the generation that sees these things happen, by no method will pass away, until it is all fulfilled. (33) Heaven and earth shall pass away, but My Words shall never pass away. (34) Pay attention and be careful that you are not caught up in drunkenness, indulgences, self-pleasure or the cares of this life and allow this time to come on you unexpectedly! (35) It will be a trap set for all who dwell on the earth. (36) Pay attention and pray without ceasing, that you may be made worthy to escape all these things and stand (unashamedly) before the Son of Man (Yahshua)." Here is one more Scripture I would emphasize could mark when the end of the age is. Yahweh (God) talking in Joel 3:1-2 says, "(1) Behold, *in those days* and *in that time* (Hebrew idiom for the Day of the Lord), I will bring again the captivity of Judah and Jerusalem. (2) I will also gather all nations and will bring them down in the valley of Jehoshaphat, (A valley near Jerusalem) and will plead with them there for My people and My heritage Israel, whom they have scattered among the nations and they have divided up *(Parted) My land.*" When you see the parting of Jerusalem and the dividing of the land to make a false peace with the Palestinians (They divide the land and will say peace, peace but there will be no peace) you can know we have arrived because God's judgments will come quickly on those men and countries that facilitated this.

> ***You can make your own decision and draw your own conclusions whether or not we have arrived at the End of the Age.***

Remember, we are Commanded to *not* fear, but to pay attention and hear and obey our loving Creator through Messiah Yahshua! If you are fearful after reading these Scriptures along with the following dreams and visions, I would caution you to turn off your television and all other distractions and spend time studying the Word of God, praying and worshipping. I would also caution you to consider the destinies for believers during this stressful time of growing our faith and trusting Him found in Revelation 13:9-10. This Scripture promises that if you help lead men into captivity, you will also be taken into captivity and if you use weapons to kill, by weapons you will be killed, and this is the *patience and faith* of the believers. Again, what is the faith and patience of the believers? Keeping the Commandments and trusting Yahshua to make us worthy to escape and endure these trials coming on the earth that we may stand at His appearing unashamed. We will need His supernatural directions and power to escape and endure. The glaring omission here, the point begging for our utmost attention is the theoretical nonsense of a pre-tribulation or pre-trial rapture of the believers before any trouble starts. Please notice that the Scripture says to *escape* and *endure*. If there were a pre-tribulation rapture like so many erroneously are prepared for (no preparation required except to be born again) then there would be no requirement by this Scripture to *endure*. We would just escape only with no endurance required. However, a pre-tribulation rapture would not have you prepared without spot or blemish to meet your bridegroom, Yahshua. What profit would it bring us to escape only to then be cast out unworthy and unprepared to enter the Kingdom? Enduring and escaping is required to survive and produce fruit for the Kingdom of Heaven. Notice the Scripture does not say to stand and defend yourself. It says to *escape and endure*. Do not think that you can kill others and be supernaturally protected during this time. Many think that they will be able to defend themselves. I would suggest to them that it would be wiser to trust Yahshua for one ten foot angel for protection. Do not think that you can arrange the betrayal of others to be arrested and led captive, while protecting and bringing favor to yourself, and have supernatural protection from God during this time. I would suggest that all who betray and facilitate other people's destruction and captivity will end up in captivity. It is a Scriptural guarantee. *Patience and faith* is interestingly then defined by the Word of God in Revelation 14:12, "Here is the patience and faith of the believers; they will *keep the Commandments and trust in Yahshua.*"

Dreams and visions are the evidence of a merciful God showing us things to come. One of the end time's events before the Day of the Lord is Joel 2:28-32, "(28) It shall come to pass afterward, I will pour out My Spirit on all flesh, on your sons and your daughters, and they shall prophesy, your old men shall dream dreams and your young men shall see visions. (29) Upon my servants and handmaidens, I will pour out My Spirit in those days. (30) I will show wonders in the heavens, and in the earth blood and fire and pillars of smoke. (31) The sun shall be turned dark and the moon blood red before the great and terrible Day of the Lord. (32) It will come to pass that whoever calls on the name of Yahweh will be delivered, for in Mt. Zion and in Jerusalem there will be deliverance, as Yahweh has said, and in the remnant whom Yahweh calls." With these instructions in place, let us look at what believers are having visions of and dreaming.

Vision on the Recent G8 Summit

By Kato Mivule

July 8, 2005

Foremost, I wish to extend my deepest sympathy and prayers to the families of the victims of the London attacks. I include in my prayers all those injured and suffering because of the attacks, that Jesus Christ will be their comfort and healer. I also wish to make note at this point to all who are still blinded by the left and right politics that I am none of that and I categorically reject such partisan nonsense, and nothing of what I write today is in support of such. After the London attacks on July 7, 2005, I sensed heaviness in my heart, but at the same time, I was not surprised by the attacks. Therefore, I went to the Lord in prayer and asked for His thought on this situation before I slept... the Lord then gave me a Scripture in Isaiah....

Isaiah 40:15-17 (15) Behold, the nations are as a drop of a bucket, and are counted as the small dust of the balance: behold, He takes up the isles as a very little thing. (16) And Lebanon is not sufficient to burn, nor the beasts thereof sufficient for a burnt offering. (17) All nations before Him are as nothing; and they are counted to Him less than nothing, and vanity.

I was then woken up at 1:00 am on July 8, 2005. This was after I had a dream concerning the welfare of my family. I knew that The Lord wanted to speak to me because He will always interrupt my sleep when He has something to say to me. I thought I would begin by prayer and intercession but the Lord stopped me and compelled me to get a paper and pen and just wait on Him.

The inverted Pyramid

The first vision I say was a pyramid on the One US Dollar bill. It was brought before me and the eye in the pyramid was alive and staring at me when suddenly a man dressed in a white robe came and inverted and turned it upside down. The base was on top and the top on bottom and the base pressed upon the inverted top with great pressure crashing the pyramid. The base became so heavy that the top, which was on the bottom, could not handle the pressure of the base and pressure exerted on it by the hand of the man dressed in a white robe. The eye that was looking at me was taken by the sudden move, caught unaware, and horrified. The

Man who I later realized was the Lord told, "I am going to overthrow the pyramid, there is going to be a revolt." The vision ended, so I wrote it…

The G8 Summit Forgot About God and Gog…

After this, I had the second vision. I was with the same man who I later realized was the Lord. He told me "You have been writing an article about the G8 summit" (I was writing a short piece about my own opinion on the G8 Summit and the London attacks on the evening on July 7, 2005). In the vision, I said "yes." Then the Lord told me, "The G8 have been caught with their pants down." I knew He was referring to the London attacks. In the vision, I was carried over Europe, as if I could see Europe from space but very close. It was as if someone was taking me on a tour of Europe. The Lord proceeded to say, "I will expose their nakedness for all to see, and the blood of the innocent is placed at their feet." Then I was shown the photo up at the G8 Summit but all did not have trousers on but boxers (underwear) on and no shoes on (half-naked). The Russian President was skinny but grew fat because of the anger and bitterness he stored as the British Prime Minister read out the solidarity statement against the London attackers. The Russian President seemed to come to the microphone to say something but could not; he was held back and in the photo stood alone at a distance from the leaders who did not even notice. The Lord then said, "they forgot about God and Gog, Gog will revolt."

The Lord's tone towards the G8 was not a favorable one, I instantly knew that the G8 are His enemies and The Lord spoke to them as a people who were given to judgment. I know the Lord is very angry with them and they would not escape His judgments. I was made to feel the Holy Anger of the Lord against the G8. However, the Lord's anger towards the G8 seemed to be a kind of protection for His people. He was angry with the G8 because He loved His people.

Word for London...

I was then taken over London and I saw the people get angry and begin a revolt against the rulers; they discovered on the radio that their rulers, including the US, orchestrated the attacks. (Disclaimer: Please do not attack me, this was just a vision and dream, I am only sharing a vision and dream... will you kill the dreamer?) However, they seemed to join the revolt against the pyramid on the US dollar bill. After this the Lord said to me, "Let the people in London prepare places of refuge." I knew he was referring to the Christians. Therefore, I saw Christians in London prepare hidden shelters secretly. So I thought well, would they have another attack? The Lord said, "They will have refugees from America, they will see America burn." I was then told to read Psalms 28.

Psalms 28:1-9 "(1) Unto thee will I cry, O LORD my rock; be not silent to me: lest, if Thou be silent to me, I become like them that go down in to the pit. (2) Hear the voice of my supplications, when I cry unto Thee, when I lift up my hands toward Thy Holy oracle. (3) draw me not away with the wicked, and with the workers of iniquity, which speak peace to their neighbors, but mischief is in their hearts. (4) Give them according to their deeds, and according to the wickedness of their endeavors: give them after the work of their hands; render to them their desert. (5) Because they regard not the works of the LORD, nor the operations of His hands, He shall destroy them, and not build them up. (6) Blessed be the LORD, because He hath heard the voice of my supplications. (7) The LORD is my strength and my shield: my heart trusted in Him, and I am helped: therefore my heart greatly rejoices; and with my song will I praise Him. (8) The LORD is their strength, and He is the saving strength of His anointed. (9) Save Your people, and bless Your inheritance: feed them also, and lift them up for ever."

Technology Center Shifts From US to London...

The Lord showed me a shift of technology from the USA to London. It was as if a huge database was now stationed in London. The U.S. technology diminished until America was burned with fire. However, not all technology was under the control of the British Government. Those who revolted against the Pyramid used part of the technology based in London in their revolts.

American Refugees in Africa...

After this, the Lord showed me Africa, with the wasteland turning to springs and wells and people rejoicing. American refugees were fleeing to Africa and some people were fleeing France to hide in Africa. They were kept there and welcomed by the locals. The Lord said to me "I was in Africa as a refugee until Herod died, I will hide some of My people from America and France in Africa until their Herod dies." I knew He spoke about Joseph and Mary escaping to Egypt with Jesus and being protected there until Herod died. (Disclaimer: I am not saying that everyone should run to Africa... seek the face of God concerning these matters, don't simply run to Mexico, Canada, Israel, because your friends are doing so, seek God's will as to where He wants you to be personally). This is the second vision that the Lord showed me of American refugees in Africa, however in both of my visions, the locals welcomed the Americans.

France, Chirac, and the Eiffel Tower...

After this, I was taken over France. The first place was at the Eiffel Tower. Then the Lord said to me in a commanding voice "Son of man, pull that Tower down!" I was, like, well, how do I do it, and He said "I said pull that Tower down!" So, I simply prayed against the Tower in the name of Jesus Christ saying, "I pull you down in the name of Jesus Christ." After, I saw saints in France underground in prayer, the prayers were so fervent that I then suddenly saw the foundations of the tower crumble, then suddenly a naked Chirac carried the huge tower over his head and began running towards the French people, the people ran away from Chirac and there was another revolt. The people were angry at Chirac, they were betrayed by him so they ran away from the burden of the Tower, Chirac grow darker and darker till his body became black as coal, no one helped him with the burden of the Tower, and they all laughed at Chirac for he is not a person for the people.

Civil unrest in France...

Then The Lord said to me, "There is going to be civil unrest in France, they rejected God and laughed at My church and offended God. Chirac, to whom will you turn to with the burden of the Tower? I hate their Towers; they are an abomination before Me. Paris will be overthrown. There are God's faithful in France and God will protect them. The French decided to build a Tower instead of fountains of water, the land is now dry and there is no water."

Demonic Beings Land in Paris...

The Lord then proceeded to say to me, "I gave France 1978 to 2008". Then I was shown beings landing over France that looked like demonic beings. The demonic beings communicated to each other saying, "Landing in Paris 2008." Then I heard the words Darkness comes over Paris 2008. I do not know anything about the dates and meanings here, the timings and seasons belong to God. All I am humbly narrating was a vision the Lord gave me, surely demonic darkness and gloom are moving towards France in the near future.

University of Paris...

After this, I was taken over to the University of Paris, and then the Lord said to me "The University of Paris is an abomination, it will be overthrown. They have poisoned many of My children in America with their doctrines. The French will surely be overthrown." Then I saw Gog ready to attack, the enemy of France came from the North. I do not know if the attack will come from Gog or not, but for sure, God has set His judgment on France. I pray if anyone knows any intercessor and prayer warriors from France, they can forward these visions and they can begin to pray for God's remnant in France. The Lord is very serious about France.

Back to the Pyramid..." Strike at the Pyramid"...

After this I had another vision, I was taken back to the Pyramid with the revolt going on and the pressure was now turned towards the top of the Pyramid which was now upside down. The Lord said to me "Son of man, get the hammer and strike at the eye on the pyramid." Therefore, I got the hammer, which I knew was God's True Holy Word, and hit at the wicked eye in the pyramid that was staring at me.

Therefore, the visions ended and that was at 3:00 a.m. I pray that God will bless you all as we draw close to Him daily. Silver and gold do not save; only Jesus Christ can save you. The storms have already begun gathering, the G8 meeting was an abomination before God, the saints and angels in Heaven denounce the beast and his system... they rejoice over God's judgment on the beast and his system... The blood of all those who have been killed by the orchestrated "terror" attacks lies at the feet of the New World Order who have declared war against God and His Anointed One, Jesus Christ, our only place of safety is Jesus Christ. So together, we can sing Psalm 91 with all who truly love Jesus Christ.

July 9, 2005 Encouragement...

I was praying in the morning because of the visions I had against the G8 (The G8 are very diabolic). The Lord gave me a Scripture and an encouragement to all who are receiving word from God concerning these last days.

Daniel 2:20-28 "(20) Daniel answered and said, Blessed be the name of God for ever and ever: for wisdom and might are His: (21) And He changeth the times and the seasons; He removeth kings, and setteth up kings: He giveth wisdom unto the wise, and knowledge to them that know understanding: (22) He revealeth the deep and secret things: He knoweth what is in the darkness, and the light dwelleth with Him. (23) I thank Thee, and praise Thee, O Thou God of my fathers, who hast given me wisdom and might, and hast made known unto me now what we desired of Thee: for Thou has now made known unto us the king's matter... (28) But there is a God in heaven that revealeth secrets, and maketh known to the King Nebuchadnezzar what shall be in the *latter days*. Thy dream, and the visions of thy head upon thy bed, is this..."

Race War and Genocide in America Dream

Disclaimer: I am NOT a Moslem terror sympathizer neither am I a Moslem murderer.

On July 1, 2005, The Lord gave me a dream about a Post Terrorist Attack Genocide in America. However, because of the heaviness of the dream and its message, I prayed to God as to when He would allow me to release this dream. The Genocide Spirit is from Hell, and has been released from the bottomless pit to Babylon America, so that is why I was hesitant to release the dream but waited for the Lord's timing. With the attacks I got from releasing the G8 Visions, I now know it takes the Lord's leading in releasing some of these dreams, Satan hates being exposed. He hates light because then he flees, where the light shines darkness flees. However, the Lord placed a very heavy burden on me today, even as I was at work to release this dream today. I had decided to rest from the attacks I received from the release of the G8 Visions but the Lord encouraged me by reminding me that this is a war and I had better get back to work.

For we wrestle not against flesh and blood but principalities, powers and rulers in the high and dark evil places. The evil spirits behind the G8 and evil spirits are behind the coming American genocide of true

Christians who truly love Jesus Christ from a pure heart. In my dream, I saw the USA had just undergone major terrorist attacks in a major city that brought about an economic crash in the nation. Millions of people were no longer working. I was out of work too and living on the few foods I had stored. Everyone was told to stay in their houses and there was a semi-curfew in America. Then something began to happen, neighborhoods were separated and demarcations done. The white people were placed alone, and the black people alone, Mexicans alone etc, and the other group were the Moslems; they were separated and placed in their own quarters. This was happening across American cities and towns.

The most disturbing pictures in the dream, was that the people who carried out the separation were Christians who worked as secret service agents for the government. They accused the American Moslems of carrying out the deadly terrorist attacks and then begun slowly and calmly taking *ALL* Moslems to concentration camps. I saw the American Moslem men who I work with at my job, being lead on buses to concentration camps and told that they were being taken for safety. However, a group of white worship leaders from the churches begun to object and then people realized it was a lie, the American Moslems were being taken to be killed without trial, and people realized that they did not carry out the attacks. In the dream, the Christian Secret Service Agents convinced Christians in churches that they had to fight back for their nation against Moslems who were said to be responsible for the terrorist attacks.

Then a resistance among the American Moslem citizens began, but they were overpowered, rounded up, and taken handcuffed to concentration camps. Now, the Christian Secret Service Agents begun doing it openly with no fear, they had guns, they supplied food to the unemployed and they had power. All American Moslems who resisted were shot and killed even before they were bused to the camps. In the dream, Christians from churches were participating in the murders and street killing of their Moslem neighbors whom they saw as terrorists; they saw this act of murder as patriotic but were deceived by the Genocide Spirit. Now at the same time when the Moslems were being rounded up, riots were going on between white and black, black and Mexican, Mexican and whites and all races, each accusing the other of collaborating with terrorists.

However, the Christian Secret Service Agents got backing sadly from the UN. In the dream, I saw them come to churches with secret service badges and UN Badges and they began to arrest all white worship leaders who had refused to engage in the arrest of the Moslem "terrorists." These were beaten and some were killed. They were taken and accused of collaborating with "terrorists." The white church worship leaders had arranged joint worship services between blacks, whites and other races... all who engaged in this were rounded up by their fellow church members who served in the Secret Agent Army... these were beaten severely and some killed. The churches were allowed to worship but not mix with any other race. The worst scenario was the whites that began killing fellow whites, accusing them of treason.

In the dream, we were defiant with a group of Christians, so we went on praying in this free abandoned church with all other races but knowing anytime the Christian Secret Service Agents would arrest us. They did come and broke into the church meeting and began the beatings and torture but the most severely beaten and tortured people were white church worship leaders who were seen as traitors. (I do not know why the Lord chose to use the worship leaders and not pastors in the dream). The spirit of genocide was all over the place with people killing each other, accusing each other of supporting the Moslem "terrorists." However, in my dream, the Moslems who were arrested and murdered, were innocent, everyone seemed to know they were not responsible for the terrorist attacks (Please do not get mad at me, this was only a dream, I am not a Moslem supporter nor a supporter of murder and genocide, I hate all evil).

The Lord showed me that the evil spirit of genocide has been released from Hell and is about deceiving people into a race war to kill each other. Some Christians will be deceived that killing Moslems and Christians who refuse to engage in the race wars is serving God and being patriotic. The Lord gave a warning that those who are Christians should not participate in that spirit of the world, the spirit of hate and genocide; we are called to be separate from such unto the Lord in holiness and righteousness. The Lord revealed to me that the "Christian" Secret Service Agents were already at work in the churches. The Lord also showed me the economic crash. I saw in the vision two switches, one for the NASDAQ and the other for the Dow Jones. The one for the NASDAQ was the first to be turned off by someone I recognized was an angel. Then chaos began, but not until the Dow Jones was turned off too, and people went into riots and begun to blame the terrorists and engage in hunting for the Moslem terrorists.

The Lord gave me a stern warning to all who call themselves Christians *NOT* to engage in any riots and race wars, and murder of Moslems, if you do, His protection will not be on you. He does not delight in the shedding of innocent blood. Please, Jesus Christ knows Moslems are not Christians and knows they can only be saved through Him. Do not send me hate e-mails; this genocide is orchestrated by the New World Order. If you participate in it you will be guilty of murder and you will be heading for HELL. Those who live by the sword will surely die by the sword. In the dream, I was compelled to tell the Moslems to leave. Those who left the US survived but *all* who stayed were killed during the riots. The Angel who turned off the NASDAQ switch showed me a number, 06/06/2006; Please, again I refrain from going into dates, let the times and seasons belong to God, whatever that date means, let all who love Jesus Christ discern.

Word of Caution and History (It is said history repeats...)
During the Rwanda Genocide in 1994, I was still living in Uganda at the time, which is just North East of Rwanda, I knew many Rwandese refugees in Uganda at that time. However, The Lord began to show people dreams and visions of the coming genocide and told the Christians to pray. Many Christians in Rwanda did not take it seriously; others heeded, and left Rwanda. In Uganda, preachers would tell us how the Lord showed them an evil spirit from hell attacking Rwanda and many people dying, others ignored them until bodies begun to float on Lake Victoria from Rwanda to the shores of Uganda.

Christians begun to pray that the same evil spirit from hell would not attack Uganda. In Rwanda, the Pastors who survived the genocide told stories of Jesus Christ visiting some of them to warn them but they ignored and enjoyed the elite lifestyle of a typical rich African. Many were warned, but few received the warnings. In Uganda, we could feel in our spirits, something was wrong. All intercessors and prayer warriors knew that evil was set in our neighboring country, and we prayed.

I feel the same way today, that should one of those NASDAQ and or Dow Jones switches be turned off with combined terrorist attacks, the genocide spirit will take over the streets of America. Those who can warn your friends do so; do not engage in the New World Order bias, segregation, racism, tribalism, prejudice, and race war spirits; they are not from the Father, these spirits have been released from HELL. Please do not send me e-mails with an idiot mentality thinking I support Moslem terrorists or condone their acts. The picture here is bigger than that, what we are seeing is a genocide spirit that was thrown back in the pit in

Rwanda in 1994 and being released in America, it knows no religion and race, only those in Jesus Christ can be safe from this evil spirit of hate.

Sadly, in Rwanda, Christians engaged in killing each other, The Hutu Christians, both Catholic and Protestants engaged in the murder and slaughter of their fellow Christians who ran to churches for help but were turned over to state agents for slaughter. Catholic priests turned over hundreds of innocent Tutsi Christians who ran to them for protection only to be murdered by Hutus. The West, including America, stood by and watched.

> *This has happened before and is scheduled to happen again, this time in America.*

In 1994 after the Rwanda Genocide, the churches in Uganda rushed to go minister in Rwanda. Therefore, I went with my pastor and a team from our Church in Entebbe with a mission to preach forgiveness, reconciliation and minister to the survivors. However, we found forgiveness was a very hard topic to speak about. We interviewed some people who were involved in the murders and the victims who had survived. Those who had engaged in the murders spoke of how some demonic evil beings took over their minds and found themselves killing mercilessly their neighbors and best friends for no apparent reason. The demonic spirit from Hell had taken over. These were some of the most religious people but did not escape the Genocide Spirit.

This Warning Goes Out To All Christians in America...
This warning goes out to all Christians in America. I know pathetic and drunk American pastors will reject this warning but only those who love Jesus Christ and love His true word will be protected from the coming genocide on the American streets. Please do not engage in any type of hate. Truly, like the Bible says, hate is murder and it will happen soon in

Babylon America. These will be some of her first pains to her death, for she will be burned with fire in one hour.

I know this is a very tough word and I pray peace and protection for all who will release this word or forward and e-mail it. I pray that you are covered in Jesus Christ. Proclaim Psalms 91. I love Psalms 91 because it is for us Christians who love Jesus Christ in these end times. Fear not, the Lord is with us and will never leave us alone. I also ask for your prayers, some of the words I get are very direct at times. Sometimes, the Lord will reveal the evil secrets of world leaders and I will listen to all the evil plans they say in dreams and visions, I know many have had similar experiences but Jesus Christ is with us and will protect us. I see the dark clouds of genocide on American soil as I witnessed in 1994 as those same winds blew towards Rwanda. Watch and pray that you will escape all these things... the times are hastened.

A new prophetic anointing has been released. God will continue to reveal secrets hidden in dark places. The New World Order and Babylonian secrets will *not* go unrevealed to the righteous and the wise, they shall know. In addition, many more revelations will be released to many people, including Christians, concerning our times. God will warn all, for what is coming on America is also a chastising of all nations that have committed whoredoms and fornications with America. The warnings will increase as Babylon approaches her death.

In the ancient times, they depended on Joseph with his dreams and interpretation to save Egypt from famine, Daniel in Babylon to help the kings understand their future and judgments... they will come for you because the hearts of men will fail. Their science and engineering will fail, and they will rush to those who are filled with the Holy Spirit and love Jesus Christ and have experienced the wilderness of the Lord. They will rush to you to give them answers when all what we have been saying begins to happen. Do not think they are not following these dreams and visions; they are recording them in their databases. Nevertheless, wisdom will fail and God's children will arise, do not be afraid when that time comes; arise and be a witness for Jesus Christ.

Daniel 2: 19-30 "(19) Then was the secret revealed unto Daniel in a night vision. Then Daniel blessed the God of heaven. (20) Daniel answered and said, Blessed be the name of God for ever and ever: for wisdom and might are His: (21) And He changeth the times and the seasons: He removeth kings, and setteth up kings: He giveth wisdom unto the wise, and knowledge to them that know understanding: (22) He revealeth the deep and secret things: He knoweth what is in the darkness, and the light dwelleth with Him. (23) I thank Thee, and praise Thee, O thou God of my fathers, who hast given me wisdom and might, and hast made known unto me now what we desired of Thee: for Thou hast now made known unto us the king's matter.....(27) Daniel answered in the presence of the king, and said, The secret which the king hath demanded cannot the wise men, the astrologers, the magicians, the soothsayers, show unto the king; (28) But there is a God in heaven that revealeth secrets, and make the known to the King Nebuchadnezzar what shall be in the latter days. Thy dream, and the visions of thine head upon thy bed, are these; (29) As for thee, O king, thy thoughts came into thy mind upon thy bed, what should come to pass hereafter; and He that revealeth secrets maketh known to thee what shall come to pass. (30) But as for me, this secret is not revealed to me for any wisdom that I have more than any living, but for their sakes that shall make known the interpretation to the king, and that thou mightiest know the thoughts of thy heart."

Oh America, I hope you hear America, the genocide clouds and bloodshed are gathering and moving towards you. The world will look with horror and marvel that such a thing could happen even in America, the envy of nations. America, you will be shown naked, all will watch and see your nakedness because you have forsaken the Lord your God. This is because of sins you have committed around the world; you have sown the wind in nations with your wars, greed, sorcery, and war crimes, and now you will reap the whirlwind. The sword of the Lord is stretched out against Babylon America. Her judgments have begun, even though not being noticed by fools but only noticed by the wise. The time to seriously pray and consider is now! Ask Jesus Christ, where He wants you to be and what to do there. However, for some you will have a mission here; pray that God will direct your steps. These are matters of life and death. I ask for all your prayers for God's protection even after I have released this word.

Word and Vision
Christendom Time is up...

As I was praying today, I had a clear vision from The Lord. I saw someone with a measuring rod and this person measured a building in shape of a dorm... later I realized He was The Lord. After the measurements, He said to me, "I have given 100 days to Christendom to repent and her time is ended. It is now time to leave Christendom, everything in Christendom will fail."

The vision then ended...

I do not know what the 100 days stand for but I know the call is out for all those still in the Babylon Church system... and it is individual between you and the Lord... but I know Christendom's time is up! I was later given a Scripture in the book of John...

John 12:20-26 "(20) And there were certain Greeks among them that came up to worship at the Feast: (21) the same came therefore to Philip, which was of Bethsaida of Galilee, and desired Him, saying, Sir, we would see Jesus. (22) Philip cometh and telleth Andrew: and again Andrew and Philip tell Jesus. (23) And Jesus answered them, saying, the hour is come, that the Son of Man should be glorified. (24) Verily, verily, I say unto you, except a corn of wheat fall into the ground and die, it abideth alone: but if it die, it bringeth forth much fruit. (25) He that loveth his life shall lose it; and he that hateth his life in this world shall keep it unto life eternal. (26) If any man serves Me let him follow Me; and where I am, there shall also My servant be: if any man serves Me, him will My Father honor."

Babylon America's Days will not be prolonged...
Greetings,

Today I was blessed of the Lord just to spend the whole day in His presence in prayer, fasting, and waiting on Him. I did spend a long time praying in the spirit and interceding for the saints too. I did take time to lift you in prayers too. It was a blessing being in His presence. As I lay down just taking a time of silence before the Lord, I was given a quick vision. I was like fallen asleep quickly but for a short time...

Africa...
I had prayed for Africa too and the famine there. In the vision, I saw the hunger spread from other parts of Africa and grow dramatically. The little places where there was food; pests and insects began eating the harvest. I was again shown the little rations of food left in Uganda. However, I saw pests called banana weevils destroy a large harvest in Western Uganda. Therefore, pests eating the harvest exasperated the famine and drought. I saw also the South Africans gather into their storehouse's maize (corn) that again was being attacked and eaten by pests. I know this is just a confirmation of a previous starvation dream I had about famine in Africa. I know it is going to be more severe in the days to come. I also saw many rich people in Uganda again pack their African Prado's (SUVs) because of gas prices and scarcity of gas. I could see chaos and people running to

places they thought would have gas and found none. The nation came to a standstill.

America...

After, I was shown Isaiah 13 and Isaiah 56, which these were to be fulfilled in America soon. After reading, a word was given to me, these were to be fulfilled soon and quick, that there was no more delay. One message was for Babylon America and the other for the saints chosen by God to endure. In Isaiah 13, The Lord is to bring judgment on Babylon America very soon and her destruction will no longer delay, her days have been numbered. The hearts of men will fail. I do not have any more interpretations but the chapter itself is self-explanatory, a confirmation of many things the Lord has shown many of His servants.

Isaiah 13:1-22 "(1) The burden of Babylon, which Isaiah the son of Amoz did see. (2) Lift ye up a banner upon the high mountain, exalt the voice unto them, shake the hand, that they may go into the gates of the nobles. (3) I have commanded my sanctified ones; I have also called My mighty ones for Mine anger, even them that rejoice in My highness. (4) The noise of a multitude in the mountains, like as of a great people; a tumultuous noise of the kingdoms of nations gathered: the LORD of host mustereth the host of the battle. (5) They come from a far country, from the end of heaven, even the LORD, and the weapons of His indignation, to destroy the whole land. (6) Howl ye; for the day of the LORD is at hand; it shall come as a destruction from the Almighty. (7) Therefore, shall all hands be faint, and every man's heart shall melt: (8) and they shall be afraid: pangs and sorrows shall take hold of them; they shall be in pain as a woman that travaileth: they shall be amazed one at another; their faces shall be as flames. (9) Behold, the day of the LORD cometh, cruel both with wrath and with fierce anger, to lay the land desolate: and He shall destroy the sinners thereof out of it. (10) For the stars of heaven and the constellations thereof shall not give their light: the sun shall be darkened in his going forth, and the moon shall not cause her light to shine. (11) And I will punish the world for their evil, and the wicked for their iniquity; and I will cause the arrogance of the proud to cease, and will lay low the haughtiness of the terrible. (12) I will make a man more precious than fine gold; even a man than the golden wedge of Ophir. (13) Therefore, I will shake the heavens, and the earth shall remove out of her place, in the wrath of the LORD of Hosts, and in the day of His fierce anger. (14) And it shall be as the chased roe, and as a sheep that no man taketh up: they shall every man turn to his own people, and flee every one into his own land. (15) Every one that is found shall be thrust through; and every one that is joined unto them shall fall by the sword. (16) Their children also shall be dashed to pieces before their eyes; their houses shall be spoiled, and their wives ravished. (17) Behold, I will stir up the Medes against them, which shall not regard silver; and as for gold, they shall not delight in it. (18) Their bows also shall dash the young men to pieces; and they shall have no pity on the fruit of the womb; their eyes shall not spare children. (19) And Babylon, the glory of kingdoms, the beauty of the Chaldees' Excellency, shall be as when God overthrew Sodom and Gomorrah. (20) It shall never be inhabited, neither shall it be dwelt in from generation to generation: neither shall the Arabian pitch tent there; neither shall the shepherds make their fold there. (21) But wild beasts of the desert shall live there; and their houses shall be full of doleful creatures; and owls shall dwell there, and satyrs shall dance there. (22) And the wild beasts of the islands shall cry in their desolate houses, and dragons in their pleasant palaces: and her time is near to come, and **her days shall not be prolonged**." (This verse was highlighted to me... *her days shall not be prolonged.*)

Isaiah 56 is a prophetic message of encouragement to the saints of God. It is also a stern warning to the leaders of the American church who continue to get drunk with all kinds of blindness and self- imposed stupor from Satan.

Isaiah 56:1-12 "(1) Thus saith the LORD, keep ye judgment, and do justice: for My salvation is near to come, and My righteousness to be revealed. (2) Blessed is the man that doeth this, and the son of man that layeth hold on it; that keepeth the Sabbath from polluting it, and keepeth his hand from doing any evil. (3) Neither let the son of the stranger, that hath joined himself to the LORD, speak, saying, The LORD hath utterly separated me from His people: neither let the eunuch say, Behold, I am a dry tree. (4) For thus saith the LORD unto the eunuchs that keep My Sabbaths, and choose the things that please Me, and take hold of My covenant; (5) Even unto them will I give in Mine house and within My walls, a place and a name better than of sons and of daughters: I will give them an everlasting name, which shall not be cut off. (6) Also the sons of the stranger, that join themselves to the LORD, to serve Him, and to love the name of the LORD, to be His servants, every one that keepeth the Sabbath from polluting it, and taketh hold of My covenant; (7) Even them will I bring to My Holy mountain, and make them joyful in My house of prayer: their burnt offerings and their sacrifices shall be accepted upon Mine altar; for Mine house shall be called a house of prayer for all people. (8) The Lord God, which gathereth the outcasts of Israel saith, yet will I gather others to him, beside those that are gathered unto him. (9) All ye beasts of the field, come to devour, yea, all ye beasts in the forest. (10) His watchmen are blind: they are all ignorant, they are all dumb dogs, they cannot bark; sleeping, lying down, loving to slumber. (11) Yea, they are greedy dogs, which can never have enough, and they are shepherds that cannot understand: they all look to their own way, every one for his gain, from his quarter. (12) Come ye, say they, I will fetch wine, and we will fill ourselves with strong drink; and tomorrow shall be as this day, and much more abundant."

May 2005 Wormwood Vision...

However, as I was seeking the Lord through prayer and fasting through this past May 2005, the Lord showed me a powerful vision. I was taken to the heavens above the earth and I could see the earth in a distance not so far but clearly. Suddenly I heard a very loud sound and vibration with a very heavy zoom sound coming my way, hundred times louder than that of a Boeing 747 Jet. I then saw a very huge rock almost the size of the moon zooming past me at a very high speed with a large tail of fire besides and behind it. In The vision, I was made to feel the waves of vibrations and the heat it generated that hit me but I was protected. It was as if someone was holding me by my collar and snatched me out of its way to a safe distance. I then could see other splintering rocks falling off this huge burning object and catching fire themselves.

I looked to see where it was directed, I knew it was headed for planet earth. I thought well, I hope it lands in the ocean, so not many people will die. However, it seemed targeted to the ocean and the United States. I was like, no Lord no! However, it kept its course targeting the ocean and the United States, it seemed as though someone was controlling its path unhindered and sure to hit its target. The vision ended. I shared the vision with a prayer warrior sister who then told me I had a vision of Revelation 8:10-11.

June 27, 2005 Wormwood Vision...

However, I simply wrote the vision down and well, as we do with many visions, I kept this one and did not give much attention to it until this morning. This time I had a series of visions early in the morning as I got up to pray and they were all related.

Shown the Calendar...

First, I saw someone dressed in a white robe holding a calendar and said to me, "The date has been set back for Wormwood" which I understood as forward...he then showed me the calendar with September/October written on it and the number 7. I did not see the year but I instantly knew it was the Fall Season. I do not know if the number 7 represents 2007, I do not know the meaning but I know it is not that far.

Then I was shown the second vision. People were having their usual life, for some reason I saw people going to get movies at blockbuster and did not seem to care about what was coming. People were busy watching movies. No one was warning anyone, life was going on as normal.

At Chiefs Football Stadium...

Then in the same vision, I was taken to the Chiefs Football Arrowhead Stadium, here in Kansas City. I knew it was Fall and the beginning of the football season. In the vision, it looked like evening and the stadium was packed to capacity with everyone putting on their red Chiefs outfits, the stadium was all red as it normally is here with chiefs games in Kansas City. The game was going on as usual and suddenly there was a very huge loud bang in the sky. Then a huge object I had seen previously in my May vision lit the sky with red fire and zoomed passed across the sky, with very powerful vibrations that threw everyone off their seats and shook the stadium.

Everyone in the stadium began to scream and go hysterical, and run to and fro but could not leave the stadium. The huge ball of fire flew from the east across to the west. I knew it was Wormwood. The stadium officials seemed to have had a clue about the coming disaster but did not warn anyone and also they locked the stadium doors and no one could go out. I then saw something amazing, people began to fall on their knees and pray to God, they knew they were going to die anytime soon. I even saw young toddlers who had come to the game with their parents praying too. I was then taken back to the blockbuster place and people saw the object and heard the band and vibrations but seemed not to care about it, some said, "I will die watching a movie."

Saints Protected, Rise of fierce end-time Preachers of the Word...

After this, I saw another vision, I was taken to a place where I saw believers gathered and protected, I don't know where, but I knew they were Christians because I was given a Bible and I was preaching to them and encouraging them with God's Word. Many other people were encouraging the saints too. However, these who were preaching did so in much more powerful authority than I have ever seen or heard before. They were men and women of authority, as if Jesus Christ had given them His authority. All who were preaching were dressed in white robes with a Bible in their hands. These preachers were powerful and fierce in the face of the devils and they hated all types of evil. They had authority and they commanded judgments on all who stood in their way.

People are always offended at real Bible truth preaching preachers and some times calling them "harsh," unkind or unloving. In this vision, these guys were no joke guys, they were very tough and fierce, they meant what they said, and a powerful Elijah anointing was upon them. They had authority so powerful it shook world leaders and Presidents and they dared not to answer these preachers back. These preachers had such love and passion for the saints and Christ, they seemed to do everything in care for the saints. They spoke with such authority to world leaders and Presidents that they never begged them but just commanded what they wanted done and none of the Presidents dared get into their way for fear of judgments. The preachers seemed to be perfectly in accord with Jesus Christ; they could hear His Commands and do likewise. The believers were protected in a secret place and I know they did survive Wormwood.

Debris more destructive than 2004 Dec Tsunami...
After this, I was shown the debris and damage floating all the way on the Atlantic Ocean because the force of the moving star caused the debris of destroyed buildings to float all the way from Europe and dumped it at the east coast of America with damage that is more excessive. I remembered the Tsunami, it looked like very small compared to the Wormwood damage.

Angels High Tech Room...
I was then taken to a room where I saw men around some very high tech gadgets with screens that looked more like flat screen computer panels, but this was the most advanced technology I had ever seen. I knew the men here were angels, they were all dressed in white robes and they turned on one flat screen panel and showed me the trajectory of the Wormwood star. I was then shocked to look behind Wormwood and find another star following the same trajectory, just a small distance behind Wormwood. This star was also headed for the ocean and the United States; they all seemed to have the United States in their path.

Uganda/Africa...
After this, I was then taken to Africa, in Uganda where I come from. I was shown people, very sad looking to the destruction in the West. In Uganda, the staple food is bananas (Matoke in Luganda, a Ugandan Language); people grow different types of bananas and plantains. However, the path of Wormwood dried up all the banana plantations. There was already a drought before Wormwood and now the little food was gone. People cried because the West that had provided them food was in destruction, fiercer hunger loomed on the horizon. However, I saw the saints gathered for Jesus Christ in numbers. I was encouraging the saints there. I did not see as much destruction from Wormwood in Africa as I saw in the West in the visions, apart from a fierce hunger and famine across the continent.

Encouragement...

I pray that everyone will get deeper into loving Christ Jesus; because He loves His saints and will fight for them. No one knows really what great things He has prepared for those who love Him. Jesus Christ will protect and provide for His own, even in the midst of judgments, even if we die, we go home to be with Him forever.

There is nothing to hold us back from loving the Lord. There is NO HOPE in the things of this world. The silver and gold will be cast into the streets as useless. It is time to reconsider ALL your priorities and what is of value to you. I speak this to American Christians. DON'T waste your time on money, silver, gold and the riches of this world. GO SELL WHAT YOU HAVE AND GIVE TO THE POOR and come follow Jesus Christ. Store and invest in heaven now because the days of your riches, America, are numbered. I say this with sorrow and sadness, please do not be foolish and build your house on sinking sand, build your house on the rock, Jesus Christ. The storm is surely coming, not very far away but very soon to test and beat against both houses and only those who have built on the Rock, Jesus Christ, will withstand the coming days.

However, our faith in Jesus Christ is more precious than gold, though tested, will endure and we shall be with Christ Jesus forever. I cannot wait for those times to come. My spirit is excited, because Wormwood is not for our destruction but we should learn to rejoice in God's Judgments upon the wicked. The saints in heaven sing hallelujah at the unleashing of God's judgments upon the earth, lets get in agreement with them and sing also as Jesus Christ exalts His Holy Name and brings vengeance on all who hate God and practice evil. The saints of the Lord can freely claim Psalms 91 without fear; this is not a time to fear but a time to walk by faith in God.

Persecution and Martyrdom in America...

I had a dream in which there was a very intense persecution of Christians here in America. In this dream, I saw Christians here in Kansas City arrested with all their families and taken to underground locations here in Kansas City. The locations served as a very huge jail and execution house. However, I saw a revival of prayer and repentance in these jailhouses, the prison guards dressed in black uniforms allowed us to pray and have these meetings and even share the Word while in chains and awaiting execution. The men were separated from women and children. They executed both children and parents. Everyday there were people executed and I knew my turn was soon. Many people I knew were executed. However, I was amazed at the guards asking some of the Christians what method they preferred to be executed, lethal injection or beheading, people were given choices.

During this time, an evil President had made a decree that all Christians in America be arrested and executed. However, in the dream I was anticipating meeting Christ Jesus. I woke up and later shared with some of my fellow church people and of course, they dismissed this dream. However, Kansas City, Missouri has some of the largest storage underground facilities being used now by companies to store Data Servers and Data Storage Centers and also by the Post Office. Across the state line in Kansas, especially in Salina, it is known for its underground cities, not mentioning Nebraska where we had the President hide during 911. This Mid- West area has some large underground facilities, I was surprised to find. The Lord spoke to me when I was about 16 years and I was to prepare myself to suffer for Him even to death, so I am not afraid to tell Christians about what is coming.

Kissing Serpents...

I had a dream in which I was shown two former Presidents, Clinton and Bush Senior going on the Tsunami tour of Asia. However, instead of going to Asia, the plane diverted and went to a tropical forest some place here in the USA. However, in the dream, everyone saw them on TV go to Asia but I was disturbed in the dream when the plane diverted and went to this secret tropical forest in the USA. I grew up in Africa so I know very well how tropical forests look like. I was amazed that such a tropical forest existed in the USA with all the huge big tall trees and thickets. The forest was well guarded, and manned, no one was allowed entrance except secret members.

The plane landed in this forest and these two former presidents went on to meet their counterparts from China, Japan and Russia. In this forest, they had some of the best exclusive houses, I had seen. Huge tropical snakes, mainly Cobras and Black Mambas, were raised in this private forest. I was so disturbed again, with what I was seeing. The snakes did no harm to the members but could strike any intruder. I also saw flying snakes that would jump from tree to tree but did no harm to the visitors.

I was following these men and they could not see me nor did the snakes get any sight of me. The Presidents then sat down with their counterparts from these nations and began performing rituals, of which one was smoking cigars. After which I saw them perform a second ritual that was very disgusting, gross, and nauseating. They all gathered and sat down in the living room around an exclusive and expensive coffee table. In the middle of this coffee table, one of the Cobra snakes would pop up its head from an outlet in the coffee table and then each of those men and their counterparts from China, Japan and Russia would kiss the head of this serpent. The ritual went on and on and I was so disgusted mainly because on TV, they showed pictures of these men visiting Tsunami victims but I was seeing them kissing heads of very poisonous and deadly serpents. I was so sickened at the hypocrisy. These men were signing pacts with serpents while TV showed them in Asia helping Tsunami victims. I woke up from the dream shaken with my heart beating so fast at 3:00 a.m. in the morning and I prayed about this dream. I do not have any clear meaning of that dream but I certainly know there is a scheme that is very true going on for the rich men of the earth to rule with power from the chief Serpent who is Satan.

Economic Disaster and Fever Epidemic in Asia...

I had another dream about the economic disasters coming to the world soon. In this dream, I was taken to Asia and in the dream, I visited Vietnam. Again, the Asian economy has collapsed and caused great havoc all over but the most hit country in this dream was Vietnam and India. There was hunger in Asia with scarcity of food due to a drought that came with the economic catastrophe. I saw many Asians this time die from malnutrition and lack of food. Most disturbing of all, was the outbreak of a type of fever not known before. This was caused by a large swarm of big mosquitoes twice the size of a normal mosquito that spread across Vietnam and other parts of Asia especially India. Many people died because the cure was not readily available.

In the dream, I was taken to India and shown bodies on the street of people that had died due to this fever spread by mosquitoes and hunger. In the dream, I began to pray for missionaries who were working in these areas that God would protect them and the communities they worked in from this deadly fever. I also saw many Asian University students some of whom I went to school with here in the USA preaching the gospel from village to village at this time in Asia. I was amazed that they had finally met Jesus Christ. I was then taken to Africa and I saw large numbers of Africans who lived in Europe and America leave the USA and Europe and they headed back to Africa. I saw many expatriates of African origin who came to study here in the USA go back to Africa after this worldwide economic crash. There were no more jobs in the USA; so many people returned to Africa, these included doctors, engineers, teachers, professors and many people. In the dream, I know an event had occurred that changed the world forever. I again was woken up at 3:00 a.m., as usual after such dreams, and I prayed about those events.

Military Draft in USA...

I had this dream in which I saw a huge military draft in the USA. I saw families separated, husbands leaving their wives and then when they learned they were not to come back, many refused to go. Therefore, there was a huge chaos all over. America was at a looming war with a nation I did not get clearly. However, the draft caused huge internal chaos because people refused to go and fight. Troubling in the dream was that the guy heading and pushing this draft was a rebel leader with characteristics of many African ruthless rebels and militiamen. In the dream, I was disturbed that such a rebel junta leader was allowed to lead the United States forces. In the dream, I was praying against this draft because it was time to go preach the gospel all around America and the world. In the dream, I could see many men refuse to go because they were going to preach the gospel and not fight.

The Two Towers...
Tower I...

I had a frightening dream in which I was praying with other Christians here in America. I then saw the Eiffel Tower of Paris grow so tall into the sky and became the tallest tower in the world.

At the top of the tower was a five-pointed star. The Eiffel Tower then had some kind of life in it that it could see all around the world by simply bending its head, which was this five-pointed star. The Eiffel Tower then faced west and begun to walk and come towards Christians who were praying in the USA. I could see that the Eiffel Tower was so furious at the praying Christians. When the tower came to me, it stood and begun to attack and kick the praying Christians. However, there was more fervent prayer and many Christians were repenting and getting deep in prayer. As the Eiffel Tower tried to attack and kick the Christians, it was unexpectedly held back by mighty Angels sent by the Lord. The Eiffel Tower was so stubborn that it tried to fight against the Angels but to no avail. It was thrown down, and could not stand ever again. I woke up shaken and frightened and I prayed about the events in the dream.

Tower II Atlanta Georgia...

After I had dozed off again, I got another vision, this time I was in Atlanta, Georgia. The vision was so frightening more than the first one. I saw a tower this time being constructed, and it was being built in the likes of the Tower of Babel. The construction workers included engineers and many construction companies. Disturbing was that among the construction workers were very evil creatures and demons from hell. I hated these creatures on seeing them; they were very evil, dirty, and filthy and had hate for anyone who did not help in construction of this tower in the center of Atlanta. The construction workers did not care but continued building the Tower that went up all the way to the heavens. I hated the sight, it was so evil but the people in Atlanta did not seem to care.

The dream got so disturbing; these evil creatures among the construction workers would go and feed on the hearts of people. They would go and kill people, take out the hearts of people along the streets in Atlanta and eat the hearts; their food was human heart. However, the only people I saw protected were Christians who were fighting with swords and cutting these evil creatures to pieces. These creatures dreaded anyone with a sword but never the less tried stubbornly to see if they would eat a Christian's heart, only to be cut in pieces by a sword. I woke up again and just got into prayer about the events in the vision, that God would have mercy on the City of Atlanta.

Last Card and Housing Burst

I had a dream in which I was in a classroom with other students. The teacher was a guy well versed in End Times events, he told us that the current President was just playing his cards and that there was a final card, he was to play that would set a domino effect. In the dream I could see the President playing his cards with some other folks, I saw his cards and he had one last card he was about to play that would set events in motion and everyone in the room seemed to know it. For some reason in this dream, this teacher also showed us how this President loved to sing songs taught to him by German teachers while he was young. After this, the teacher took us on a tour of very exclusive American suburbs. However, I began to see the houses in these areas turn very ugly. The Houses seemed to have life in them and these houses hated the people living in them. The houses changed shape from their former beautiful and exclusive state and I could tell they became overweight houses and extremely ugly. The houses were so ugly that people who passed by did not want to look at them.

I was then given Psalms 82 to Psalms 86 and told to share this with Mark. (Mark Watson has a great website at www.markwatson.com) I woke up and prayed. I do not know if the ugly houses have to do with the coming burst in the housing market but I felt that it had to do with that after this dream. I was compelled to tell you that Psalms 82 and 86 would be a confirmation to you and God would surely give you a sign by confirming some of the things He has been telling you. However, the sign means a catastrophic event coming on the earth that would be judgment on the wicked but joy for those who love Christ. Psalms 82:5... all the foundations of the earth are shaken. Psalms 86:17... Show me a sign... that word 'sign' in Greek is 'ot' meaning a visible illustration (forgive my small knowledge of Greek but I am learning), also means a portent, ensign, signpost, a miracle, a mighty deed or event. This word appears 78 times in the Old Testament and used to describe the ten judgments on Egypt... Exodus 10:2.

I believe that when these events begin to happen at greater levels, this will be a confirmation to God's people that God would not release His judgments without first warning His people and showing His servants the prophets. I would like to encourage you that whatever the Lord has been showing you is about to come to pass and that a sign will soon come of a catastrophic event that will be a confirmation about these events perhaps to awake the church further. Well, that is what I had to share with you. I pray that God will continue to bless your ministry and God's protection over you. I need your prayers too. I appreciate every bit of them. I have lots of spiritual warfare going on, especially with the building of my site.

Mushroom Cloud in Memphis

B. H. July 13, 2005

I had this dream back in August 2003, but certain circumstances have brought it to the forefront of my mind over the past few months. A plant that towered over my head in the dream (I am 6'-3") was non-existent back in 2003, but is now right where it was in my dream, and two days ago, went from sagging and blocking our walkway, to standing straight up. I was not the one who did this, and the person who tied it up was not aware of this aspect of the dream. Seeing that plant standing up like that sent chills down my spine and this is why:

> In this dream, I was in my backyard facing west, the direction of the river (I live in Memphis, TN, about 5 miles or so from the river). I was standing directly next to the towering plant I described above. There were no shadows, but I could feel the

sun's warmth (midday?), and the sky was a clear blue. Suddenly, there was a bright flash in the southwest and as a mushroom cloud rose into the sky; the roar of the blast hit me, soon followed by a blast of hot wind. I felt the air grow hot very quickly and I hit my knees. I awoke in a cold sweat, tears streaming down my cheeks.

In addition, two nights ago when I saw that the plant had been bound up like that, as I sat there staring at it, the phrase "it's on a barge" popped into my head. From experience, I have learned to pay close attention when this happens. Today I took out my map of the city and traced a line from my street toward the southwest and the line ran directly between the two bridges. It is quite apparent that an event like this would sever the supply lines across the Mississippi River as well as kill many people in the surrounding area.

I hesitated to write to you about this dream, but when I saw that plant standing tall two nights ago, I had to tell you. Forgive me for waiting as long as I did to pass this on to you. God willing, I will be proven wrong.

Revelation 8:10-11 "(10) And the third angel sounded, and there fell a great star from heaven, burning as it were a lamp, and it fell upon the third part of the rivers, and upon the fountains of waters; (11) And the name of the star is called Wormwood: and the third part of the waters became wormwood; and many men died of the waters, because they were made bitter."

Destruction upon the South, USA

LaTonya N. Malinconico

March 2005

Destruction in the City

Dream One: I was in the middle of tall downtown buildings and a huge flood was coming so a group of people and I decided to hold on to the buildings inside of this tall see-through building. We were a little high up in the business building. The wind was huge and swept away almost anyone who was not holding on to something. And if you were holding on to something, you had to pray and hold as tight as you could because the wind came, then a big wave of water came. Then when people thought they were safe and were starting to get off the buildings, another wave came. I remember I was in the street and I looked to my left side and saw the buildings shaking and slowly water started to come. I started to run back to the building but the dream was in slow motion. I barely made it before the water hit. I think I was in New York because the buildings were so huge. Somehow, we got on a train and were leaving and I remember green grass but there was no conductor and everyone on the train looked tired. Then I woke up. I had forgotten about this dream until I started to research and write about my dream concerning the destruction of the south. So that is why it is posted along the destruction for the south dream. This dream along with many other people's dreams about New York could mean that God is not playing when He shows us the things that will happen. If we do not warn the people, God's judgment will be on us for being bad watchmen. It also serves as a reminder that if we do not have Jesus Christ as our foundation, we will be swept away by the wind and water like a house built on sand. So let us be prepared.

Destruction upon the South, USA

Dream Two: My husband and I were together at my Aunt's House and I was telling them that something was happening outside. It was dark all of a sudden and loud thunders were everywhere suddenly. Then we went through one of the doors in the house and I was outside by myself and there were remnants of water everywhere. There was lightening. Huge lightening and I could tell where they would hit. Very loud!!!! Everything was flooded and desolate. I was looking around and I could see people scattered and homeless people. A few trees still stood tall. I went under one tree because I did not want to be hit by lightening but a woman came and told me not to stand under the tree because there was a huge puddle of water there and the lightening was coming straight for it. In slow motion, she grabbed me and the lightening struck and I felt it a little but it hit her instead. There were people in trenches and they were all scattered everywhere. I woke up and went to the bathroom. There I was just starting to think about the interpretation when God gave me an open vision. It was a map of the United States and zoomed in to the south and there appeared what seemed to be a fault line that spread across the tip of California to the East coast of Florida & Georgia. Under the line, everything was flooded, destroyed or devastated. Then He said that the South would be destroyed because she used to be the Bible belt and now she is a whore! Immoral in sex sins and letting everyone run over her. I walked away and tried to go back to sleep but I couldn't and I felt sad for the South so I prayed to God that He would forgive the sins of the south and prolong her judgment. "(18) Come now, and let us reason together, saith the LORD: though your sins be as scarlet, they shall be as white as snow; though they be red like crimson, they shall be as wool. (19) If ye be willing and obedient, ye shall eat the good of the land: (20) **But if ye refuse and rebel, ye shall be devoured with the sword: for the mouth of the LORD hath spoken it**. (21) How is the faithful city that became a harlot! It was full of judgment; righteousness lodged in it; but now murderers." (Isaiah 1:18-21)

Vision to Evangelist A.A. Allen In the 1950's

As I stood atop the Empire State Building, I could see the Statue of Liberty, illuminating the gateway to the new world. Here, spread before me like an animated map, is an area 60 or 80 miles in diameter. I was amazed that the Spirit of the Lord should so move me, there atop the Empire State building. Why should I feel such a surge of His Spirit and power there?

Suddenly I heard the voice of the Lord. It was so clear and as distinct as a voice could be. It seemed to come from the very midst of the giant telescope; but when I looked at the telescope, I knew it had not come from there, but directly from Heaven. The voice said, 2 CHRONICLES 16:9, "For the eyes of the LORD run to and fro throughout the whole earth, to show Himself strong in the behalf of them whose heart is perfect toward Him. Herein thou had done foolishly; therefore, from henceforth thou shalt have wars." Immediately when I heard the voice of God, I knew this was a quotation of Scripture; but never before had a thing come to me so forcibly by the power of the Spirit.

The ticking of the telescope stopped. The man before me had used up his dime's worth. As he stepped away, I knew that I was next. As I stepped to the telescope and dropped in my dime, immediately the ticking started again. This ticking was an automatic clock, which would allow me to use the telescope for a limited time only. As I swung the telescope to the north, suddenly the Spirit of God came upon me in a way that I had never thought of before. Seemingly, in the Spirit I was entirely caught away. I knew that the telescope itself had nothing to do with the distance, which I was suddenly enabled to see, for I seemed to see things far beyond the range of the telescope, even on a bright, clear day. It was simply that God had chosen this time to reveal these things to me, for as I looked through the telescope, it was not Manhattan Island that I saw, but a far larger view.

That morning much of the view was impaired by fog; but suddenly as the Spirit of the Lord came upon me, the fog seemed to clear until it seemed that I could see for thousands of miles, but that which I was looking upon was not Manhattan Island. It was the entire North American continent spread out before me as a map is spread upon a table. It was not the East River and the Hudson River that I saw on either side, but the Atlantic and the Pacific Oceans; and instead of the Statue of Liberty standing there in the bay on her small island, I saw her standing far out in the Gulf of Mexico. She was between the United States and me.

I suddenly realized that the telescope had nothing to do with what I was seeing but that it was a vision coming directly from God; and to prove this to myself, I took my eyes away from the telescope so that I was no longer looking through the lens, but the same scene remained before me.

There, clear and distinct, lay all the North American continent with all its great cities. To the north lay the Great Lakes. Far to the northeast was New York City. I could see Seattle and Portland far to the northwest. Down the west coast, there were San Francisco and Los Angeles. Closer in the foreground laid New Orleans at the center of the Gulf Coast area. I could see the great towering ranges of the Rocky Mountains and trace with my eye the Continental Divide. All this and more I could see spread out before me as a great map upon a table.

As I looked, suddenly from the sky I saw a giant hand reach down. That gigantic hand was reaching out toward the Statue of Liberty. In a moment, her gleaming torch was torn from her hand, and in it instead was placed a cup; and I saw protruding from that great cup a giant sword, shining as if a great light had been turned upon its glistening edge. Never before had I seen such a sharp, glistening, dangerous sword. It seemed to threaten the entire world. As the great cup was placed in the hand of the Statue of Liberty, I heard these words, "Thus saith the Lord of Hosts, drink ye and be drunken and spew and fall and rise no more because of the sword which I will send." As I heard these words, I recognized them as a quotation from Jeremiah 25:27.

I was amazed to hear the Statue of Liberty speak out in reply, "I WILL NOT DRINK!" Then as the voice of the thunder, I heard again the voice of the Lord saying, "Ye shall certainly drink." (Jeremiah 25:28) Then suddenly the giant hand forced the cup to the lips of the Statue of Liberty, and she became powerless to defend herself. The mighty hand of God forced her to drink every drop from the cup. As she drank the bitter dregs, these were the words that I heard: "Should ye be utterly unpunished? Ye shall not be unpunished, for I will call for a sword upon all the inhabitants of the earth, saith the Lord of hosts." (Jeremiah 27:29)

When the cup was withdrawn from the lips of the Statue of Liberty, I noticed the sword was missing from the cup, which could mean but one thing. THE CONTENTS OF THE CUP HAD BEEN COMPLETELY CONSUMED! I knew that the sword merely typified war, death, and destruction, which is no doubt on the way.

Then as one drunken on too much wine, I saw the Statue of Liberty become unsteady on her feet and begin to stagger and to lose her balance. I saw her splashing in the gulf, trying to regain her balance. I saw her stagger again and again and fall to her knees. As I saw her desperate attempts to regain her balance and rise to her feet again, my heart was moved as never before with compassion for her struggles; but as she staggered there in the gulf, once again I heard these words: "Drink ye and be drunken and spew and fall and rise no more because of the sword which I will send among you." (Jeremiah 25:37)

As I watched, I wondered if the Statue of Liberty would ever be able to regain her feet, if she would ever stand again; and as I watched, it seemed that with all power she struggled to rise and finally staggered to her feet again and stood there swaying drunkenly. I felt sure that at any moment she would fall again, possibly never to rise. I seemed overwhelmed with a desire to reach out my hand to keep her head above water, for I knew that if she ever fell again, she would drown there in the gulf.

"Thou shalt not be afraid for the terror by night, nor for the arrow that flyeth by day, nor for the pestilence that walketh in darkness, nor for the destruction that wasteth at noonday." (Psalms 91:5-6)

Then as I watched, another amazing thing was taking place. Far to the northwest, just out over Alaska, a huge, black cloud was arising. As it rose, it was as black as night. It seemed to be in the shape of a man's head. As it continued to arise, I observed two light spots in the black cloud. It rose further, and a gaping hole appeared. I could see that the black cloud was taking the shape of a skull, for now the huge, white, gaping mouth was plainly visible. Finally, the head was complete. Then the shoulders began to appear; and on either side, long, black arms. It seemed that what I saw was the entire North American continent, spread out like a map upon a table with this terrible skeleton-formed cloud arising from behind the table. It rose steadily until the form was visible down to the waist. At the waist, the skeleton seemed to bend toward the United States, stretching forth a hand toward the east and one toward the west—one toward New York and one toward Seattle. As the awful form stretched forward, I could see that its entire attention seemed focused upon the United States, overlooking Canada at least for the time being. As I saw the horrible black cloud in the form of a skeleton bending toward America, bending from the waist over, reaching down toward Chicago and out toward both coasts, I knew its one interest was to destroy the multitudes.

As I watched in horror, the great black cloud stopped just above the Great Lakes region and turned its face toward New York City. Then out of the horrible, great gaping mouth, began to appear wisps of white vapor, which looked like smoke, as a cigarette smoker would blow puffs of smoke from his mouth. These whitish vapors were being blown toward New York City. The smoke began to spread until it had covered all the eastern part of the United States. Then the skeleton turned to the west and out of the horrible mouth and nostrils came another great puff of white smoke. This time it was blown in the direction of the West Coast. In a few moments' time, the entire West Coast and Los Angeles area were covered with its vapors.

Then toward the center came a third great puff. As I watched, St. Louis and Kansas City were enveloped in its white vapors. Then on they came toward New Orleans. Then on they swept until they reached the Statue of Liberty where she stood staggering drunkenly in the blue waters of the gulf. As the white vapors began to spread around the head of the statue, she took in but one gasping breath and then began to cough as though to rid her lungs of the horrible vapors she had inhaled. One could readily discern by the coughing that those white vapors had seared her lungs. What were these white vapors? Could they signify bacteriological warfare or nerve gas that could destroy multitudes of people in a few moments' time?

Then I heard the voice of God as He spoke again: "Behold, the LORD maketh the earth empty and maketh it waste and turneth it upside-down and scattereth abroad the inhabitants thereof. And it shall be, as with the people, so with the priest; as with the servant, so with his master; as with the maid, so with her mistress; as with the buyer, so with the seller; as with the lender, so with the borrower; as with the taker of usury, so with the give of usury to him. The land shall be utterly emptied and utterly spoiled, for the LORD hath spoken this word. The earth mourneth and fadeth away. The world languisheth and fadeth away. The haughty people of the earth do languish. The earth also is defiled under the inhabitants thereof because they have transgressed the Laws, changed the ordinance, broken the everlasting Covenant; therefore, hath the curse devoured the earth, and they that dwell therein are desolate; therefore, the inhabitants of the earth are burned and few men left." (Isaiah 24:1-6)

As I watched, the coughing grew worse. It sounded like a person about to cough out his lungs. The Statue of Liberty was moaning and groaning. She was in mortal agony. The pain must have been terrific, as repeatedly she tried to clear her lungs of those horrible white vapors. I watched her there in the gulf as she staggered, clutching her lungs and her breast with her hands. Then she fell to her knees. In a moment, she gave one final cough, made a last desperate effort to rise from her knees and then fell face forward into the waters of the gulf and lay still as death. Tears ran down my face as I realized that she was dead! Only the lapping of the waves, splashing over her body, which was partly under the water and partly out of the water, broke the stillness. "A fire devoureth before them, and behind them a flame burneth; the land is as the Garden of Eden before them, and behind them a desolate wilderness, yea, and nothing shall escape them." (Joel 2:3)

Suddenly the silence was shattered by the screaming of sirens. The sirens seemed to scream, "RUN FOR YOUR LIVES!" Never before had I heard such shrill, screaming sirens. They seemed to be everywhere—to the north, the south, the east, and the west. There seemed to be multitudes of sirens; and as I looked, I saw people everywhere running, but it seemed none of them ran more than a few paces, and then they fell. And even as I had seen the Statue of Liberty struggling to regain her poise and balance and finally falling for the last time to die on her face, I now saw millions of people falling in the street, on the sidewalks, struggling. I heard their screams for mercy and help. I heard their horrible coughing as though their lungs had been seared with fire. I heard the moaning and groaning of the doomed and the dying. As I watched, a few finally reached shelters, but only a few ever got to the shelters. Above the moaning and the groaning of the dying multitudes, I heard these words: "A noise shall come even to the ends of the earth, for the Lord hath a controversy with the nations. He will plead with all flesh; He will give them that are wicked to the sword, saith the Lord. Thus saith the Lord of hosts, Behold, evil shall go forth from nation to nation, and a great whirlwind shall be raised up from the coasts of the earth, and the slain of the Lord shall be at that day from one end of the earth even unto the other end of the earth. They shall not be lamented, neither gathered, nor buried; they shall be dung upon the ground." (Jeremiah 25:31-33)

Then suddenly I saw from the Atlantic and from the Pacific and out of the Gulf rocket-like objects that seemed to come up like fish leaping out of the water. High into the air they leaped, each headed in a different direction, but everyone toward the United States. On the ground, the sirens screamed louder, and up from the ground I saw similar rockets beginning to ascend. To me these appeared to be interceptor rockets although they arose from different points all over the United States; however, none of them seemed to be successful in intercepting the rockets that had risen from the ocean on every side. These rockets finally reached their maximum height, slowly turned over and fell back toward the earth in defeat. Then suddenly the rockets, which had leaped out of the oceans like fish, all exploded at once. The explosion was ear splitting. The next thing, which I saw, was a huge ball of fire. The only thing I have ever seen which resembled the thing I saw in my vision was the picture of the explosion of the H-bomb somewhere in the South Pacific. In my vision, it was so real that I seemed to feel a searing heat from it. As the vision spread before my eyes and I viewed the widespread desolation brought about by the terrific explosions, I could not help thinking. While the defenders of our nation have quibbled over what means of defense to use and neglected the only true means of defense, faith and dependence upon the true and living God. The thing which she greatly feared has come upon her! How true it has proven in Psalms 127:1 "Except the Lord builds the house, they labor in vain that build it; except the Lord keep the city, the watchman waketh in vain."

Then as the noise of battle subsided, to my ears came this quotation: "(1) Blow ye the trumpet in Zion and sound an alarm in My Holy mountain; let all the inhabitants of the land tremble, for the day of the Lord cometh, for it is nigh at hand. (2) A day of darkness and of gloominess, a day of clouds and of thick darkness, as the morning spread upon the mountains, a great people and a strong, there hath not been ever the like, neither shall be any more after it, even to the years of many generations. (3) A fire devoureth before them, and behind them a flame burneth; the land is as the Garden of Eden before them, and behind them a desolate wilderness, yea, and nothing shall escape them. (4) The appearance of them is as the appearance of horses; and as horsemen, so shall they run. (5) Like the noise of chariots on the tops of mountains shall they leap, like the noise of a flame of fire that devoureth the stubble, as a strong people set in battle array. (6) Before their face the people shall be much pained; all faces shall gather blackness. (7) They shall run like mighty men; they shall climb the wall like men of war, and they shall march everyone on his ways, and they shall not break their ranks. (8) Neither shall one thrust another; they shall walk everyone in his path; and when they fall upon the sword, they shall not be wounded. (9) They shall run back and forth in the city; they shall run upon the wall; they shall climb up upon the houses; they shall enter in at the windows like a thief. (10) The earth shall quake before them; the heavens shall tremble; the sun and the moon shall be dark, and the stars shall withdraw their shining." (Joel 2:1-10) Then the voice was still. The earth too, was silent, with the silence of death.

Then to my ears came another sound—a sound of distant singing. It was the sweetest music I had ever heard. There was joyful shouting and sounds of happy laughter. Immediately I knew it was the rejoicing of the saints of God. I looked, and there, high in the heavens, above the smoke and poisonous gases, above the noise of the battle, I saw a huge mountain. It seemed to be of solid rock, and I knew at once that this was the Mountain of the Lord. The sounds of music and rejoicing were coming from a cleft high up in the side of the rock mountain. The saints of God were doing the rejoicing. It was God's own people who were singing, dancing, and shouting with joy, safe from all the harm, which had come upon the earth, for they were hidden away in the cleft of the rock. There in the cleft they were shut in, protected by a great, giant hand which reached out of the heavens and which was none other than the hand of God, shutting them in until the storm over passed.

The Crash of the U.S. Stock Market

Stephen Hanson... You will see the **stock market crash** more than it did during the deep depression.

Thomas Gibson... You stand on the verge of the greatest destruction of the economy of this earth. When the great crash (in America) occurs, it (the World Economy) shall come down. You stand on the verge of the greatest economic collapse in the history of mankind.

Harold Eatmon... I saw the **Stock Market soar and then crash**. After the [first] crash, many big business corporations and private parties bought up stocks because of the low cost to buy in. Then I saw *the market begin to climb again in a short period of time. Then it crashed again* bringing tremendous loss, ruin, and devastation to all who bought in the first time. This is what I have labeled "**Two Black Mondays**." The time period between the Two Black Mondays was very close together. I could not tell exactly how close. It could be a couple of days to a couple of months. *There are some telltale signs indicating the season and the setting. *I saw the season to be when 'the leaves fall to the ground' then the first crash would occur. *I also saw the Yen fall dramatically just before this sudden and inexplicable crash.*

Robert Holmes... There will shortly come a time when *Wall Street will collapse.* NO longer shored up by public confidence, it will swagger under the weight of national debt. On a day of frenzied trading, it shall tumble the nation into turmoil and depression. The attention of the creditor nations will be drawn to America. I saw a time of conferences and meetings, international concern and intervention by prominent international organizations in domestic economics and affairs. For the first time in US history, international organizations will intervene in domestic affairs. I saw international troops on US soil. A national economic crisis and localized crises will be announced, and utilizing certain powers, the US President will call FEMA (Federal Emergency Management Agency) into action. You will see black helicopters on television and this will be a sign. When she (America) is weakest, a set of disasters will befall the nation.

David Wilkerson... **The great holocaust follows and economic collapse in America.** The enemy will make its move when we are weak and helpless. America is going to be destroyed by fire! Sudden destruction is coming and few will escape. Unexpectedly, and in one hour, a hydrogen holocaust will engulf America – and this nation will be no more.

I SAW THE RUSSIANS ATTACK THE UNITED STATES

A Vision Given to Henry Gruver

AMOS 3:7 "Surely, the Lord God will do nothing, but He revealeth His secret unto his servants, the prophets."

2 CHRONICLES 20:20 "Believe in the LORD, your God, so shall ye be established; believe His prophets so shall ye prosper."

MATTHEW 18:16 "But if he will not hear thee, then take with thee one or two more, that in the mouth of two or three witnesses every word may be established."

I was in Wales on December 14, 1985. I went up on top of the Eagle Tower in the Caernarvon Castle. It had eight points on it. Each of the points on it were eroded eagles. This castle was built in the 12th century.

I was overlooking the Irish Sea toward the North Sea, Norway, Sweden, Denmark, the tip of Scotland, Greenland, Iceland, in that area. All of a sudden, I was up above the earth looking down upon the earth like a globe. As I looked down on the earth, I saw all of these massive amounts of all kinds of ships and airplanes. They were coming from up above Norway, out of this inlet. They headed down between the United States and Europe. They literally covered the whole Atlantic.

Then I wanted to see what was happening to the United States. I looked over on the globe at the United States. I saw coming out of the United States these radio communication towers. I saw the jagged lines like they draw to show that communications are coming out. All of a

330

sudden, as I was looking down on them, they began to sprinkle down on the earth like dust. I thought, Oh, no! They are not getting through! They are not getting through! They do not know what is happening! They are totally oblivious!

Then I began to see all of these submarines emerging from under the surface. I was surprised at how close they were to our borders! They were in our territorial waters. Then I saw the missiles come out of them. They hit eastern coastal cities of the United States. I looked over across the country where my family was over in the northwest side, and I saw the submarines. I saw the missiles coming out and hitting the western coastal cities. I cried out and said, "Oh, God! Oh, God! When will this be, and what shall be the sign of its coming?" I heard an audible voice speak to me and say, "When Russia opens her doors and lets the masses go. The free world will occupy themselves with transporting, housing, and feeding and caring for the masses, and will let down their weapons and cry peace and safety. Then sudden destruction will come. Then it will come." That was December 14, 1985. Glasnost and Perestroika were unheard of at that time!

1 THESSALONIANS 5:3 "For when they shall say peace and safety, then sudden destruction cometh upon them, as travail upon a woman with child; and they shall not escape."

EZEKIEL 38:10-13 "(10) Thus saith the Lord God: It shall also happen that at the same time shall things come into thy mind, and thou shalt think an evil thought. (11) And thou shalt say, I will go up to the land of unwalled villages; I will go to them that are at rest, that dwell safely, all of them dwelling without walls, and having neither bars nor gates. (12) To take a spoil, and to take a prey, to turn thine hand upon the desolate places that are now inhabited, and upon the people that are gathered out of the nations, which have gotten cattle and goods, that dwell in the midst of the land. (13) Sheba and Dedan (Saudi Arabia) and the merchants of Tarshish (Britain) with all the young lions thereof (the nations that have come from the British Empire-Canada, etc.) shall say unto thee, Art thou come to take a spoil? Hast thou gathered thy company to take a prey, to carry away silver and gold, to take away cattle and goods, to take a great spoil?"

VISION BY A. C. VALDEZ

In 1929, I was preaching in Vancouver, British Colombia. I had gone to the 6th Avenue Church that seats 1,000 people. The old building is gone. I sat down on the platform and looked down at the congregation for the Sunday morning service. There were 18 people. I had crossed the continent from Los Angeles to get to that meeting – 18 people in my first service. My first thought was, My Lord and my God, the nerve, asking me to come across the country to stand here in front of 18 people. Now, that was my first thought. Now, I no sooner thought that when God spoke to my heart and said, "Son, I want you to comfort these people."

They needed comfort, Brother. He gave me the capacity to comfort them. I started preaching comforting words. If I had given way to the human, Brother, I would have skinned them alive and tacked their hides up on the wall. People in a condition like that do not need a skinning; they need comfort. God helped me. He poured in the oil and the wine. He helped me to comfort those people. They began to cry all over the place, as they needed comfort. The tears began to stream down their cheeks. They had gone through a terrible trial in that city, the name of "Pentecost" was in the newspapers of that city, and it was not very good. The things that they had put into the newspapers were enough to keep most anybody away. I had 18 people in the inside and thousands on the outside.

God began to work, and the Spirit began to come forth. By the following Sunday the place was well filled. The Holy Ghost began to bring them in. By the end of the third week, they had to take down the partition that separated the coatroom from the main auditorium to put more seats in that auditorium that seated a thousand. It packed out. They packed the place, standing up and down the winding stairs and outside of the church building and even out into the street. The glory of God came down. Souls began to get saved, and the sick were healed. We had a glorious victory over the world of flesh and the devil. The ministers were so happy. They said, "Lord, in spite of that death, you've given us victory." Right in the middle of that victory, I stood in 6th Avenue Church one day with the power of God on me. All of a sudden the ceiling just disappeared. Now, when I say "vision," my friends, I know that some visions are what the Bible calls "night visions," like in a dream. You will find that in the Bible. Dreams are also called "visions." Generally speaking, a vision is differentiated by what you see with your eyes open, that which you see when you are not asleep.

In this particular case, I was standing on my feet, when all of a sudden the walls and the ceiling just faded right out. I began to see this vision, and the Lord showed me. I looked up and saw what answers to the description of an ICBM (Inter-Continental Ballistic Missile), just as real as any picture that you would see—or the real thing if you've ever seen one of those missiles. It was just as real as you would look upon one if it were right in front of you, two or three feet away! I saw it. It was passing over a skim of clouds, not heavy clouds, but a thin skim of clouds. I was standing on the side of this mountain, a residential district. I was looking over into a bay area. It would appear like I was in Berkeley, if you've ever been to Berkeley, and the Berkeley hills. I was looking into the bay area toward San Francisco, the San Francisco Bay region, that direction.

I saw the freeway. I do not say that it was the Oakland freeway that is there today. I do not know where it was, my friends. I do know this, I was standing on the side of this mountain, overlooking a huge metropolis, when I saw this missile directed toward the city; and suddenly, being electronically controlled, no doubt, it plummeted right down into the city and then exploded. Then I saw the fireball, which answers to the description of what I have seen in a civil defense film release of the first hydrogen bomb explosion. This happened in 1929! The atom was not split until 1932! Yet I saw it as clear as I see you here tonight. There was a purpose in it. I have been warning people ever since that this thing is coming!

As the day approached, my friends, I feel more vibrant than ever before! I must bear testimony to what I saw with my eyes! I must warn God's people that they must live in the Spirit and walk in the Spirit and be filled with the Spirit if they want God's protection in these last days! I saw this thing blossom out in all of its beautiful colors. Did you ever see a picture of it? It is a beautiful sight, but it is a horrible sight. All of the colors of the rainbow you can see in that big ball as it swells out. Then the pressure that it creates following the explosion, it demolishes everything before it. It leaves a crater over 300 feet deep and over 2 miles across. It is capable of destroying a huge metropolis the size of New York City in one blast. Even though there were no freeways in 1929, I saw freeways. I saw them run and jump in their cars to escape, but there was no escape! I saw the aftermath of this explosion. I saw all of the details.

The Spirit of the Lord picked me up. Like St. Paul, whether in the body or out of the body, I do not know! All I know is, my friends, God took me and whisked me across that area where the bomb hit in the midst of that huge metropolis. There was nothing left. The center where it struck was molten, like molten glass. It was not, my friends, until I was carried

334

way beyond the residential area that I began to see any sign of debris. Finally, I came to what looked similar to snow or sand drifts piled up against the fences and buildings. I saw piles or iron, like broom straw, only much finer than broom straw. It was in piles and in patterns—everything destroyed! Finally, way, way out, beyond what I felt was the residential area, I began to find signs of human beings, only in pieces—torsos, heads, hands, arms, and legs. They were scattered around everywhere!

The Spirit of the Lord carried me out farther. I began to find signs of life. People were running. Everybody was blind. (I did not know in 1929 that if you are 35 miles away from the explosion and you happened to be looking in that direction, you would never see again. I did not know that at that time.) Everybody was blind, my friends. They were running and screaming and bumping up against this, that, and the other, bouncing back, children blind and screaming and crying out for their parents and parents for their children. The farther I went, the more the confusion, and the cries increased. My friends, even tonight, while I am speaking to you, I can hear those cries! I can hear those cries, children and parents screaming out for one another! It was a terrible sight to behold! If I were to live 10,000 years, I know I could just close my eyes and hear those screams and see the terror that was written all over the faces of parents and children! It was a terrible sight, indeed.

Then, my friends, The Spirit of the Lord took me. Oh, I wonder how fast I was going. I could see the mountains and the hills just passing before me. I came sweeping down over a large valley. In the distance I could see, as I began to approach, a body of people that looked like tens of thousands. I do not know how many were there. It was a sea of people. Long before I got there, I could see. As I came down closer, I could discern them. They had their handkerchiefs. They were wiping their tears from their eyes. Then for the first time I began to hear heavenly anthems. I could hear the

Hallelujahs, in bass and tenor and soprano and alto, voices blending. That mass of humanity was lifted together by the heavenly music. I came right down in the midst of them. There they were, God's people. This is what I saw, friends. They were all dressed up as if they were ready for the Sunday service. Their hair was parted. Nothing was disturbed. There was no soil on their shirts. They were cared for so perfectly that everything was in order, my friends. Their faces were clean. Their clothing was clean. Everything was in order! The only word you could use to describe them would be "meticulous" Meticulous! Glory to God! What a wonderful thing to be in the hands of God! I say that God is going to protect His people in these last days IF ...they live in the Spirit, walk in the Spirit, and keep filled with the Spirit!

Florida To Be Hit By Mega Hurricane?

Here is an excerpt of Al Cuppett (Retired Joint Chiefs of Staff-U.S. Military) on Frankly Speaking Radio talking about Florida's coming destruction (from part 3 of broadcast aired 7/25/05).

I'm writing this, with little hope that you'll heed or take any action on this admonition. However, maybe if I set the parameters into context properly, when you see them coming to pass, you will have time to escape. Florida will be almost completely destroyed by two "super cell" hurricanes, which will form up, concurrently, from six separate storms. I do not know which year, however, Sept. '05 is not out of the realm of possibility.

To wit, there will be a hurricane come from the Cape Verde Islands, combining as a "super cell," with two already-formed storms somewhere S-SE of Florida. At the same time there will be a hurricane come across Central America into the Gulf; as recently happened, for the first time ever.

This storm will combine with two smaller storms which will have formed in the Gulf; the three forming another "super cell."

These two "super cells" will then move to NE and SW positions off the Florida coasts; before converging and combining together over the state. The resultant destruction will literally be apocalyptic in scope. I have known terrible destruction was coming for years; however, recently, in the past two years, there have been four separate individuals who have been given visions or dreams, by the Holy Spirit, regarding this destruction. The one brother, a personal friend, has never been wrong in the last 11 years.

I am sure that none of you will want to believe the above warning, however, when you see the Pacific storm materialize, then crossing Central America, as well as the Cape Verde Islands-born storm moving westward, you should have time to leave. If you wait no less than about 24 hours before they give the evacuation order you may be able to escape; say like at 1:00 AM. However, be advised, this weather cataclysm will, in the final stages, accelerate quickly, leaving little or no time for National Weather Service evacuation warnings. The destruction will be without precedent over the entire state. Be advised I have at least five Holy Ghost witnesses to this event; plus the Hebrew Bible Code. Warmest regards, in His glad Service, the Lord Jesus Christ, Alex "Al" Cuppett (Retired member of the Joint Chiefs of Staff- US military) another description of the storms Al sent to friends in Florida:

> There will be six storms closing/forming at once. One from the Pacific, across Central America into the Gulf of Mexico, and one from Africa. These two will join four smaller depressions/storms, two on the SE quadrant and two on the west side of Florida. They will combine, eventually, into one huge storm; it is this "monster" storm which will doom the state. If you wait until the storms are

in the form of TWO "super cell" storms, each one threatening Florida directly, you will be caught; unable to evacuate.

Warned to Leave Florida

Renae Gregoire in St. Petersburg, FL

The Lord is leading my family to go to NC... quickly! Over several days from June 20th, 2005 until June 22-23 (?) I sensed the eyes of the Lord upon me. I did not see anything, but sensed like a pair of wings with eyes hovering above me and to my right. The first time, it happened outside. I went into my office and the eyes followed me. I obviously could not work so I asked the Lord why He came. He said, in response to my fears about my salvation, "Do not worry. You are My child. I selected you and chose you before the beginning of time."
END OF DREAMS/VISIONS

I should mention that I read several (at least four) dreams/visions that were sent to me from different people, and I found and read one on my own, that told of a reshaping of America. These particular dreams and visions showed maps that showed California mostly in the ocean, Oregon mostly in the ocean, and a large portion of Washington State in the ocean. In addition, the largest part of Florida was in the ocean and much of the East Coast including the bottom half of the state of Texas. They all showed Texas underwater with Austin, Texas being ocean front property. These parts of the U.S.A. had dropped into the ocean due to natural and man-made disasters, i.e. earthquakes, tsunamis, meteor strikes and or nuclear attacks. The two interesting underlying points that seemed to confirm these dreams and visions were that all their maps were almost identical and it seemed apparent that these four people did not know each other and were unaware of the others dreams and visions. Second, these disasters seemed to follow fault lines in the earth. I would be remiss not to mention at least one of the wonderful deliverances of our Lord for believers during these times. One of hundreds of dreams/visions that stands out in my memory was about a young woman with a baby/small toddler running from wicked soldiers and without food. It was a time of winter and there were no leaves or fruit on the trees, and she was walking in a wilderness area in snow. She stopped and put the little one down, raised her hands to heaven and worshipped Yahweh. The trees started blooming and producing fruit immediately and they stopped and ate! These experiences will be a regular occurrence for true believers during the tribulation time.

These dreams and visions are an awakening blast, a trumpet call to sleeping believers. This is the time of our testing by Yahshua with a refiner's fire, as He is not preparing to marry a whore. His bride will be refined with fire (trials and testing) and be without spot or blemish (trusting Him and being forgiven by repenting, i.e. coming apart from the pagan traditions of Babylonian sun-god worship which spiritually is whoredom to YHWH) when He arrives for marriage. You could not hurt yourself by fasting before your King either. The reason the Scripture indicates all men will hate you because of His Name is that they hate that you have intimacy with Him, the hate is against the relationship you have with Him. Because of that intimate relationship with Yahshua, you will not bow to them and the antichrist system of the world. You cannot live in drunkenness, worldliness, and the cares of this life and receive any help or protection from your Creator! However, obedience and trust in Yahshua guarantees His supernatural protection and favor. He hears heart rendered prayers and He promised to never leave nor forsake you. The problem with most of us is that we have left Him, never spending time with Him. The more words from the Prince of Peace you digest into your spirit, the more peace you will have. The daily confessions in the back of the book have been designed to help you acquire faith and trust so that you will abolish fear, and have His peace.

Where Did You Come From?
And Where Are You Really Going?

Chapter Eighteen:
Recent Bible Code Findings

I have researched many Bible Code findings and code researchers and have found one that I believe has somewhat mastered the research. His name is Roy A. Reinhold. With his permission,, I have included his findings, which I believe are extremely important and helpful. The Bible Codes I have determined are relevant and have a profound effect on the days just ahead are: The Torah (Law/Instructions which are the first five books of the Bible) teaching the Torah is pointing to the Name of YHVH (pronounced Yahweh) in Leviticus, which is the middle Book in the Torah and The End of Days Matrix. At the end of the matrix studies, I will give my take and comments on the Bible Code findings. I have not included the matrixes themselves as these include Hebrew letters with graphs and charts, which my publisher cannot reproduce. These matrixes are freely available for your study and review via the internet at http://biblecodes.us/ and/or http://ad2004.com

TORAH MATRIX

This code is based on what are called ELS or Equidistant Letter Sequences found in the traditional Masoretic Hebrew text of the Torah or Five Books of Moses. The idea is a simple one. According to its supporters there is encoded within the plain text of the Hebrew Torah hidden messages and information. Imagine the entire 304,805 Hebrew letters of the traditional Torah fed into a computer in perfect sequence, much like the sequenced chemical strand of a DNA double helix. The computer then looks for meaningful words and phrases occurring at various intervals or equal distant letter skips; say every 50 letters, or 75, or 100 letters, or really any number one chooses to use, forward or backward in the text.

For example, if you start with Genesis 1:1, go to the first occurrence of the letter Tav (which is at the end of the first word *bereshit*, "In [the] beginning"), count 49 letters, and you come to the letter Vav (50th letter); count another 49 letters and you arrive at Resh; and 49 letters again and you come to the letter Heh—put these together: Tav, Vav, Resh, Heh and you spell a Hebrew word: TORaH (see illustration). It is most interesting that the same thing happens with the first lines of Exodus, the second book of Torah. If you begin with the first Tav (the end of the second word *shemot*), count 49 letters, you come to a Vav, another 49 letters to a Resh, and a fourth 49 letters you end up with a Heh—again TORaH in Hebrew. The third book of the Torah, Leviticus, has a similar pattern, but this time the sacred Name of God (YHVH/Yod, Hey, Vav, Hey) is spelled out every *seven* letters, beginning with the first Yod. Numbers and Deuteronomy continue the pattern, but with the word TORaH spelled *backwards*, every 49 letters. The sacred Name YHVH also is found at the end each of these five books, also at intervals of 49 letters. The question is, are we dealing with a phenomenon that can be explained purely by chance and random sequence, *or* is there some "pattern" that has somehow been inserted by the Author or authors of these texts? Given the number of letters in Genesis (about 78 thousand), one would expect the letters Tav, Vav, Hey, and Resh, to appear in sequence, at various letter intervals, at least two or three times based on chance distribution alone. What is interesting here is the way in which these key terms: Torah and YHVH, appear precisely where they do; at the opening and closing of the Five Books of the Torah, and in a balanced sequence of forward and backward spelling, with YHVH opening Leviticus, at a sequence of seven letters. Such number patterns, of seven and forty-nine, have mystical and historical significance in Hebrew tradition.

The phenomenon is also found in much more complicated ways. Prof. Rips, for example, found that in the single section of Genesis 1:29-3:3, one can find encoded, at various letter sequences, not only the names of the seven edible species of seed-bearing fruits in the land of Israel (barley, wheat, vine, date, olive, fig, and pomegranate), but also the names of the twenty-five trees of the Garden of Eden, delineated by tradition (chestnut, acacia, willow, etc.)—again, all hidden at various equal distant letter skips (5, 18, 9, 14, and so forth). There is no other segment of Genesis of similar length where these words occur at such short intervals (less than 20 letters).

By Roy A. Reinhold, April 2004

The End of Days matrix was first publicly seen on the History Channel TV show, The Bible Codes: Predicting Armageddon, premiering in late 2003 and repeated periodically. In fact, they named the show after this matrix. I looked for the matrix on request by the show's producers, and only had a couple of weeks in my spare time to look for and develop the matrix before filming. You should view this matrix as preliminary, since there is far more in it than shown. However, what is shown in the matrix is sufficient to make the case for the coming of the Messiah in the fall of 2010 (end of Hebrew calendar year 5770).

No, the Governator (The Terminator) does not have anything to do with my matrix, but was a Hollywood movie about the end of days (end-times) which came out in 1999. (There was a picture of The Terminator Movie, which could not be included here)

I think even Hollywood recognizes that we are in unusual times, when predictions from the Revelation (Apocalypse of John) appears to either be occurring or be about to appear.

We have North Korea threatening a showdown unless they receive massive payoffs of food and oil. We have extremist Muslims on a worldwide Jihad. And we have strange new diseases such as SARS, threatening population centers. And strangest of all, we have the VeriChip for chipping people in their hand as John prophesied in Revelation 13. We live in interesting times.

One issue I'd like to address from the History Channel special is something they showed me saying on-air, "that one way we could recognize that the matrix is valid is if my understanding of the scriptural prophecies is true, where 7 years before the coming of the Messiah there would be a peace treaty between Israel and the Palestinians and surrounding Arab nations." I went on to say, "that since the matrix shows the Messiah coming in the fall of 2010, then 7 years prior would be the Fall of 2003. If my understanding of prophecies is correct, then the Peace Treaty should occur in the Fall of 2003."

Actually, this Fall of 2003 issue IS NOT in the matrix. What the matrix shows is the Messiah coming in the Fall of 2010. My offhanded remark while filming was used on-air, perhaps giving the impression that the matrix predicted a Peace Treaty in the Fall of 2003. It does not predict it. Since then, I went back and carefully looked at the prophecy in the scriptures (only 1 verse, in Daniel 9:27), and the verse doesn't necessarily say that the peace treaty begins the end-times 7 year period. It reads in English:

> Daniel 9:27 *"And he will make a firm covenant with the many for one week (period of 7), but in the middle of the week (period of 7) he will put a stop to sacrifice and grain offering; and on the wing of abominations will come one who makes desolate, even until a complete destruction, one that is decreed, is poured out on the one who makes desolate."* (NASB)

The first thing to notice about Daniel 9:27 is that the verb "higbir" is used, which is a Hifil 3ms verb. The Qal (simple active) verb root is "gavar" meaning "to become strong." The Hifil form of the root ver is "causative," meaning in 3ms "he causes to become strong." In other words, nowhere does it say that the "he" initiates the peace treaty (firm covenant with the many for a 7-year period). What it does say is that the beast (antichrist) will come along AFTER the peace treaty is in existence and agree with it, and enforce its provisions so as to cause it to be made strong. We see similar occurrences when there is a new president, and the new president initially signs an Executive Order at least temporarily extending all the treaties and Executive Orders of his predecessor. The new President agrees with and enforces what the previous president had done, until they can study and modify anything, which might need to be changed. Similarly, Daniel 9:27 makes the point that the "he" (antichrist) agrees with and enforces an already existing treaty.

My second point is that the NASB English translation does a poor job in Daniel 9:27, and is wrong in saying, *And he will make a firm covenant...*, since the verb "make" is wrong. The KJV English translation does a much better job of translating "higbir:" as, **and he shall confirm a covenant with many**.

(Comment: By author Thurston McCutchen: I suggest the Covenant referred to in Daniel 9:27 is not anything about a peace deal confirmed by the anti-messiah but is The Covenant that Messiah will confirm with many as the Messiah is the "He" referred to and the subject is His Covenant- and this misunderstanding by many has permeated erroneous thought and conclusions of the church!)

I deliberately used the NASB, because it is wrong on the verb translation, while the KJV is correct in saying "confirm the covenant." The "he" will confirm an already existing peace treaty, agree with its provisions, and enforce it so that it is made strong.

The third point is that the firm covenant with the many (peace treaty), has treaty provisions delineating 7 years of intermediate goals before full, final ratifications. Nowhere does this prophecy say that the peace treaty begins the end-times 7-year period. Yes, the treaty has terms of 7 years, and there is a final 7-year end-times period, but the verse DOES NOT say that these two 7-year periods start and end at the same time. It could mean that it does start the 7- year period, but it doesn't have to. I've come to the conclusion that my matrix is correct and my previous understanding, which I was taught throughout the years, may have led me astray.

My present stance is that the peace treaty has to occur in the next couple of years or else I have made a mistake in understanding what the End of Days matrix is showing me. I can reconcile that Daniel 9:27 does not say that the peace treaty starts the end-times 7-year period only that it has to be done in the first 3.5 years, so that the stopping of sacrifices and grain offerings occurs in the middle of the 7-year period. Therefore, I believe my End of Days matrix is correct in predicting the Messiah coming at the end of 5770 (Fall of 2010).

All the terms in the End of Days matrix are sentences, and the statistical odds of the matrix are 1 chance in 7.3 times 10 to the 97th power. Additionally, 3 terms in the matrix have 5770 in them, related to end-times prophetic events. I am not relying on one term in the matrix, but 3 terms to verify the year. For those not statistically inclined, 10 to 97th power means: 7.3 with 97 zeroes after it. All scientists in the world agree that chance in the universe cannot exceed 1 chance in 10 to the 50th power, so this matrix is well beyond chance in the universe. It is a matrix with terms that are sentences and all the thematically related (they are on the same topic).

The following is the matrix report.

1. In 5770 (fall of 2010), a lion (Lion of Judah) is against Har Megiddo. He laid it waste. You are finished. **12488** 20.558 22.22 1 Leviticus Chapter 2 V5 Letter 23

2. Gather yourselves together, that I may tell you that which shall befall you in the last days. Gather yourselves together, and hear, you sons of Yaakov, and hearken to Israel your father. **1** 0.0000.000 Genesis Chapter 49 V1 Letter 21

3. And the evil divisiveness (is) indeed of 5770 (Fall of 2010), of its towns; and He purified the heart for me a people. **37466** 15.094 16.757 Leviticus Chapter 13 V45 Letter 41

4. He covered the coldness of 5770 (Fall of 2010); command "Days of HaShem" **24970** 11.575 13.238 Genesis Chapter 30 V32 Letter 55

5. He anointed your perfection to give a sea with Him. With power, YHVH (Yahweh) subdued them. A mountain of them

I will answer, "Enough." -**12488** 3 1.602 33.265 Genesis Chapter 39 V4 Letter 8

6. Who comes from them? He scorned Bel of Sheol, the head of it. **12488**   12.384 14.047 Numbers Chapter 28 V3 Letter 52

The ELS reference is 12488 characters between rows. There are 6 displayed terms in the matrix. The matrix starts at Leviticus 13 V44 Letter 37 and ends at Genesis 39 v5 Letter 6. The matrix spans 811819 characters of the surface text. The matrix has 66 rows, is 99 columns wide and contains a total of 6534 characters.

Matrix odds (as shown above): Total matrix R-value = 97.865. That translates to matrix odds of 1 chance in 7.328 times 10 to the 97th power. (Add 97 zeroes to 7.328)

The main term has two key sub-terms in it: 1. 5770 (2010) 2. Har Megiddo (Armageddon of Revelation). It is a telling term with 24-letter reading, "In 5770 a lion is against Har Megiddo. He laid it to waste. You are finished." As a Christian, my understanding of the Bible is that the Messiah is referred to as the "Lion of Judah." The prophecies tell us that the Messiah will not come again as a meek and mild mannered individual, but as a victor in battle riding a white horse. In Revelation 19, He is shown leading the armies of Heaven on white horses and He has a sword proceeding out of His mouth, which is symbolically the sword of the Spirit of God, which is the Word of God. Isaiah 63:3-4 NASB reads, *"I have trodden the wine press alone, and from the peoples there was no man with Me. I also trod them in My anger, and trampled them in My wrath; and their life blood is sprinkled on My garments, and I stained all My raiment. For the Day of Vengeance was in My heart, and My year of redemption has come."*

Messiah as a lion, Hosea 11:10-11, NASB (also Isaiah 31:4-5, Hosea 13:7; 5:14 to 6:2) *"They will walk after the Lord, He will roar like a lion; indeed He will roar, and His sons will come trembling from the west. They will come trembling like birds from Egypt, and like doves from the land of Assyria, and I will settle them in their houses, declares the Lord."*

The Valley of Megiddo is in the middle of Israel, due east from Mount Carmel/Haifa. It is a broad plain and the old ruins of the city of Megiddo lies on top of a hill or small mountain (har means mountain) on the south side of the valley, midway between Haifa and the Jordan river. The armies of the earth will assemble themselves in the Valley of Megiddo to fight against Messiah and the armies of Heaven. The battle is over very quickly and the Messiah will reign over all the earth. That is why the term "har megiddo" is very important in the matrix. The Lion of Judah will conquer the forces of the antichrist there.

As you can see, the main term in the matrix sets the theme and is in agreement with the prophetic scriptures. What is also important in the term is that it identifies 5770 (end of which is the Fall of 2010). I should mention that I looked for 30 years from 2004 to 2034 to see if any of these years were in the same term with Har Megiddo, and only 5770 was there.

Next, term 3 also has 5770 in it. It reads, "And the evil divisiveness (is) indeed of 5770, of its towns; and He purified the heart for me of a people." The Messiah is coming in a time of evil when people have turned away from God the Creator. The Messiah will prophetically fulfill appointed time of Yom Kippur (The Day of Atonement or Judgment Day). He will purify the hearts of the people towards and for God. Again, it mentions this happens in 5770 (end of 5770 in the Fall of 2010).

The third term with 5770 is term 4. It reads "He covered the coldness of 5770;" command, "Days of HaShem." HaShem is what the Jewish people use for the name of God, YHVH, and it means, "the name." The coldness of 5770 is the rebellion of the peoples of the earth in their hearts against God. Again it identifies this in 5770, and the Messiah will cover the cold hearts of the peoples towards God. The last part, "command, Days of HaShem," also is extremely meaningful in identifying this time as the beginning of something special called the Days Of HaShem. It will happen in 5770.

I included the long surface text (Genesis 49:1-2) because "akharit hayamim," meaning the end of days, was one of my search terms. It just happened to go right through the middle of my main term. Genesis 49:1-2 is the beginning of the blessings that Jacob (Israel) gave to his sons before he died.

Genesis 49:1-2 NASB, "Then Jacob summoned his sons and said, Assemble yourselves that I may tell you what shall befall you in the end of days. Gather together and hear, O sons of Jacob; and listen to Israel your father."

I said it just happened to occur there, but.....is it really coincidence given all the rest that is in the matrix? Terms 5 and 6 add to the matrix by corroborating the theme and delineating new pieces of information. In term 5, the one anointed with perfection is the Messiah. It tells us that the appointed time has come when YHVH, our God says, "Enough." Enough of the rebellion from your freewill misused enough of mistreatment of others, enough of the mistreatment of God's people. In term 6, the spiritual leader of the forces who oppose Messiah is identified as Bel of Sheol. Sheol is hell or the pit, and Bel is the ancient god who rebelled as a watcher and was cast out of Heaven.

I have developed the matrix more, but <u>what is shown is sufficient to make the case for the Messiah coming at the end of 5770</u> **(Fall of 2010)**. ***SEE NOTE BELOW***

If you have questions or comments, feel free to visit my website at *http://ad2004.com*   *Roy A. Reinhold*

** Author Thurston McCutchen's Note:

My own take on this matrix does not confirm his exact conclusion. I expect <u>Messiah's judgment falls</u> on Judah and Ephraim (All Israel) in the Fall of 2010 (September-October) at the Feast of Trumpets. This will be <u>seven biblical months after Aviv one</u> when the new biblical year starts in March or April of 2010. (14 days before Passover). This is when I believe the judgment of Ephraim, the scattered tribes for remaining in pagan traditions- lawlessness; and Judah for rejecting Messiah Yahshua. <u>ALL</u> Israel's scales are removed because judgment is finished for pagan traditions and lies we inherited. The times of the Goyim or Gentiles is fulfilled. We all are mercifully given 7 months to repent and come apart from the pagan traditions and be sober and alert! The Jews are likewise given the same seven months to repent and accept Messiah Yahshua who is the Jewish Messiah of all. These rockets flying will indeed be the only pre-trib rapture many have erroneously taught. The main problem with this "rapture" is that **it is thermonuclear!** Rockets fly and most of unrepentant and sleepy Ephraim (Christians) will be separated from their bodies and be present with the Messiah! *(Comment: I call most of the church "sleepy" because they are mainly interested in their own welfare and getting away in some pre-trib rapture myth/wish when in truth YHWH will deliver us in the tribulations not from it!)* Then they may be in the presence of YHWH with no righteous robes to wear. We are to produce fruit for the Kingdom or be ashamed at His appearing, as our righteous acts provide the robes of righteousness in the Kingdom of YHWH. I expect His second coming at the last Jubilee at the Feast of Trumpets 2017. Here are the scriptures again to help you understand why judgment falls on sleepy and <u>drunk Ephraim</u> (in lieu of sober and alert!) for your consideration as *those that divide*

Jerusalem (Part His land) will be quickly destroyed and the USA (The crown of pride drunk and asleep Ephraim) is and has played a key role in forcing this! (Joel 3:2) I will also gather all nations, and will bring them down into the valley of Jehoshaphat, and will plead with them there for My people and *for* My heritage Israel, <u>whom they have scattered among the nations</u>, and **parted My land**.

Isaiah 28:3-22 "(3) The **crown of pride**, the **drunkards of Ephraim**, (mainly USA) **shall be trodden under feet:** (4) And the glorious beauty, which *is* on the head of the fat valley, shall be a fading flower, *and* as the hasty fruit before the summer; which *when* he that looks upon it sees, while it is yet in his hand he eats it up. (5) In that day shall YHWH of hosts be for a crown of glory, and for a diadem of beauty, unto the residue of his people, (6) And for a spirit of judgment to him that sits in judgment, and for strength to them that turn the battle to the gate. (7) But they also have erred through wine, and through strong drink are out of the way; the priest and the prophet have erred through strong drink, they are swallowed up of wine, they are out of the way through strong drink; they err in vision, they stumble *in* judgment. (8) For all tables are full of vomit *and* filthiness, *so that there is* no place *clean. (Comment: traditions inherited of sun god and Easter fertility goddess worship)* (9) Whom shall he teach knowledge? And whom shall he make to understand doctrine? *Them that are* weaned from the milk, *and* drawn from the breasts. (10) For precept *must be* upon precept, precept upon precept; line upon line, line upon line; here a little, *and* there a little: (11) For with stammering lips and another tongue will he speak to this people. (12) To whom He said this *is* the rest *wherewith* you may cause the weary to rest; and this is the refreshing: yet they would not hear. (13) But the word of YHWH was unto them precept upon precept, precept upon precept; line upon line, line upon line; here a little, *and* there a little; that they might go, and fall backward, and be broken, and snared, and taken. (14) Wherefore hear the word of YHWH, **you scornful men, that rule this people which** *is* **in Jerusalem**. *(Comment: This is not just Israel's rulers but more likely the rulers of the USA and others of the world elite who are determined to set up their own New World Order and Kingdom that they, not YHWH, will rule)* (15) Because you have said, we have made a covenant with death, and with hell are we at agreement; when the overflowing scourge shall pass through, it shall not come unto us: for we have made lies our refuge, and under falsehood have we hid ourselves: (16) Therefore thus says YHWH, Behold, I lay in Zion for a foundation a stone, a tried stone, a precious corner *stone*, a sure foundation: he that believes shall not make haste. (17) Judgments also will I lay to the line, and righteousness to the plummet: and the hail shall sweep away the refuge of lies, and the waters shall overflow the hiding place. (18) And your covenant with death *(Comment: Oslo accords and Oslo in Modern Hebrew means toilet seat)* shall be disannulled, and your agreement with hell shall not stand; when the overflowing scourge shall pass through, then you shall be trodden down by it. *(Comment: I believe the overwhelming scourge is rockets flying in the Fall of 2010- first to USA and simultaneously to Israel which YHWH leaves a remnant of 1/3: (Zechariah 13:9) And I will bring the third part into the fire, and will refine them as silver is refined, and will try them as gold is tried. They shall call on my name, and I will hear them: I will say, It is my people; and they shall say, YHWH is my God.) YHWH alone will be Israel's help- who are His people!)* (19) From the time that it goes forth it shall take you: for morning by morning shall it pass over, by day and by night: and it shall be a vexation only *to* understand the report. (20) For the bed is shorter than that *a man* can stretch himself *on it*: and the covering narrower than that he can wrap himself *in it*. (21) For YHWH shall rise up as *in* mount Perazim, He shall be wroth as *in* the valley of Gibeon, that he may do his work, his strange work; and bring to pass his act, his strange act. (22) Now therefore be you not mockers, lest your bands be made strong: for I have heard from YHWH of host's consumption, **even determined upon the whole earth**."

*Remember when the world says **PEACE AND SAFETY**-sudden destruction comes on them! It will come on the world like a thief in the night, but we are children of the light- it will not surprise us! Prepare.*

Blessings- Thurston

For the serious Bible student of YHWH I want to recommend a book by a dear brother in Yahshua you may order at www.Amazon.com:

EPIDEMIC! By Dr. Russ Houck

This book will stimulate and challenge everything you think you know about God and how He wants to be known and worshipped!

By Thurston McCutchen

It is nothing less than astonishing to me, as I have prayed and studied these scriptures, dreams, visions, and yes, even these Bible codes seem to help make sense of the warning messages given. It is astonishing in that they predict or tell of time frames that just happen to match up perfectly with the Feasts of the Lord, which were prophetically given as rehearsals for believers. These Feasts of the Lord are given to us to teach the *appointed times* that YHVH has pre-determined for all events to take place. This includes End Time events. Isaiah 42:8-9 has Yahweh Speaking, "(8) I am YHVH (Yahweh): that is my name, and my glory I will not give to another, neither my praise to graven images. (9) Behold, the former things are come to pass, and the new things I declare: before they spring up I tell you of them." Yahshua speaks the same promise in John 13:19, "Now I tell you before it comes to pass, so that when it does come to pass, you may believe that I am He." As far as the 7-year peace agreement is concerning the end of days, I believe it is the Oslo accords that were signed in 1993 at the same time the "one world" church came into existence whose bylaws exclude any God or Deity being the ONLY WAY to heaven. The One World Religion's Charter declares the penalty for any religion declaring their way is the only way is loss of citizenship in the world. Of course, without citizenship you have no rights and can be killed without breaking any law. Much like they did to the Jews during WWII, they will declare us less than human. Of course, the Word declares that the covenant of death (as Yahshua calls this peace agreement in Isaiah 28:18) will not stand, that He will annul it, and of course He did just that in 2000.

What is the visible and prophetic event that will occur to partially verify this code? I believe it is the nuking of Damascus according to the scripture passage in Isaiah 17:1, "The burden of Damascus, Behold, and Damascus is taken away from being a city and shall be a ruinous heap." It is pretty well a foregone conclusion that much of the other information supplied in this code has already been verified by intelligence sources. Why would Israel or America (the ships from the West or the Coastlands) want to attack Damascus? Because that is where the weapons of mass destruction are stored and where the so-called Muslim party of God, "Hezbollah" operates from, which does the training for most of the Muslim terror organizations throughout the world. They will do something so horrible, probably a suitcase nuke or biologicals or both, here in the USA or Israel that leaves the USA and/or Israel not caring what the world opinion is concerning this nuking of them. Later in the year, or at least by the Feast of Trumpets 2010 (September/October time frame), I believe that a nuclear and biological surprise strike will occur. Armies will surround Israel but the nearly simultaneous attack will occur first against the USA and then Israel by China, Russia, Cuba and many Muslim countries. How does this tie in with the End of Days Matrix Bible Code? The End of Days Matrix shows that the Messiah destroys His enemies in the Fall of 5770 (Hebrew or Jewish year) which would give us the time frame of September/October 2010 and be on the Feast of Trumpets also known as the Day that no man knows the day or hour. It is a Hebrew idiom. Even so, I do not believe it is out of the realm of speculation that we will have an economic collapse prior to these attacks mentioned in the Bible Codes. Satan will always create disorder so that the antichrist can bring order and be the answer and remedy for many. So, how then should we prepare if we see these things come to pass? We should repent of all transgressions, ask for forgiveness and study the word daily that we may have faith in our Messiah who has told us the end from the beginning. Turn off the television and all distractions and find time to learn of this Messiah and eat the bread of life, which is His word. If you are fearful at this point, then you need to take the time to receive the knowledge or a revealing of His love for you. Remember, faith comes by hearing and hearing the word of Yahweh (Scriptures) according to Romans 10:17. Hear the Word and hear the Word until it is written in your mind.

Perfect love casts out all fear. A great way to help build your faith also is to hear and see the testimony of other believers who have overcome based on the scripture promises and www.sidroth.org is a great website for doing that. According to 2 Timothy 1:7, "Yahweh has not given us a spirit of fear, but a spirit of power, love, and a sound mind." And Matthew 10:28-31 where Yahshua reminds us, "(28) Fear not them that can only kill the body and not the soul; but rather fear Him who can destroy both body and soul in hell. (29) Are not two sparrows sold for a little? And not one of them shall fall to the ground without your Father. (30) But the hairs of your head are all numbered. (31) Do not fear, therefore, you are of more value than many sparrows." He has promised that whoever calls on the name of the Lord

(Yahshua) shall be delivered. Remember Yahshua hears heart rendered prayers, and the Holy Spirit will guide you into all truth and teach you of things to come. Finally, remember Yahshua's instruction to pray that you be made worthy to escape and endure all these things coming on the Earth to test those of us living on the Earth and that we may stand at His appearing unashamed. It is not a question of just living, as there would be little purpose for that, but the goal here is to produce much fruit for the Kingdom of Heaven and accomplish the purpose and destiny for which we were created. Any goal short of our Creator's plan for us is unacceptable!

Now give Him thanks, as you have whatever you ask for that is according to His word. A thousand may fall at your left and ten thousand at your right hand, but the pestilence shall not come near you or your house, family and friends. Only believe, for all things are possible to the one who believes. As you submit to the word of life, the devil will flee from you. Lastly, remember that Yahweh (YHWH) inhabits the praises of His people and the spirit of fear cannot stay around His presence. So enter His gates with thanksgiving and enter His courts with praise! If these codes are accurate, then where is the safe place to be? Should you flee to another country? Maybe, but only if you feel led by His peace, <u>NOT BY FEAR</u>! Wherever you have His peace and are doing what Yahweh has called you to do. ***Being in His perfect will by worshipping, hearing and obeying is your safe zone!*** If these codes are correct, and the numbers are mathematically literally millions of times past the number assigned to random chance possibilities, then as my friend Michael Rood says, "I'll see you when the smoke clears!" Hopefully, in the Messiah's Kingdom back home in Israel.

Of course, we should be aware of the real possibility and hopefully a probability; that the codes, dreams, and visions may have been delivered

100% accurate and still misunderstood, misinterpreted and incorrectly presented here!

If these Bible Codes, dreams, and visions are all wrong, then we can give thanks and praise Yahweh that we have more time to share His love with others and get to know Him better ourselves! *Either way, let us be active about our Heavenly Father's business.*

Shalom and Blessings,

Thurston Ben McCutchen

TIMELY UPDATE FOR YOUR CONSIDERATION!

Remember we get progressive revelation, i.e. as we have a need to know and seek Him with all our hearts, He will answer and reveal to us. This is what I believe YHWH has shown me but of great importance is your understanding that no matter what I was shown or told, the room for error in interpreting is colossal. Please pray (and possibly fast) and ask for confirmation before accepting any of this.

**THIS UPDATE IS THE WRITTEN ACCOUNT THAT HAS BEEN DISCUSSED PREVIOUSLY IN THE THIRD NEWSLETTER-SHABBAT SHALOM LOVED ONE!

The Warning

Praise YHWH, He does not give us a spirit of fear!

I give this information as personal revelation. It was given me on the 40th day of a 40 day fast the end of June 2008. I **do not** give it to you guaranteed as thus says YHWH. Obviously, I believe it was from my Messiah Yahshua and the Ruach Ha Kodesh (Holy Spirit) but only YHWH can give you your interpretation. I freely admit if it was truly from YHWH, it is still filtered and written down by an imperfect servant of His, namely myself. I urge you to pray, fast and seek for yourself His timeline and plans He has for you and never rely on someone else's personal revelations. Remember His promise for the end of the age believers in **Ezekiel 14** concerning our deliverance and ability to help deliver our own sons and daughters from the trials during the times of Jacob's trouble or the Great Tribulation of the saints and followers of Messiah Yahshua mentioned in Revelation. Remember that only those who seek Him with all their hearts and call on His name will be delivered. He alone will be the sole deliverer of the believers.

Act 2:16-22 "(16) but this is that which hath been spoken through the prophet Joel: (17) And it shall be in the last days, says YHWH, I will pour forth of My Spirit upon all flesh: And your sons and your daughters shall prophesy, And your young men shall see visions, And your old men shall dream dreams: (18) Yes and on My servants and on My handmaidens in those days I will pour forth of My Spirit; and they shall prophesy. (19) And I will show wonders in the heaven above, and signs on the earth beneath; Blood, and fire, and vapor of smoke: (20) The sun shall be turned into darkness, And the moon into blood, Before the day of the Lord come, That great and notable *day*. (21) And it shall be that whosoever shall call on the name of the Messiah Yahshua shall be saved, delivered and healed."

After you read these scriptures for us living at the end of the ages (you and I reading this) I will share what I believe I was shown as a partial and incomplete timeline for the last day believers.

The Scripture Warning
Ezekiel 14:7-20 "(7) For every one of the house of Israel, or of the strangers that sojourn in Israel, that separates himself from Me, and taking his idols into his heart, and putting the stumbling block of his iniquity before his face, and comes to the prophet to inquire for himself of Me; I YHWH will answer him by myself: (8) and I will set My face against that

man, and will make him an astonishment, for a sign and a proverb, and I will cut him off from the midst of My people; and you shall know that I am YHWH. (9) And if the prophet be deceived and speak a word, I, YHWH, have deceived that prophet, and I will stretch out My hand upon him, and will destroy him from the midst of My people Israel. (10) And they shall bear their iniquity: the iniquity of the prophet shall be even as the iniquity of him that seeks *him*; (11) that the house of Israel may go no more astray from Me, neither defile themselves anymore with all their transgressions; but that they may be My people, and I may be their Elohim, says YHWH. (12) And the Word of YHWH came unto Me, saying, (13) Son of man, when a land sins against Me by committing a trespass, and I stretch out My hand upon it, and break the staff of the bread thereof, and send famine upon it, and cut off from it man and beast; (14) though these three men, **<u>Noah, Daniel, and Job</u>**, were in it, they should deliver but their own souls by their righteousness, says YHWH. (15) If I cause evil beasts to pass through the land, and they ravage it, and it be made desolate, so that no man may pass through because of the beasts; (16) though these three men were in it, as I live, says YHWH, they should deliver neither sons nor daughters; they only should be delivered, but the land should be desolate. (17) Or if I bring a sword upon that land, and say, Sword, go through the land; so that I cut off from it man and beast; (18) though these three men were in it, as I live, says YHWH Elohim, they should deliver neither sons nor daughters, but they only should be delivered themselves. (19) Or if I send a pestilence into that land, and pour out My wrath upon it in blood, to cut off from it man and beast; (20) though Noah, Daniel, and Job, were in it, as I live, says YHWH, they should deliver neither son nor daughter; they should but deliver their own souls by their righteousness." We can be guaranteed by these Scriptures that we can deliver only ourselves by the righteousness given us by

Messiah Yahshua. **Needless to say only the true children of YHWH (those born again who will seek His face) will be delivered and even be able to follow Him to safety.** I want to touch on one more set of Scriptures about the destiny of the saints (believers and followers of Yahshua). We are Commanded to pray (being sober and alert) that we be made worthy to escape and endure, producing fruit for the Kingdom of YHWH and stand at His (Yahshua's) appearing unashamed. We will need to produce fruit to have robes of righteousness at the wedding supper of the Lamb. (Even invited, it wouldn't be much fun to be thrown out with no wedding clothes on.)

Luke 21:36 "But you watch at every season, making supplication that you may prevail to escape all these things that shall come to pass, and stand before the Son of Man."

2 Timothy 2:12-13 "(12) If we endure, we shall also reign with Him: if we shall deny Him, He also will deny us: (13) If we are faithless, He remains faithful; for He cannot deny Himself."

Here are the destinies prepared for the saints: Revelation 13:9-10 "(9) if any man hath an ear, let him hear. (10) If any man is for captivity, into captivity he goes: if any man shall kill with the sword, with the sword must he be killed. Here is the patience and the faith of the saints."

One: Whoever leads men toward captivity (probably thinking they go free and save themselves if they will turn others in) into captivity YHWH promises they will go.

Two: Whoever thinks they can kill others and defend themselves (defensive or offensive-by the sword, guns, or other means) they will be killed in a like manner. Remember we are cautioned to escape.

Three: The faith and patience of the saints (many obedient believers) will **escape and endure** and **stand at His appearing unashamed**. We can be unashamed if we give ourselves to producing fruit for His Kingdom-even at the risk of certain death.

Timeline I believe I was told to write down

July 2008- March 2010 is preparation time for the sober and alert believers. Make sure you are about the Father's business. Anti-messiah is preparing his means of tracking and destroying the saints of YHWH as they consolidate world currencies. Remember there will be no buying and selling if you don't take the anti-Christ's mark I expect by Passover 2014. If you are sober and alert and have "Come out of her my people that you do not partake of her plagues" you will have a means to survive by farming, bartering and especially angelic host feeding and protecting you. Remember here that **Babylon the whore** that rules over the people (Earth) is a religious system (spiritual), a mindset and attitude of the world (soul); and a physical country or countries (body) mainly USA. So we have spirit, soul and body. Whoever takes the mark of the beast will be condemned to the fire of hell for eternity. Remember you are a spirit being, you have a soul or mind, will, and intellect, and you live in a body which is physical. Your spirit is the real you as Peter (Kefa) called this the "hidden man of the heart," and your spirit will be eternal and live somewhere forever: the lake of fire for the unrepentant and rebellious and the Kingdom for those who endure to the end as born again- even unto death and do not deny Yahshua and His Kingdom, nor take the mark of the beast or pledge allegiance to the anti-Christ. Please understand that "**no man knows the day or hour**" is a Hebrew idiom for the Feast of Trumpets- the only Feast of the Lord there is no preparation time for! I expect March 2010 to be the last safe time to easily and safely exit the USA.

October 2008- October 2010 economic failure; USA stock market and currency failure causes worldwide problems, famines, diseases, and civil unrest. The civil unrest in the USA will be catastrophic and lead to martial law, forced vaccinations from the elite power brokers of the world and many millions dead. The world elite are determined to bring in AMERO currency to Mexico, USA, and Canada. This has been done by international treaty in 2005 to be installed in 2010 and citizens and legislators will have no say. Martial law likely and congress will be disbanded. During this time Israel will strike Iran's nuclear facilities and Isaiah 17:1 will likely happen toward the end of this time and Damascus will be taken away from being a city, and become a ruinous heap. Common defense treaties between the Arab countries and Russia spark the wars below.

September or October 2010 (FEAST OF TRUMPETS) Russia and a large Muslim and Chinese army will attack Israel and the scattered tribes (believers in USA) regarding **Ezekiel 38 and 39**. The USA will become a divided and second rate nation and will have no desire, will, or ability to stand up for Israel again, as the Russian led federation of Muslims' army come for the food and gold (spoil) which is mainly the livestock and grain farms in the midst of the land (heartland of USA) which are the un-walled villages of those dwelling safely gathered from all the earth. All but 1/6th of this Russian led Muslim army will be destroyed by brimstone and fire (their eyes will melt in their sockets before their bones hit the ground in the mountains of Israel) I believe this is simultaneous attack on the USA and then Israel. The USA will not be the deliverer of Israel, only YHWH will. Judgment of Ephraim and Judah (Unrepentant Christians and Jews) begins at YHWH's house first. (1 Peter 4:17) For the time *is come* that judgment must begin at the house of God: and if *it* first *begin* at us, what shall the end *be* of them that obey not the gospel of God?

Feast of Trumpets 2010 (This Feast of Trumpets is in September-October timeframe of 2010 above to the Feast of Trumpets 2017

September-October timeframe 2017) - burying the bones of a destroyed army in Israel, and using fuel of a destroyed army for 7 years.

Feast of Trumpets 2010- For 7 months cleaning the Temple mount until Passover 2011 which will be April-May timeline of 2011 and will start the sacrifices on the Temple mount again. (DO NOT speak against these sacrifices as a believer even if you do not understand; YHWH sends out an angel and commands him to measure His temple- **whose temple you are**- to see who agrees with these things- remember it is the **anti-Christ who STOPS the sacrifices DO NOT AGREE WITH THE Anti-Christ!** Next YHWH sends another angel and says slay all those who disagree with their tongues with my sacrifices (which are a sweet aroma to YHWH). All of the Muslim countries who hated Israel and wanted Israel destroyed and drowned in the sea will be annihilated and be no more by YHWH. YHWH declares He will get honor for His great name again from this event from the whole world. He also declares that the sons of Esau and Ishmael will be destroyed totally due to their "hamas" terror and blood thirstiness for the innocent.

Passover (April-May) 2014- The anti-Christ or anti-messiah will declare he is god and sit on the throne (Ark of the Covenant that is currently under the cross holes on the Temple Mount where Jeremiah hid it in the earth over 600 years before Messiah's crucifixion) This Ark or throne will be brought up and used as a throne of the anti-messiah or some other statue or image of himself (antichrist) that is an abomination to YHWH. I expect the orthodox Jews in Israel will flee to Jordan and Petra and a great flood (people) will be about to slaughter them and will be swallowed up by the earth opening up, much like Korah and his rebellious followers. The anti-messiah is given power to make war against and destroy the saints for 42 Hebrew months. The saints (believers and followers of Messiah) will be hidden, fed and cared for in the wilderness in a place prepared before the foundation of the earth. The "**mark of the beast**" law will be passed in North America. Many will be beheaded and not deny His great name. Many will call on His name and be delivered as they escape as mighty angelic forces will be at work on their behalf.

Feast of Trumpets 2017 (September-October 2017) This is what I believe is the end of the last Jubilee or set of 120 fifty year periods that were promised mankind (the first Adam ruled or had dominion; this rule was stolen by Satan in the garden of Eden and he ruled the remainder of mankind's reign on the Earth; the last day or 1000 years will be the Sabbath millennium and YHWH rules the Earth and the garden of Eden is restored and the curse removed. I questioned the revelation about the Jubilee and the capturing and deliverance of Jerusalem by Messiah from Father YHWH but I believe I upon questioning I was told "look it up!" I thought for a moment as I questioned this thought, "Look it up?" I answered with another question, "How?" I immediately thought of "Google it" which meant to me to see if there had been any other signs of deliverance for Jerusalem every 50 years prior. "There must be some record Father for me to agree," although I did not quickly remember any. Using Yahoo Search Engine, I typed in **Jerusalem 1967** which would be exactly 50 years prior to Messiah coming in 2017. Surprisingly, I saw that Jerusalem was liberated by the Jews in 1967! I was sure nothing else would be in line with another step backwards 50 years for anything happening regarding Jerusalem in 1917. Surprised again, I saw that General Allenby captured Jerusalem and all Israel that year. The British forces liberated Jerusalem from the Ottoman Empire (Arabs). This was the first time Israel's arch enemies had NOT ruled Jerusalem for thousands of years! The Greeks, Romans, and Arabs had controlled Jerusalem for thousands of years. Now YHWH is getting my attention, but I reminded Him quickly, "You promised three witnesses if I ask for them!" Next I load Jerusalem 1867 in the Yahoo Search. Confident that there was no record of anything about Jerusalem I hit the search button on the computer. Amazingly, two items popped up. First was the reference of Mark Twain (Author Samuel Clemens from USA) visiting Jerusalem and proclaiming, "This is a desolate place, Jesus could not have lived here!" (Exactly what the scriptures teach they would say in the last days- the tribes would be scattered and Israel would be desolate!) Secondly, Captain Warren (Then a young Lieutenant) of the British Expeditionary Forces surveyed Jerusalem! I have concluded that Messiah had shown me or led me to a truth- 2017 Feast of Trumpets our Deliverer is coming!

I also expect: **Author's Note on Power to Overcome**: As the Holy Spirit Early Rain Outpouring was given at the conclusion of the Spring Feasts of the Lord; (Feast of Weeks or Shavuot called by many Pentecost) it stands to reason that the Latter Rain Outpouring of the Holy Spirit will be the conclusion of the Fall Feasts of the Lord; (The Last Great Day or eighth and last day of the Feast of Tabernacles in 2010). We can be assured when more evil is poured out we will receive more Heavenly help from our merciful God!

Messiah comes and YHWH makes judgment against the anti-messiah and throws him and the false religious leader that helps the anti-Christ into the lake of fire and Satan their King is locked away for 1000 years and the Day of the LORD (The Sabbath reign of Messiah) is underway. We will sit at the feet of Messiah Yahshua (Jesus) and learn how to submit and obey Him as He teaches us Kingdom principles (Torah).

Blessings and Shalom to you! Thurston

For the serious Bible student of YHWH I want to recommend a book by a great friend and brother in Yahshua at www.amazon.com:

EPIDEMIC! By Dr. Russ Houck

This book will stimulate and challenge just about everything you think you know about God and how He wants to be known and worshipped! (www.amazon.com)

Where Did You Come From?
And Where Are You Really Going?

Chapter Nineteen:
Yahweh's Medicine

Recommended Dosage: Read these Scriptures (or record them and listen to them) three times daily until perfect health manifests in your body. If conditions worsen, increase the dosage as there are only beneficial side effects, which are guaranteed heavenly results of healing and health. Maintain health by continuing the "dosage," at least once daily after health is achieved. Find other Scripture promises to manifest heavenly results in all areas of your life. Please note that these are not direct quotes of Scripture, but they are Scripture promises personalized for you.

Heavenly Father, I attend to your Words. I pay close attention and meditate on them. I do not let them depart from my eyes. I keep them in the midst of my heart, for they are life to me and healing to all my flesh. (Psalm 119:11) Your Word is a lamp to my feet and a light to my path. (Psalm 119:105) The wicked one tries to destroy me, but I consider Your Words on the matter. (Psalm 119:95) Forever, Yahshua is Your Word settled in heaven. (Psalm 119:89) Therefore, I establish Your Word in my life on the earth! I have abundance in all things; for You came that I have life more abundantly. (John 10:10) I bless Your Set-Apart and Holy Name with my soul, Yahshua, and forget not all Your benefits. You forgive all my iniquities, and heal all my diseases. You redeem my life from destruction, and crown me with Your loving kindness and tender mercies. You satisfy my mouth with good things, and my youth is renewed like the eagles. (Psalm 103:2-4) For as heaven is high above the earth, so great are Your mercies to us who hold You in high esteem and worship You. As far as the east is from the west, unending, You have removed our sin from us. (Psalm 103:11-12) Give us understanding, and we shall keep the Commandments and Instruction of Your Law with our whole heart! (Psalm 119:34)

I enter Your gates with thanksgiving, and enter Your courts with praise, for I am thankful and praise Your Holy Name, Yahweh! (Psalm 100) I believe You; therefore I have spoken agreement with You, for I was greatly afflicted. You have delivered my soul from death and my eyes from tears, and my feet from falling, for Your truth endures forever and I praise you! (Psalm 116:8-10) Whoever trusts in You shall never see shame. Some trust in their wealth, some trust in their careers, some trust only in hospitals, doctors, and drugs, some trust in their fame, some trust in horses and chariots, but I will trust in You and Your promises. You sent forth Your Word and healed me, and rescued me from destruction. (Psalm 107:20) No weapon formed against me shall prosper, and I refute every tongue that accuses me. The accuser of the believers is Satan, and he has no power over me. I forgive all that do evil against me, for I am a doer of Your Word, Yahshua. (Isaiah 54:17) You Command Your angels concerning me and my family and friends. They are ministering spirits to us who are the heirs of Your deliverance and salvation. No disease or calamity will come near us, for we only see the reward of the wicked. (Psalm 91) Yahshua, You have borne all my sickness and diseases and You carried all my pain and sorrows. Therefore, Satan has no legal right in the courts of heaven or earth, to put any sickness or disease on me, or my family and friends. You were wounded for my transgression, bruised for my iniquities, and the punishment that was due me was put on You, and by Your stripes I am healed. I receive you, Yahshua, as my healer and deliverer! (Isaiah 53:4-5) You desire above all things that I prosper and be in good health, even as my soul prospers from receiving Your engrafted Word. (3 John 2) You heal me, O Lord, and I shall be healed. (Jeremiah 17:14) Your Word is health to me, and healing to all my bones. (Proverbs 3:8) Now my health springs up speedily because I fast and pray and obey You. (Isaiah 58:8) I put away from me a deceitful mouth and perverse words I put far from me. (Proverbs 4:24) I keep Your Words in front of my eyes; I pay attention to Your Words, for they are life to me and healing to all my flesh. (Proverbs 4:20-22) I hear and receive your sayings, O Lord, and the years of my life shall be many. Your pleasant Words shall be like a honeycomb, sweet to my soul, and healing to my bones. I listen and diligently pay attention to Your Words, and I do that, which is right in Your sight, and give ear to Your Commandments and keep them. You allow no diseases on me, for You are the God that heals me. (Exodus 15:26) My body is the temple of the Holy Spirit. Yahshua, Your life permeates my spirit, soul, and body, because I present my body as a living sacrifice by renewing my mind in Your Word. I know and obey Your perfect will. (Romans 12:1-2)

Heavenly Father, Your Word has become part of me, and Your life flows throughout my body in my blood. For life is in the blood. Therefore, my blood is free from all impurities, and flows to every cell of my body restoring life and health abundantly. It destroys all sicknesses, including cancers, aids viruses, tumors, arthritis, swine and all types of flu, dementia, blood disease, diabetes, and all manner of diseases, because it carries the engrafted Word of life from the source of all life! The same Spirit that raised Yahshua from the dead is in me, therefore; every bone, joint and organ of my body is filled with Your life Yahshua, and You send healing throughout my body. Every cell of my body supports life and health, therefore; I will not die, but I will declare the marvelous works of the Lord! (Psalm 118:17) Body, I command you, be healed in the name of Yahweh!

I have commanded perfect health and long life to this body, and I command every spirit of infirmity and disease to go from this body! Disease, you have no place on this body. I break your power, Satan, for Yahshua has destroyed all your works. I do not doubt in my heart, I only believe those things which I have said shall come to pass, and I will have whatever I say. Therefore, I have prayed Your Word over whatever I desired, and I shall have them. (Mark 11:23-24) Thank You for health and healing, Yahshua! Great and marvelous are Your works! I thank You for my healing! I thank You Yahshua who has bought and paid for my perfect health!

Chapter Twenty:
Daily Confessions

Man doesn't live by bread alone but by every Word from the mouth of Yahweh (God). I hunger and thirst for Your righteousness and truth, and therefore I am filled. You write Your Word on my heart, and the meditations of my heart and the words of my mouth, are pleasing in Your sight Yahweh! I meditate on Your Word continually, and am careful to do everything in Your Word, and I am prosperous and successful in all things. Because I am diligent to hear and obey Your Commands, all these blessings overtake me; I am blessed in the city and I am blessed in the country. Blessed are my children and blessed is my harvest. I am blessed coming in and blessed going out. Yahweh, You cause all my enemies that rise up against me to fall before my face. They shall come against me one way and flee from me seven ways. Yahweh You Command Your blessing on the land You give me, and upon all my storehouses.

Yahweh, because I keep Your Commandments and walk in Your ways, all the people of the earth shall see that I am called by Your Name and fear me. Yahweh, You shall make me plenteous in goods, and You open Your treasure and prosper all I set my hand to do. I shall lend to many, but shall not borrow. You make me the head and not the tail, above and not beneath, and You give me rain in its season. I attend to Your Words for they are life to me and healing to all my flesh. My body is the temple of the Holy Spirit so I eat only those foods that are healthy and drink water and those liquids, which promote healing, and health. I honor You with my body. I exercise my body and soul daily and maintain perfect health. I do not allow any addiction on my body in Yahshua's Name! I confess my sin and You are faithful and just to forgive me of all my iniquity! I plead and apply Your blood Yahshua, for You are the Passover Lamb, and Your blood protects me from all the power of the destroyer. You rebuke the destroyer for me and You are my protection. I am free from all curses, including generational and family curses! I am delivered from all food addictions, overeating, sugar, caffeine, carbonated colas, tobacco, alcohol, drugs, sexual perversions, pornography, witchcraft and all areas of deceit and the occult! I speak Your Word daily Yahshua, for it will not return void, but will accomplish the purpose for which You sent it. It is the bread of life to me. Mighty is Your Word, and excellent is Your Name in all the earth! I do not let it depart from my eyes, and I renew my mind with Your Word daily. I do not conform to this world, but I am changed to Your image day by day. You do not change, for You are the same yesterday, today and forever, therefore, I submit to Your Word and I change, because I follow and obey You. I resist the devil and he flees, because I submit to Your Word and worship You! I hear and listen to Your voice for You are the Good Shepherd, and I know and obey Your perfect will.

I enter Your gates with thanksgiving and enter Your courts with praise! I meditate on Your Word continually, and think on whatever is honest, pure and lovely, and just, the good report that agrees with You, Yahshua! Therefore, I am in perfect health and prosper in all that I do. No weapon formed against me prospers, for You Command Your angels concerning me and my house (Family and friends), and no evil, sickness or calamity shall come near my house, but I will only see the reward of the wicked and disobedient. I hear the voice of the Good Shepherd and I will not listen to the voice of the thief- Satan. I bring forth fruit worthy of repentance and I win souls for Your Kingdom Messiah Yahshua! I am not ashamed of You or Your Word. It is Your power to save and deliver everyone who believes it, and I believe it! I speak Your Words, for they have destroyed, and do continually destroy, the works of the devil! I believe them, and therefore, I speak them with authority! I cast out devils in Your precious and Holy Name, Yahshua! I do not get drunk on wine, but I am filled with Your Spirit!

I speak with unknown tongues and pray in the Spirit often, because I love You and trust You. I pray in the Spirit and also pray with understanding. I sing praises in the Spirit and also sing praises with understanding. Freely, You give to me and freely I give abundantly! Your anointing breaks every yoke of bondage from me, so that I am free to minister to the hurting and lost with Your compassion, love, and power! I am free from what people think. I concern myself with what You think, Yahshua! I have Your power over all the power of hell, and by no means shall anything harm me or my house (Family and friends)! You Command Your angels concerning us, and they minister to us as heirs of Your deliverance and salvation. I lay hands on the sick and they recover, because You watch over Your Word to perform it! I worship and pay my vows to You by helping the down and out, the widow, the orphan, the homeless, and those ministers that increase Your Kingdom, that teach and do Your Word; as You Command and lead me. Therefore, my faith works. Wealth and riches are in my house, because I pay my vows where You tell me to, and I worship You in Spirit and Truth. I worship You and am a doer of Your Word, and therefore, my children shall be mighty upon the earth! As I give with great measure, You cause men to bring back into my bosom wealth and riches, to increase Your Kingdom!

I fear not because Your perfect love casts out all fear! The supernatural gifts of Your Spirit flow through me as You will. I receive words of wisdom, words of knowledge, gifts of supernatural faith, gifts of healings, workings of miracles, prophecies, discerning of spirits, diversities of unknown tongues, and interpretations of tongues from You as You will. I do not control Your gifts, but they flow through me as You direct. I ask You for wisdom and You give it to me abundantly. I have Your mind, Yahshua, and I allow no demonic oppression or confusion. I crucify my flesh and am lead by Your Spirit. I no longer live, but You, Yahshua, dwell in me. The life I live in this body I live by Your faith, because You love me and gave Yourself up for me. You guide me into all truth and teach me of things to come. One thousand may fall on my left, and ten thousand at my right hand, but the pestilence will not come near me or my house (Family and friends)! I meditate on Your Word and produce fruit for Your Kingdom. It is Your good pleasure to give me the keys to Your Kingdom. You are The Way, The Truth and The Life, and You are trustworthy, therefore, I am trustworthy! I am led by Your Spirit and You renew a right spirit within me, and create in me a clean heart. I count my blessings and see good in all things, for You bless me. I worship and adore You, Yahshua! You alone are worthy to be praised and glorified! There is none like You! You are my healer, the lifter of my soul, and my provision seen! Your peace and anointing guards my heart and mind and I can do all things through You who strengthen me. You supply all my needs according to Your riches in glory, Yahshua! I give You thanks, and praise Your precious and Holy Name!

I do exploits and miracles in Your Name, because You confirm Your Word with signs and wonders following! You are no respecter of persons, but You honor doers of Your Word who give thanks and trust You. I give You thanks in all situations, and praise Your Holy Name! I trust and obey

You! You are the same yesterday, today, and forever! You came to set captives free and I am free! I am free to worship and adore You! Whom the Son sets free is free indeed, and I am free! I humble myself and obey Your Word and the devil flees from me. I submit to You and I change, for You change not. I trust You unto death in all things, and therefore I trust You with my children. You continually draw us (Family and friends) to intimacy with You, and protect us because we love You and obey You! For as for me and my house (Family and friends), we will serve the Lord Yahshua the Messiah!

I pray and only believe that those things I pray will come to pass, and therefore, I shall have whatsoever I say. All things are possible to me, because I believe and therefore speak Your Word, Yahshua, in faith and nothing doubting. I believe Your Word and promises in my heart, and do not doubt but I confess Your Word with my mouth unto deliverance and salvation, which is You bringing it to pass. You make me worthy to escape and endure all the troubles coming on the earth to test the earth, and I will stand at Your appearing unashamed. You were and are and are to come, Yahshua! I worship and give You thanks! In my pathway is life and there is no death. I honor Your Shabbat (Sabbath) and all Your Feasts. I do not do my own pleasure on Your Set-Apart Day, but I rest and allow You to minister life to me! I study and rightly divide Your Torah (Word). You teach me and guide me into all truth! I ask for, and receive Your wisdom abundantly! I put my body in subjection, I fast and pray and rid myself of all unbelief. I walk by the Spirit and not by the flesh. I quickly forgive those that curse me, and pray for those that spitefully use me, for I am a doer of Your Word. I am not ashamed of You or Your Word, for it is Your power, Yahshua, for us who believe, and I believe!

I resist you devil and you flee from me! I will not allow any oppression, bondage, headaches, sickness, disease, or heaviness to come

377

on me! I resist you devil and cast you away from me in Yahshua's Name! Your power is broken off of my life, and I live for Yahshua the Messiah, and Him alone will I worship! Yahshua You are the truth, therefore, I speak only truth. I do not deviate from the truth in any way. I do not depart from You. Lying devils, you have no place on me! Lust of the flesh devils go from me! I give no place to unclean thoughts! Pride, I command you to flee from me! Covetousness and jealousy go from me! All unclean spirits, I cast you out in Yahshua's Name! I break your power Satan, because Yahshua has destroyed all your works. You are condemned, but there is no condemnation on me, for I remain in Yahshua and walk by the Spirit, and not the flesh! Yahshua, I am in You and Your Words remain in me, and I produce fruit that will remain! I ask what I wish and You provide abundantly. I worship you! You have framed the worlds with Your spoken Word. I agree with You, and frame my world by Your spoken Word. Your Word is established in heaven and therefore I establish Your Word on the earth. I give you thanks and praise for victory! You confirm Your Word with signs and wonders following! Mighty are you, and excellent is Your Name in the earth! I worship and adore You! I love and obey You! I worship and give You thanks!

There is none like You! You have given me all things that pertain to life, health, and Godliness! You were pierced for my transgressions, bruised for my iniquities, the punishment for my peace was on You, and by Your stripes I am healed and made whole! Thank You for saving me and my house (Family and friends)! Through the shed blood of Yahshua I am righteous and without spot or blemish! Yahweh, You are my Father and I come to Your throne room with confidence, and receive mercy and grace in my time of need. I worship You and You inhabit the praises of Your people! HaleluYah! HaleluYah! HaleluYah! You alone open doors that no man can shut, and close doors that no man can open! I praise and adore You! I forgive all that do evil against me and therefore I am forgiven! I worship and adore You! You are the author and finisher of my faith! You are perfect in all Your ways! You continually bless me and my house (Family and friends)! There is none like you! HaleluYah! I am who You say I am, and I do those things You say I can do in Your Holy and Set-Apart Torah (Word)! I walk in Your compassion, power, and love and minister Your life to others as You direct me each day! I lift up Holy hands in surrender, Yahweh! Heavenly Father, You are so good to me and I worship You! HaleluYah!

Chapter Twenty One:
Daily Confession Short Version

I hear and obey You Yahshua. I love and submit to Your Word, I am honored to keep Your Sabbath, and Your Feasts, for You guide me into all truth and show me things to come. I am healthy and receive Your wisdom as You direct my steps each day. I continually forgive and am continually forgiven. I have abundance in all provision, for You care for me. Freely I receive and freely I give, therefore, I walk in the gifts of Your Spirit and pray in the Spirit and unknown tongues often, for You pray for me as I yield my tongue to allow You to direct my prayers and offer You mysteries in the Spirit. I give abundantly and I receive abundantly for I trust You, Yahshua. I cast all my cares upon You for You are The Way, The Truth and The Life to me. I speak only truth. All things are possible for I remain in You, Your Words remain in me, I ask what I wish, and it is given to me. I am blessed to be a blessing and have all power over the power of hell; by no means shall anything harm me or my house, my family and friends. I pray and only believe those things I say shall happen; therefore, I shall have whatsoever I say. I say only good that agrees with Your Word of blessing for me and my house, family and friends.

No weapon formed against me or my house, family and friends prospers. You Command Your angels to guard and protect me and my house, family and friends. You rebuke the devourer for us, guard us, and hide us from the enemy. You make me and my house, family and friends worthy to escape and endure all troubles that come on the earth and we shall stand at Your appearing unashamed, Yahshua! We are not ashamed of Your Word and we produce fruit for Your Kingdom! Praise Your Set-Apart, Holy, and precious Name Yahshua! HaleluYah! HaleluYah! HaleluYah! You prepare a table for me in the presence of my enemies and my cup runs over. You anoint me with oil, which is the precious Holy Spirit! Surely, goodness and mercy shall follow me, my house, family and friends always, and we shall dwell in the house of Yahshua forever! HaleluYah! HaleluYah! HaleluYah! I fight the good fight of faith, taking hold of what I speak and enter in to the total victory You paid for! There is none like You, Yahshua! HaleluYah! HaleluYah! HaleluYah! All Praise and honor I give to Yahweh!

EPILOGUE

As a testimony to the goodness of Yahshua and His power to protect us when we put His Word in our spirits, I will share a recent experience. My wife Bonnie and I had traveled Europe for five weeks ministering and meeting people, and had promised many that we would send them the book you have just read. Daily, He protected us and we unquestionably experienced divine appointments. We prayed daily and asked several other believers to pray for us for protection and divine appointments. Every day we also read the above confessions to build our spirits in faith. I heard a great preacher say one time that if it is the truth then it is worth practicing what you preach. In other words, if it's good enough to share with you, then it better work for me also! We were in Paris and had taken the metro to the large center where all the trains came together, the busiest part of their subway system. We were warned that there were professional thieves (pickpockets) there, so I shifted my billfold to my front pocket. It carried all our credit cards, cash, and maybe more importantly our list of names of new friends and contacts we had met and promised to send this book to. If this were ever lost or stolen, I would not have been able to keep my promises to them.

As we stepped on the train many people were getting off and many more crowded onto the train. I thought I heard the Lord say, "check your wallet." It was gone! How could that be possible, I frantically thought? Looking around quickly, there were about forty people getting off, and probably as many crowding onto the train car we were in. The Lord spoke and said, "That man there took your wallet." I grabbed at one of the many leaving the train and said, "You took my wallet!" He answered in broken English, "No, I saw the man who stole it running up the stairs!" There were probably over one hundred people moving in front of me. Then again, I heard from our Messiah who is very much alive, "No- this man took your wallet. Shake his arm!" Meanwhile, the train door had closed, as I had quickly followed this man off the train. Away Bonnie sped into Paris, waving frantically! As I shook him violently, down came my billfold, credit cards, and hundred dollar bills floating to the ground! Still shocked, as this had all taken less than one minute, I reached to pick up everything the man had stolen, and the exposed thief bolted away into the stunned and disbelieving crowd. I took the next train to where YHWH led as we had not determined where we would go. I thought and hoped Bonnie would be there, and she was there, nearly in tears. The Lord had put a nice couple with her, who waited for me with her. She said she had seen me shake the man, and watch the money fall out as she disappeared down the tracks, but she did not know what had happened after that. The couple, along with many others, told us they had never seen anyone get their funds back. The whole episode had taken less than ten minutes, but it was a testimony of the power of His protection, and Him still watching over His Word to perform it!

These sorts of experiences were commonplace during our whole trip of ministry. The last day, as we drove to the Frankfurt airport, we were looking for diesel fuel for our rent car and asked directions from a lady standing by her home. She said she was a believer, and asked us to pray for her husband. Her words confirmed what we had continually asked for and received during the whole ministry trip. She correctly asserted, "This was an appointment by God, thank you for your prayer with me." Of course, we now have also prayed for the thief's salvation, and fully expect he has come into the Kingdom! That is the very best of blessings we could do for a deceived man who tried to do evil against us!

Remember, your Heavenly Father is no respecter of persons, and He watches over His word to perform it! He will do the same for you, as you renew your mind and spirit in His word daily! You will have the results in life that you diligently put into your spirit. In Hebrews 11:6 He promises that whoever comes to Him must believe that He exists, and that He is a rewarder of those that diligently seek Him! As you confidently speak these divine promises into your spirit, prepare yourself for a life full of blessings! Start counting your blessings!

Where Did You Come From?
And Where Are You Really Going?

About The Book

N o one person is ever given all the answers and that most certainly applies to me. We know in part and prophesy in part. Our Creator designed it so that we would rely on each other for answers and we are all growing and learning. One will prophesy, another have a word, another will have a song, etc. What I believed 4 years ago about these matters has certainly changed as I sought our Lord and grew in understanding; hence this updated version in November of 2009. The many websites, dreams, visions and Bible Codes included in the book supply a vast amount of knowledge and understanding based on the various parts of the "body of Messiah" being given their different parts of the puzzle. Of course you should realize that websites and people change, so you might have to do your own search for them. I do not pretend to have these matters all figured out so understand you will need also to hear from heaven, and you will, when you seek Him with all your heart. I encourage you to seek the King of all Kings, Yahshua! It is my prayer that you and your loved ones are made worthy to escape and endure and stand at Messiah's appearing unashamed, that we escape the judgment of Ephraim (Especially **IF** Rockets fly at Feast of Trumpets 2010) so that we may hopefully receive (expected) His latter rain outpouring of His Spirit on the Last Great Day of Tabernacles 2010 and continue to produce fruit for His Kingdom!

Shalom and Blessings to you,

Thurston Ben McCutchen

About The Author

The author of this book, Thurston McCutchen, lives with his wife Bonnie on their small ranch near San Antonio, Texas. Thurston is a husband, father, investor and businessman who has traveled the world preaching and teaching, showing the love and power of the gospel of Yahshua of Nazareth. It is his heart's desire that you are blessed with the reading of this book and understand that the gospel without a demonstration of His power and help for all who seek Him is not the real gospel at all. Thurston can be contacted for ministry dates or book orders by email at tbmccut@seedtime2harvest.com or you may visit his website at www.seedtime2harvest.com.

Are there others you want to help and prepare for the times ahead? Give these books as gifts and ministry to your family and friends!

You may order copies of the book: *"Where Did You Come From And Where Are You Really Going?"* from your local bookstore, the ISBN # is 978-0-615-33342-7

Order online at: WWW.SEEDTIME2HARVEST.COM and click on bookstore.

If you are a bookstore or want to buy large quantities, please email Thurston at tbmccut@seedtime2harvest.com

You may also order the book online at www.amazon.com.

Where Did You Come From?
And Where Are You Really Going?

Beneficial Websites

1	www.sidroth.org	Audio Video Miraculous
2	http://ad2004.com	Bible Codes
3	www.ancientpaths.org/APJTbiblecode.html	Bible Codes
4	www.yacovrambsel.com	Bible Codes
5	www.wyattmuseum.com	Biblical Archeology
6	www.biblicalastronomy.com	Biblical Astronomy
7	www.geocities.com/jsminis/	Henry Gruver Visions
8	www.younglivingworld.com	Essential Oils
9	www.e-sword.net	Free Bible Study Software
10	www.cpr-savers.com	Health
11	www.first-aid-product.com	Health
12	www.purehealthsystems.com/hydrogen-peroxide-2.html	Health
13	www.lifeextension.com	Health Answers Products
14	www.aroodawakening.tv	Hebraic Roots Bible Study
15	www.seedtime2harvest.com	Hebraic Roots Bible Study
16	www.ancient-hebrew.org	Hebraic Roots Bible Study
17	www.biblicalholidays.com	Hebraic Roots Bible Study
18	www.billcloud.org	Hebraic Roots Bible Study
19	www.coyhwh.com	Hebraic Roots Bible Study
20	www.Eliyah.com	Hebraic Roots Bible Study
21	www.elshaddaiministries.us	Hebraic Roots Bible Study
22	www.hebroots.org	Hebraic Roots Bible Study
23	www.jerusalemperspective.com	Hebraic Roots Bible Study
24	www.joinedtohashem.org	Hebraic Roots Bible Study
25	www.lionlamb.net	Hebraic Roots Bible Study
26	www.m7000.com	Hebraic Roots Bible Study

27	www.nazarite.net	Hebraic Roots Bible Study
28	www.restorationoftorah.org	Hebraic Roots Bible Study
29	www.sabbathtruth.com	Hebraic Roots Bible Study
30	www.torahzone.net	Hebraic Roots Bible Study
31	www.wisdomintorah.com	Hebraic Roots Bible Study
32	www.godslearningchannel.com	Hebraic TV
33	www.wilburministries.com	Hebraic Worship
34	www.isr-messianic.org	Hebrew Roots Bible
35	www.wildbranchministries.com	Hebraic Roots Study
36	www.copper-scroll-project.com/index.html	Israel Biblical Treasure
37	www.stevequayle.com/index1.html	New World Order Expose
38	www.fossilizedcustoms.com	Pagan Customs
39	www.arn.org	Scientific Creation
40	www.creationevidence.org	Scientific Creation
41	www.creationists.org	Scientific Creation
42	www.creationresearch.org	Scientific Creation
43	www.creationresource.org	Scientific Creation
44	www.icr.org	Scientific Creation
45	www.heirloomseeds.com	Survival Seeds
46	www.grainmaker.com	Survival products
47	www.grit.com	Rural Living
48	www.motherearthnews.com	Gardening & Rural Life
49	www.survival-warehouse.com	Survival products
50	www.survivormall.com	Survival products
51	www.heatmor.com	Survival products heater
52	www.hebcal.com/sedrot	Torah Readings Schedule
53	www.americaslastdays.com	Visions and Dreams
54	www.etpv.org	Visions and Dreams
55	www.visionsofthelastdays.com	Visions and Dreams
56	www.wnd.com	Biblical World News
57	www.pleasanthillgrain.com	Water purifiers & grains
58	www.healingwaterfilters.com	Portable water filters
59	www.prophecynewswatch.com	Current Prophecy news
60	http://watch.org	Bible World News